The Social and Psychological Acculturation

of North Korean Refugees

The Social and Psychological Acculturation of North Korean Refugees

Printed in Seoul, Republic of Korea
ISBN 978-89-521-1393-1 93300

Seoul National University Press
1 Gwanak-ro, Gwanak-gu, Seoul 151-742, Republic of Korea
E-mail: snubook@snu.ac.kr
Homepage: http://www.snupress.com
Tel: +82-2-880-5252
Fax: +82-2-889-0785

First Printing: October 10, 2014

The Social and Psychological Acculturation

of North Korean Refugees

Soon-Hyung Yi

Soo-Churl Cho

Changdai Kim

Meejung Chin

SNUPRESS

Seoul National University Press

Preface

The number of North Korean refugees who entered South Korea has been increasing since 2000. As of 2011, a total of 23,095 North Korean refugees entered and most remained in South Korea. The growing population of the North Korean refugees invoked research from the various disciplinary backgrounds.

We—as four researchers from the fields of child development, child psychiatry, educational counseling, and family studies—were interested in the refugees' way of life and their process of acculturation in South Korea. We wished to study what facilitates and hinders the process of acculturation and adaptation. Although there were some literature on North Korean refugees, a majority of the contents focused only on a limited range of topics. Consequently, we tried to investigate their lives across comprehensive areas.

Thanks to the funding from the Institute for Peace and Unification Studies, Seoul National University, we were able to begin a study on the social and psychological acculturation of North Korean refugees from the perspectives of individual and family resilience. While they have faced numerous moments of danger since they crossed the border to China, they perceived their experiences as meaningful and made significant efforts to adjust to a new environment. In the course of acculturation and adaptation, their families became their primary source of support.

We published a book based on our study in 2008, and this book was honorably awarded for its excellence by the National Academy of Sciences, Republic of Korea in the division of Basic Sciences. The stories of North Korean refugees have been featured by the media internationally. Yet, not many of books and articles on North Korean refugees were published in academia, and little has been known to international scholars and readers. For this reason, we were encouraged to translate our book in English and share our findings with international readers.

This book is based on both quantitative and qualitative research data of 44 North Korean adolescents and 195 adults who entered South Korea. These refugees recounted their experiences of acculturation in South Korea, means of overcoming difficulties, struggles in everyday life, and ideas on how we can help them to live happier lives. We hope this book can help international readers understand the lives of North Korean refugees and raise greater interests in them.

Finally, we would like to thank Sinae Han, Nam Kyung Lee, and Seung Heon Yoo for their assistance in translating this manuscript and Seoul National University Press in supporting us in publication.

October, 2012

On behalf of the authors,
Soon-Hyung Yi

Contents

Tables

Figures

I

Resilience and Acculturation of North Korean Refugees

The number of North Koreans escaping North Korea has rapidly increased after the food crisis in the mid 1990s. Exact statistics on the size of North Korean refugees (hereafter North Korean refugees or the refugees) is unavailable; yet, according to the report of U.S. Committee for Refugees and Immigrants, it is assumed that approximately 50,000 North Korean refugees resided in China in 2006. Among them, the number of refugees making entry to South Korea continually increased, and as of 2007 approximately 10,000 North Korean refugees settled in South Korea.

Until 1993, there were only less than ten North Korean refugees making entry to South Korea every year. In 1994, the number exceeded to 50, and it reached triple digits in 1999. Ever since 2002, more than 1,000 North Korean refugees per year made entry to South Korea (Table I-1). Majority of these refugees were men until the late 1990s, but their ratio was reversed after 2002, resulting that the entry of female refugees were more than that of male refugees. In 2004, the number of female refugees making entry doubled that of male refugees (Table I-2). The ages of the North Korean refugees who have settled in South Korea span widely across a broad range, but most refugees are in their 20s and 30s (Table I-3).

Rapid increase of the refugees raised issues of sociological and academical interest in their lives and adaptation. Interests from various

<Table I-1> The numbers of North Korean entrants by year

	Before 92	'93–'99	'00	'01	'02	'03	'04	'05	'06	'07	'08	'09	'10	'11	Total
No. of people	633	462	312	586	1,141	1,282	1,898	1,382	2,026	2,551	2,801	2,914	2,401	2,706	23,095

Data: Ministry of Unification's National Assembly inspection on government offices (2012); North Korea policy focus & Statistics on North Korean refugees (2012)

<Table I-2>The numbers of North Korean entrants by sex

	–'98	–'01	'02	'03	'04	'05	'06	'07	'08	'09	'10	'11	'12.9	Total
Male	831	565	511	473	626	424	514	572	608	664	589	797	303	7,477
Female	116	481	632	810	1,273	958	1,512	1,981	2,196	2,253	1,812	1,909	783	16,716

<Table I-3> The numbers of North Korean entrants by age

	Under 10	10–19	20–29	30–39	40–49	50–59	over 60	Total
Frequency	977	2,753	6,424	7,258	3,804	1,184	1,075	23,475
Percent	4	12	27	31	16	5	5	100

Data: Ministry of Unification's National Assembly inspection on government offices (2012); North Korea policy focus & Statistics on North Korean refugees (2012)

academic areas in their adaptation in South Korea are attributed to the fact that understanding their diverse experiences faced in the South Korean society will be important in preparing and forecasting the social integration process after the unification. Their adaptation itself is no doubt an important social issue, but their experiences will help estimate potential problems that would be faced by North Koreans during their adaptation in South Korean society and culture after the unification. That is, the successful adaptation of the refugees can be an essential reference in establishing psychological integration of North and South Korean society after the unification. Therefore, a majority of studies on North Korean refugees have a common goal of finding out social, cultural, and psychological challenges the refugees encounter during the settlement process, addressing causal factors of these problems and suggesting several policies that would help their adaptation.

However, studies of North Korean refugees, have some limitations and difficulties. First, a study of the refugees inevitably faces the issue of selection bias: this group cannot represent North Koreans as a whole. Although the population of the group became more diverse as the number of the refugees increased, an issue of selection bias should not be overlooked. As can be seen in previous statistics, the ages of refugees are concentrated in the 20s and 30s (60 % of total refugees). In terms of regional origins, most refugees are from the Hamgyeong province. It is possible to assume that their adaptation is related to their age and regional bias. Findings from immigrant studies also showed that an adaptation process to a new society or culture depends on an individual's age (Cho, Lee, & Han, 2005). Moreover, it can be assumed that residents of the Hamgyeong province, where there is relatively frequent exchange of visits from China due to its geographically adjacency to China, will be different from inland residents.

Second, previous researches on seeking implications of psychological integration after the unification from the North Korean refugees' psychological adaptation have overlooked the fact that the psychological adaptation of an individual and that of a society are two very different issues. In fact, of changes made from contacting a different culture, individuals' psychological adaptation and psychological integration after the unification may both be explained through an aspect of acculturation. Acculturation refers to the changes of an individual or a group resulting from a contact with a new culture. Acculturation at the group level refers to changes in economical, technological, sociological, cultural, or political systems, whereas acculturation at the individual level refers to changes in an individual's behavior, value, identity, or attitude (Williams & Berry, 1991).

Acculturation at the individual level is not an easy process. When we explore how individuals adapt to a new culture, acculturation develops through the process of selecting and modifying cultural needs from both cultures rather than absorbing the new culture or replacing the old values with the new. And yet, when there exists a dominant society, changes or adaptation become a responsibility of individuals or minority groups who are transferring into the dominant society. Moreover, a failure in adaptation, or maladaptation, is regarded as a problem of individuals or minority groups.

Social integration or psychological integration after the unification of Koreas, however, is a process of establishing a new culture by modifying each culture and norms, through compromise or conflict (Cha, 2000). That is, basic value system and norms in each Korea change and form a culture basing on a new value system. In this regard, researchers even suggest a way to merge North and South Korea through interconnecting strengths of each society (Lim & Chung, 2005). In this respect, each individual's adaptation and a society's psychological integration should be regarded as two different issues, and thus, we should be very cautious post-unification psychological integration through the refugees' adaptation process.

Even so, we should acknowledge that studies on North Korean refugees provide data on North Korea, which can be easily accessed. Given limited resources on North Korea, most studies rely heavily only on a few case studies and literature from North Korea. In this reality, the refugees provide the latest information on the North Korean society and its people. Therefore, the role of refugees in North Korean studies should not be overlooked. This book, however, intends to view North Korean refugees from a bit different perspective. It attempts to accept the special circumstances and conditions of the refugees in becoming citizens of South Korea, and explain why and how they are different from people in North Korea. For the refugees' experience during the process of becoming citizens of South Korea differentiated make them different from those remaining in the North.

Resilience of individual and family

One noticeable phenomena as North Korean refugees' entry to South Korea increases is that the cases of family-accompanied entry or sequential entry have increased. As <Table I-4> shows, as of June 2006, out of 854 North Korean refugees who have entered Korea, 267 refugees entered with their family members. That is, 31 % of the refugees have entered with the entire family, or at least some members of family. A possible reason for such increase is that whole family crossing the border increased as border-crossing (hereafter border-crossing or the crossing) became possible. Another possible reason is that as North Korean refugees' stay in China lengthened, they had more chances to help remaining family members in North Korea to cross the border (Yoon, 1999). In addition, work of professional brokers and a lump-sum payment of resettlement funds by the South Korean government made sequential entry planned crossing of remaining families in North Korea by prior refugees who left North Korea earlier, possible.

Increase in family-accompanied border-crossing raised the level of societal interest on how this phenomenon would affect the acculturation of such refugees. Prior studies showed that the acculturation of refugees who came with even a part of their families was faster and more flexible

<Table I-4> Family-accompanied entrant status

Year	Total entrants (no. of refugees)	Family-accompanied entrants (no. of refugees)	Ratio (%)
1994	52	10	19
1995	41	13	32
1996	56	27	48
1997	85	59	69
1998	71	34	48
1999	148	91	61
2000	213	97	46
2001	583	329	56
2002	1,139	409	39
2003	1,281	464	36
2004	1,894	668	35
2005	1,383	380	27
2006.6	854	267	31

Data: Constructed based on Table 2 of Kim (2001) and Ministry of Unification's National Assembly inspection on government offices (2006)

than that of refugees who came alone (Lee et al., 2001; Jeon, 2000; Han & Lee, 2002). Since family is a primary source of emotional support, family plays a positive role in relieving isolation and loneliness experienced by refugees. Moreover, with the successful border-crossing of the entire family, refugees are free from any guilt that may arise due to family members left behind in North Korea. This would be helpful for their acculturation. Stability and consolation from sharing their experiences with family members provides support, lessens acculturation stress, and stimulates acculturation. Particularly, a child or an adolescent refugee with family may have a more stable and protected life as compared to that of a child refugee without family members.

However, influence of family on an individual in the acculturation process is complex. Prior studies on North Korean refugee families pointed out various conflicts and challenges experienced by individuals within a family in the process of acculturating into a new society (Kim, 2000; Park & Lee, 1999; Lee, 2000; Jang & Kim, 2000; Jeon, 2000). These studies discussed problems associated with acculturation in a family as identified by American literature on refugees or migrant families, and emphasized that North Korean refugees may experience such problems as well. Various aspects of conflict such as individual differences in adaptation by age or gender, change in the power structure through role alteration, change in gender-role standard, and change in family culture, lie hidden within refugee families. This would become an obstacle for adaptation of an individual and a family. For these reasons, North Korean refugee families became recently a matter of concern. Yet, few studies were conducted with empirical data. Most studies discussed the problems of North Korean refugee families with contents based on interviews of a small number of refugee families (Park & Lee, 1999; Ahn, 2002; Jang & Kim, 2000).

In order to understand acculturation of North Korean refugees and their families who have undergone dangerous escape, emotionally overwhelming stress, and life-threatening societal circumstances of discrimination and isolation, we have focused on *resilience*. Acculturation is not assimilating new culture unconditionally nor replacing old values with new values. Acculturation takes place through an integrated process that selects and modifies the needs of both cultures. This process accompanies conscious or unconscious, process of reperceiving, evaluating, and choosing in regard to values, beliefs, and social customs of an individual. This acculturating process provides a context that helps to find resilience of an individual and a family.

Resilience refers to a quality that aids an individual to overcome crises and develop successfully against all odds. A concept of resilience has been used generally to explain individual characteristics or an adaption process and has expanded to a concept that explains characteristics of a family or a community and their adaptation process. Resilience, a concept that can only be applied to post-exposure of environmental stress, provides an important framework to understand North Korean refugee's acculturation process. We will discuss briefly the concepts of individual and family resilience, and present the definitive aspects of resilience of the North Korean refugees.

1) Resilience of individual and family

Resilience refers to the unexpected successful adaptation to a negative daily event, trauma, stress, or other dangers (Fraser, Richman & Galinsky, 1999). Scholars noticed and tried to explain the reason behind a phenomenon that many children who were brought up in adverse environments grew up to become successful adults. Poverty, dangerous life environments, limited educational stimulus, and a lack of opportunity have negative influences on children's development as a whole. Through various studies, it was found that children who were brought up in disadvantaged environments fell behind in the physical, psychological, cognitive, and social domains of development.

Yet, it was also found that the negative relationships between risk factors and post-adaptation are not always definitive. Scholars looked into protective factors, which help overcome risk factors and yield successful results. Protective factors buffer, stop, or prevent risks, and help people to bear or improve in times of danger (Greene, 2002). Protective factors that contribute to child development and allay stress can be categorized into three dimensions: individual characteristics of a child, characteristics related to a child's family, and the social environment beyond the family (Greene, 2002). A child's individual characteristics such as positive temperament, social reactivity, and self-esteem help the child to overcome risk factors in times of crisis, which leads to a better achievement for the child. In addition, supportive family environment, characterized as warmth and cohesion with at least one or more supportive caregivers, serves as a critical protective factor by preventing negative consequences. Formal social support systems and external social environment that strengthen the individual's belief system also function as protective factors. Evidently, resilience arises through risk factors and in times of crisis. The term resilience means "the capability of a strained body to recover its size and shape after deformation caused especially by compressive stress" (Merriam-Webster Dictionary). That is, resilience only arises in times of crisis and stress, or when exposed continuously to risk factors, not commonly appearing in everyday life.

The concept of resilience was developed in studying risk factors and protective factors in child development. At first, this concept focused on individual cases, but gradually expanded to family and community resilience (Kalil, 2003). Resilience, as a process of recovering from misfortune and maintaining a healthy life, is a valuable concept considering that it can be applied to any system beyond an individual. Not only individual, but family also undergoes many crises and difficulties. In such crisis, some families break apart, while others create stronger bonds by recovering from the crisis. What makes the difference? We focus on resilience to discover the answer to this question.

In the field of family studies, there have been many studies on how families recover and adjust to stress or crisis. In studies on how families change and adapt to financial crisis such as unemployment, recession, or the fall of farm industry (Elder, 1974; Conger & Elder, 1994), and life events such as divorce, remarriage, death of a family member, or injury, scholars have used various concepts to explain the process of recovery and to achieve a stronger family bonding after the crisis. The concepts of family cohesion, adaptation, coping, and strengths help to understand how families succeed in spite of hardships. Recently, these concepts have been combined under the broader theoretical concept called resilience (McCubbin et al., 1998).

McCubbin and his colleagues (1998) divide family resilience into two factors. First is elasticity, an ability that maintains a pattern of family functions even when challenged by risk factors. The second factor is buoyancy, an ability to quickly recover from stress or trauma, which leads to a change in family structure. Every family has the potential for self-recovery and growth, and such characteristics appear through a family's belief system, structural pattern, and communication pattern (Walsh, 1998).

2) Validity of the resilience concept

Recently, the concept of resilience has become crucial in understanding the adaptation of an individual and a family. At the same time, the validity of the resilience concept is actively discussed. To recapitulate, resilience refers to the unexpected successful adaptation to a negative daily life event, trauma, stress, or other dangers (Fraser, Richman & Galinsky, 1999). However, this is only one of many definitions of resilience. Here are some other definitions of resilience.

> Resilience refers to an overall concept of how children cope with stress and trauma. Similar to competence and adaptation as a result of coping,

> resilience deals with growth and hope. (Anthony & Cohler, 1987)
>
> Resilience deals with individual difference in responding to risk. Resilience refers to the positive end of the distribution of developmental outcomes among individuals at high risk. (Rutter, 1987)
>
> Resilience is defined by a person who restored one's ability to perform after the adversity. Resilience refers to an ability to recover to one's original competence before the extreme stress. (Garmezy, 1993)
>
> Resilience describes an individual who adjusted to the exceptional environment that brought unexpected, and yet positive result when confronted with adversity. (Fraser et al., 1999)

Definitions discussed here have a common feature of hardships and recovery. However, according to different scholars, the term resilience refers to ability, process, or output. The meaning is broad, whether it refers to an individual's tendency or an ability to recover and adapt well to adverse situations, or characteristic or suitability of interrelations between an individual and the environment, or an output as successful adaption. Tarter and Vanyukov (1999) criticized the concept of resilience by pointing out that it does not hold a unique meaning because it can be any definition that fulfills the description of a successful individual who overcame an adverse situation. In addition, they indicated that in order to apply the concept of resilience, the effect has to continue to last, and yet, none of the studies on resilience have proved the continuous effect of resilience beyond specific circumstances.

In this study, we try to address both the usability and limits of the concept of resilience. This concept provides guidance in understanding the process in which North Korean refugee families overcome many crises and difficulties, and how they change their lives. We will apply resilience in context of process in which an individual and an environment interrelate to each other throughout the life course, rather than focusing on the tendency or characteristics of an individual or a family. Human development and family development provide a foundation in our understanding North Korean refugee families. Humans and families develop throughout life, and they are, in their own way, and adaptable (Kalil, 2003). Only different degrees of resilience are displayed and found depending on the given circumstances and contexts. The same concept applies to family resilience. Each family member influences one another, forming relational resilience, which develops family resilience (Walsh, 1998).

This book explores North Korean refugees' losses and gains from their border-crossing experience. What kind of transformation processes did their values and social awareness undergo during their course of becoming a seceder from a country, then a third country refugee, and finally a South Korean citizen? How would their personalities and identities change during the process? Is it possible that despite all these experiences, their values, social perception, personalities, and identities remain the same? What are their protective factors and risk factors in adapting to South Korea? What kind of protection factors were provided to an individual in times of crisis? In searching for answers to these questions, we try to understand the adaptation process of North Korean refugees in the perspective of resilience.

II

Research Methods

1. Qualitative research

Both qualitative and quantitative research methods were utilized in this study. Data were collected from interviews on North Korean refugees and some informants who have worked for or with them, and from surveys on North Korean refugees complimentarily. The data were analyzed to examine North Korean refugee families' acculturation multilaterally. We will explain the qualitative research method first.

1) Subjects

Interviews on North Korean refugee families and relevant informants were conducted. Sixty one people from twenty three families who chose family-accompanied border-crossing participated in the interview. Of these, fifty four cases were in-depth interviews. In addition, ten informants who worked for North Korean refugee-related offices or organizations were also interviewed in-depth. In total, sixty four in-depth interviews were conducted.

We started interviews with North Korean refugees who came with a family. Also, for the purpose of diversity in families, four families formed after they entered South Korea alone were included in the study. Among these families, two were formed by North Korean female refugees marrying South Korean males, and the other two families were formed by female and male refugees who entered Korea individually.

Using random sampling and snowball sampling, interviews were conducted on North Korean refugee-related personnel-people who work for North Korean refugee-related government or non-government organizations. Participants were four educational personnel at Hanawon* who taught North Korean refugees, five personnel from a refugee-related organizations run by religious institutions, one teacher from an alternative school for children refugees, one group-home manager, and one employee from a government organization for North Korean refugees. When two interviewees were from the same organization, they were interviewed consecutively, by adding interviews of the latter person to the prior interview content.

2) Research procedure

In-depth interviews were conducted on North Korean refugee-related informants and refugee families during from January to March of 2005. Interviews were conducted by a team of two professors of Child Development and Family Studies at Seoul National University and graduate students. We visited North Korean family's home and performed separate interviews for each individual. Interviews took one to three hours, at the most, in a comfortable setting. For refugee-related informants interviews, the research team visited their workplaces and

* Translation with note: A government organization to support North Korean refugees' settlement in South Korea. It is operated by the Ministry of Unification.

interviewed the individuals in an empty office for two to three hours.

The interview was based on semi-structured questions, and questions were improvised as they were subject to the interviewee's characteristics and interview situations. After the interviews, interviewees were paid in a token of gratitude. The interviews took two hours and thirty minutes on average, and it was recorded with prior consent from the interviewees. Significant details were written down for accurate understanding. Recorded interview materials were transcribed by the interviewers and trained students, and used for data analysis after confirmation of the transcriptions by the interviewers.

3) Research scales

Qualitative research utilized in-depth interviews based on a semi-structured questionnaire. A questionnaire used in the interview on North Korean refugee family was primarily based on literature and newspaper articles. Questions were restructured after each interview for later interviews. Questions were about adaption to the South Korean society and self-identity, which included introduction of one's family, border-crossing process and route, everyday life experiences, family relationship, and psychological adaptation.

For the interviews on refugee-related informants, two types of semi-structured questionnaires were prepared in respect to the interviewee's characteristics. A questionnaire included questions for informants whose work involves refugees in general. The questions included job description, understanding of the crossing, thoughts on refugees, one's relationship with refugees, adaptation of refugees, and psychological integration.

Another type of questionnaire for informants whose work involved children and adolescents refugees was formed with questions including job description, their understanding on the crossing, similarities and differences of South and North Korean children and adolescents, third country refugee experiences of the children and adolescents refugees, experience of settlement support centers, experiences of children in the South Korean society, and futures of children and adolescents refugees.

4) Demographic characteristics of the interviewees

Regional origins of the interviewed North Korean refugee families were concentrated in specific locations, one of which was Northern Hamgyeong province. Geographically close to the border with frequent contacts from China, and with its inferior life condition, Northern Hamgyeong province is the region with the highest border-crossing rate.

There were 26 males and 35 females in the interviews. There were more female participants (Table II-1). According to the border-crossing statistics, there are more female refugees than male refugees who make entry to South Korea (Ministry of Unification, 2006). Higher number of female refugees can be explained by the following reasons: Women are under less surveillance than men because most men belong to companies where they are under severe surveillance. Most households are sustaining by women's informal labor and exchange of goods after the food crisis. Employment and survival conditions are more favorable to women in China or other third countries. Specifically, among the study participants seven cases of child accompanied entry were by mothers, and only one case was accompanied by a father.

<Table II-1> Characteristics of the interviewed North Korean refugees

Case	Sex	Year of birth	Family status	Year of crossing	Year of entry	Origin	Occupation
A-1	F	1931	single	2002	2002	N. Hamgyeong	unemployed
B-1	F/M	1970/.	wife/ husband	1997	2001	N. Hamgyeong	insurance contractor/ unemployed
C-1	F	1959	mother	2003	2004	Yang-gang	unemployed
C-2	M	1981	1st son	2003	2004	N. Hamgyeong	unemployed
C-3	F	1983	1st daughter	1998	2003	Yang-gang	student
D-1	M	1971	husband	1998	2001	N. Hamgyeong	unemployed
D-2	F	1973	wife	1998	2001	N. Hamgyeong	part-timer
E-1	M	1961	husband	2004	2004	N. Hamgyeong	unemployed
E-2	F	1970	wife	2004	2004	N. Hamgyeong	part-timer
F-1	F	1965	mother	1999	2001	N. Hamgyeong	college student
F-2	F/F	1992/ 1995	1st daughter/ 2nd daughter	1999.09/ 2001.07	2001.02/ 2001	N. Hamgyeong	middle school student/ elementary school student
G-1	M	1956	father	1999	2001	N. Hamgyeong	driver
G-2	F	1958	mother	1999	2001	N. Hamgyeong	cleaner
G-3	M	1985	son	1999	2001	N. Hamgyeong	college student
G-4	F	1987	daughter	1999	2001	N. Hamgyeong	student
H-1	F	1953	mother	1997	2000	S. Hwanghae	lecturer
H-2	M	1979	1st son	1997	2000	S. Hwanghae	office worker
H-3	M	1981	2nd son	1998	2000	S. Hwanghae	college student
H-4	M	1984	3rd son	1998	1999	S. Hwanghae	college student
I-1	M	1965	father	1998	2002	N. Hamgyeong	office worker
I-2	F	1967	mother	1998	2002	N. Hamgyeong	housewife
I-3	M	1994	son	1998	2002	N. Hamgyeong	elementary school student
J-1	F	1967	mother	1999	2001	N. Hamgyeong	unemployed

J-2	F/F	1991/ 1993	1st daughter/ 2nd daughter	2003	2003	N. Hamgyeong	elementary school student
K-1	F	1970	mother	2001	2002	.	unemployed
K-2	F/F	.	1st daughter/ 2nd daughter	2001	2002	.	elementary school student
L-1	M	1961	father	1997	2000	Pyongyang	writer
L-2	M	1988	son	1998	2001	S. Hamgyeong	high school student
L-3	F	1990	daughter	1998	2001	S. Hamgyeong	elementary school student
M-1	M/F	1945/ 1947	father/ mother	1999/ 1999	2000/ 2000	N. Hamgyeong/ N. Hamgyeong	unemployed/ unemployed
M-2	F	1974	1st daughter	1999	2000	N. Hamgyeong	college student
M-3	M	1977	1st son	1999	2000	N. Hamgyeong	college student
M-4	F	1978	2nd daughter	1999	2000	N. Hamgyeong	college student
N-1	F	1953	mother	2001	2001	.	unemployed
N-2	F	1980	daughter	2003	2003	N. Hamgyeong	unemployed
N-3	M	1983	son	2001	2001	N. Hamgyeong	convenient store part-timer
O-1	M	1984	husband	1997	2000	N. Hamgyeong	owner of conve-nient store
O-2	F	1984	wife	1998	2002	N. Hamgyeong	housewife
P-1	M	1942	husband	2004	2004	N. Hamgyeong	apartment security guard
P-2	F	1944	wife	2004	2004	N. Hamgyeong	unemployed
Q-1	M	1965	father	2003	2004	N. Hamgyeong	unemployed
Q-2	F	1973	mother	2003	2004	N. Hamgyeong	housewife
Q-3	M	1993	son	2003	2004	N. Hamgyeong	student
R-1	M/F	1973/.	father/ mother	2004 /2004	2004/ 2004	N. Hamgyeong/ N. Hamgyeong	unemployed/ unemployed

R-2	M	1974	son	1997	2004	N. Hamgyeong	unemployed
S-1	F	1949	mother	1999	2004	N. Hamgyeong	unemployed
S-2	F	1976	daughter	1998	2002	N. Hamgyeong	unemployed
T-1	F	1971	single	1997	2003	N. Hamgyeong	housewife
U-1	M	1953	father	1996	2001	Gangwon	runs refugee center
U-2	M	1982	son	1996	2001	Gangwon	student
V-1	F	1959	mother	1998	.	N. Hamgyeong	unemployed
V-2	M	1960	South Korean husband	NA	NA	NA	unemployed
V-3	F/M	1985/ 1988	daughter/ son	1998/ 2000	2003/ 2005	N. Hamgyeong	student/student
W-1	F	1970	single	2004	2004	N. Pyeongan	unemployed

Note: Alphabet indicates household identification and the subsequent number indicates household member identification. NA means non applicable.

2. Quantitative research

1) Subjects

A survey questionnaire was used for the purpose of the quantitative research for North Korean refugees. The survey respondents were mostly North Korean refugees who made entry after 2000. Data were collected through a help of a newspaper company whose subscribers were North Korean refugees. The questionnaires were distributed along with the newspapers, and were recollected by the newspaper company. A total of 300 questionnaires were distributed, and 195 were collected from March to May of 2005.

2) Research scales

The survey was composed of the following questions: post-crossing changes, value orientation and thoughts on the North and the South, adaptation problems in South Korean life, individual psychological characteristics in the process of social adaptation, community and family support, and socio-demographic characteristics.

(1) Research scales for value orientation and thoughts on North- and South-Korean society

Research on value orientation and thoughts on both North and South Korea were composed of the following questions: 11 questions on changes made post crossing, 14 questions on their value orientation both in North and South Korea, and 14 questions on their perspectives about North and South Korean society. The section on changes made post-crossing is composed of 6 questions on positive changes, 4 questions on negative changes, and 1 question on religion. The section on value orientation both for North and South Korea is composed of 4 questions on materialistic values, 2 questions on collectivist values, 2 questions on individualistic values, 4 questions on family values, and 2 questions on gender role attitudes. The section on perspectives about North and South Korean society is composed of 3 questions on characteristics of North and South Korean society, 3 questions on the compliance of rules, 4 questions on free-competition, and 4 questions on respecting authority.

For reliability of the value orientation scale, Chronbach's alpha coefficient was measured. The alphas for materialistic value orientation in North and South Korea were .61 and .50, respectively. The alphas for collectivism value were .30 and .59, respectively. For individualism alpha values were .54 and .32, respectively. The alphas for gender role in North and South Korea were .54 and .39, respectively. The alphas of thoughts on North and South Korean society were as follows. The alphas for characteristics of North and South Korean society were .14 and .33, respectively; for compliance of rules were .67 and .70, respectively; for free-competition were .61 and .81, respectively; and for respective authority alpha values were .35 and .44, respectively.

Some scales such as collectivism value orientation had low reliability which could raise concerns regarding research results. These low reliability coefficients may imply that the existing scales are not appropriate in measuring North Korean refugees' perspectives.

(2) Research scales of adaptation in South Korean life

The section on examining adaptation and difficulties in South Korean life is composed of 9 questions of what they have done in South Korea, 12 questions on adaptation problems in South Korea, and 12 questions on current difficulties. In addition to 12 questions on current difficulties, an open-ended question was provided for participants to write about their problems freely. Twelve questions on adaptation in South Korean life were constructed in accordance to a survey used in *A Study on Family Stability and Social Adjustment of North Korean Refugees and Women's Role* (Jang & Kim, 2000). Subscales of adaptation in South Korean life were composed of 4 questions on restraints in social activities, 3 questions on personal discrimination, 2 questions on psychological problems, and 3 questions on social alienation (Table II-2).

For reliability of the scale, Chronbach's coefficient was measured. The total alpha value was .80. The alpha value for difficulties in social and cultural adaptation was .72; personal discrimination was .70; psychological problems was .57; and social alienation was .65.

<Table II-2> Composition of research scales for adaptation of South Korean life

Classification	Items	No. of items	Scale/ Reliability (α)
Socio-cultural adaptation	1. I cannot participate in social activities. 2. I avoid meeting people from fear of others. 3. I have a hard time understanding unfamiliar language (Chinese or foreign language) that is used in South Korea. 4. I cannot adjust to South Korean culture.	4	.72
Personal discrimination	5. I feel discriminated by others even though people do not tell me directly. 6. I have a hard time catching up with work and work life. 7. People have biases against me.	3	.70
Emotional difficulties	8. I suffer from missing my hometown. 9. I feel guilty for the fact that I left family members and relatives in North Korea.	2	.57
Social alienation	10. I feel I have a low social status due to the fact that I came from North Korea. 11. I do not feel like I belong to South Korean society. 12. I cannot adjust to the South Korean judicial system.	3	.65

(3) Research scales of individual psychological characteristics

Scales of psychological characteristics of North Korean refugee are composed of 9 questions on self-esteem, 11 questions on depression, 5 questions on satisfaction (Table II-3), 9 questions on attribution styles, and 10 questions on identity. Nine questions in the self-esteem scale were based on the scales developed by Rogenberg (Rogenberg, 1965), and the reliability coefficient was .69. For depression and satisfaction, scales used in *The Life Course of Poor Female Household Heads* (Ok & Sung, 2004) were modified for this study. The reliability coefficient for the depression and satisfaction scales were .82 and .75, respectively. For attribution style, the Korean version of attribution scale constructed by Levenson

<Table II-3> Composition of satisfaction scale

Classification (α)	Items	No. of items	Reliability (α)
Satisfaction	1. I am satisfied with my health. 2. I am satisfied with my life at work. 3. I am satisfied with my relationship with friends. 4. I am satisfied with myself. 5. I am satisfied with my surrounding environment up until now.	5	.75

<Table II-4> Falsehood scale of MMPI

Items
1. I sometimes have extremely bad thoughts that cannot be put in words. 2. I sometimes feel like cursing at people. 3. I do not always tell truths. 4. I do not always read newspaper editorials everyday. 5. I sometimes get angry. 6. I sometimes put aside work that needs to be done today until tomorrow. 7. I feel irritated when I am not feeling good. 8. My table manner at home isn't as good as when I eat outside with others. 9. I would sneak into a movie theater if I wouldn't get caught. 10. I would rather want to win the game than to lose. 11. I want to be friends with powerful people. 12. I do not like everyone I know. 13. I sometimes talk bad about others. 14. I sometimes vote for someone I do not know well. 15. I sometimes laugh at dirty jokes.

(Ahn, 1986) was used. Internal attribution scale's reliability coefficient was .41. Ten questions on identity formation were constructed based on the previous studies and results from qualitative research.

In addition, falsehood among North Korean refugees' characteristics was examined using Minnesota Multiphasic Personality Inventory (MMPI). The falsehood test, composed of 15 questions, has two functions-as examining genuineness of the responses and measuring psychological problems (Table II-4).

(4) Research scales of social support and family resilience

A measuring scale for resilience of society and family is composed of 10 questions on social support from surrounding people and 16 questions of measuring cohesion and adaptation of family. The subscale for social support by family members is composed of 3 questions on emotional support, 3 questions on physical support, 2 questions on informational support, and 2 questions on leisure support. The Korean translated version (Ok & Sung, 2004) of FACES II, which was constructed by Olson et al., was adapted as a measuring tool for cohesion and adaptation of family.

The reliability tests for research tools were conducted. The alpha value for the scale of social support was .85. In terms of subscales, the alphas for emotional support, instrumental support, informational support, and leisure support were .60, .65, .78, and .49, respectively

<Table II-5> Composition of research scales for social support

Classification	Items	No. of items	Reliability (α)
Emotional support	1. People visit me when I am sick or lonely. 4. People acknowledge that I am an important person. 6. People are available for consultation in times of difficulties.	3	.60
Instrumental support	2. People lend me money when I am in need. 5. People lend me materials when I suddenly need them. 9. People help me when I need hands.	3	.65
Informational support	7. People provide me with information and methods to get along well with others. 8. People provide me with information when I need to make an important decision.	2	.78
Leisure support	3. People visit me without any reason. 10. People go out and eat with me.	2	.49

<Table II-6> Composition of family resilience scales

Classification	Items	No. of items	Reliability (α)
Cohesion	1. Members of my family help each other out when faced with difficulties. 4. Members of my family communicate about each other's daily lives. 6. I do whatever I want to do at home whereas I obey rules outside the house.* 10. Members of my family are more close to people other than family members.* 11. Members of my family accept a decision made by other members. 13. Members of my family like to rest or play together. 14. Members of my family like to be alone when they are at home.* 16. Members of my family are close to only a few members of the family.*	8	.38
Adaptability	2. Members of my family can easily share their thoughts to each other. 3. Every member of my family participates in deciding an important family matter. 5. Members of my family discuss a way to solve problems. 7. Members of my family share household chores. 8. Members of my family follow rules such as time of returning home or forbidding over-night stay at another place. 9. Members of my family can freely communicate with each other. 12. Members of my family share household chores and take responsibility of their work. 15. Members of my family are reluctant to share their thoughts to each other.*	8	.70

* decoded item

(Table II-5). In addition, the alpha for family cohesion was .38, and family adaptability was .70 (Table II-6). Overall reliabilities of research tools used were acceptable except for leisure support and family cohesion. Because items on shared time or activities with family are included in the family cohesion scale, it may be inappropriate to use as a tool to measure family bonding of North Korean refugee families.

The questions of research tools discussed earlier were measured using a 5-point Likert Scale consisting of "not at all" as 1 point and "very much so" as 5 points. Higher scores indicate greater tendencies of behaving in respect to the question. In addition, participants' background characteristics were included in the survey, which encompassed age, gender, religion, time of crossing, time of entry, third country before the entry to South Korea, accompanied family members, resident area in North Korea, education level in North Korea, school experience in South Korea, family income, main source of income, and current occupation.

3) Research analysis

A total of 195 surveys were encoded and then statistically analyzed using SAS and SPSS programs. Frequency, percentage, and means were calculated for the participants' socio-demographic characteristics, changes of values and thoughts in North and South Korea, current adaptation problems in South Korean life, individual psychological characteristics of social adaptation process, and family and social support. Paired t-test was conducted for examining differences of values and thoughts in North and South Korea. T-test and ANOVA were conducted to examine results from independent variables including participants' gender, age, education level, family-accompanied, time of crossing-border, time of entry, and third country before the entry.

4) Socio-demographic characteristics of the subjects

Socio-demographic characteristics of the subjects are shown in <Table II-7>. Data collected through the survey reveals the rate of missing response in each item. In general, North Korean refugees were reluctant in providing personal information in fear of getting oneself revealed. The missing response rates were high in the items on family-accompanied crossing, current occupation, family income and source of income. Missing value problems show the limitation of research with North Korean refugees through surveys. They were extremely cautious about exposing their personal information in respect to one's security and protecting remaining family members in North Korea rather than to protect personal privacy.

In the table, the socio-demographic characteristics are presented including missing responses. As for gender, the proportion of female participants (55 %) was slightly greater than that of male participants (42 %). Since there is a far greater number of female refugees, a survey research tends to oversample females. To overcome such limitations, we made a request to the newspaper company so that there would be an equal rate of male and female participants in the survey.

In terms of age, the 30s was the highest (43.59 %) followed by the 20s (24.10 %). In terms of the time of border-crossing, only 20 respondents exited prior to 1997 (10.26 %), whereas 54 respondents (27.69 %) exited in 1998 (27.69 %), and 35 in 1999 (17.95 %), adding up to about half of the total participants. This figure demonstrates the fact that the number of refugees has rapidly increased since 1998, which had the most severe food shortage. For the time of entry to South Korea, 2004 had the highest number of refugees with 60 participants (30.77 %) entered in 2004. Ninety percent of the total respondents were refugees who entered after 2001, with less than 5 years of stay in South Korea.

Among the participants, 74 people (37.95 %) made family-accompanied crossings, and 91 people (46.67 %) crossed alone. In terms of marital status, 65 participants were single (33.33 %) and 117 were married

(60 %). In respect to respondents' occupation, 39 (20 %) were employed as white-color workers and blue-color workers, 31 (15.9 %) were contingent workers, and 51 (26.15 %) were looking for employment. Thirty-five participants (17.95 %) were students at a regular school or a qualification examination preparation institution. In terms of religion, 86 people (44.10 %) were Christians, 11 (5.64 %) were Roman Catholics, 7 (3.59 %) were Buddhists, 30 (15.39 %) believed in other religions, and 40 (20.51 %) had no religion.

In terms of the source of income, 86 respondents (44.10 %) were dependent on their labor income or that of their spouse, 36 respondents (18.46 %) were dependent on settlement funds of government, and 41 respondents (21.03 %) were dependent on government subsidies for basic living expenses. It was found that only 44 % of participating refugees were living on their labor income.

The rate of missing response was high in the socio-demographic characteristics questions. The missing response was even higher in questions related to personal life such as marital status, current occupation, and source of income. Such response tendencies can be interpreted as a factor hindering the reliability of the research data. Nonetheless, due to the lack of empirical data on North Korean refugees, collected data for this research was used. In examining research questions, missing values were left out in the analysis, requiring careful interpretation of research results. Therefore, the results of this study may only be interpreted as an initial attempt to explore the experiences of North Korean refugees.

<Table II-7> Socio-demographic characteristics of North Korean refugees

(N=195)

Variable	Category	Frequency (%)	Variable	Category	Frequency (%)
Sex	Male	81 (41.54)	Year of crossing	Before 1995	1 (0.51)
	Female	107 (54.87)		1996	7 (3.6)
	No response	7 (3.59)		1997	12 (6.15)
Age	Under 20	25 (12.82)		1998	54 (27.69)
	20–29	47 (24.10)		1999	35 (17.95)
	30–39	85 (43.59)		2000	19 (9.74)
	40–49	24 (12.31)		2001	19 (9.74)
	50–59	8 (4.10)		2002	15 (7.7)
	Over 60	6 (3.08)		2003	19 (9.74)
Border-crossing status	Family-accompanied	74 (37.95)		2004	7 (3.59)
	Single	91 (46.67)		No response	7 (3.59)
	No response	30 (15.38)	Year of entry	Before 1995	1 (0.51)
Marital status	Single	65 (33.33)		1995–2000	12 (6.15)
	Married	117 (60.00)		2001	19 (9.74)
	No response	13 (6.67)		2002	39 (20)
Religion	None	40 (20.51)		2003	55 (28.21)
	Christianity	86 (44.10)		2004	60 (30.77)
	Buddhism	7 (3.59)		2005	1 (0.51)
	Roman Catholic	11 (5.64)		No response	8 (4.10)
	Others	30 (15.39)	Under-aged family members	Yes	28 (14.4)
	No response	21 (10.77)			
Current occupation	Office worker	24 (12.31)		No	167 (85.6)
	Factory worker	15 (7.69)			
	Contingent worker	31 (15.9)	Source of income	Labor income	86 (44.10)
	Unemployed	21 (10.77)		Settlement fund	36 (18.46)

Current occupation	Housework	6 (3.08)	Source of income	Government aid	41 (21.03)
	In school	29 (14.87)		Others	5 (2.57)
	Employment institute	30 (15.38)		No response	25 (12.82)
	Educational institute	6 (3.08)	Living arrangement	With family	76 (38.97)
	Others	7 (3.59)		Single	109 (55.90)
	No response	26 (13.33)		No response	10 (5.13)

III

Border-Crossing Experience by North Korean Refugees

This chapter tries to examine the process of North Korean refugees' socio-psychological changes, their resources, and factors that contribute to their resilience as they describe their border-crossing experience. Border-crossing experience can be described in various ways according to research objectives. For example, in order to understand North Korean refugees' size, motive, origin, and background or route they took to enter South Korea, one study provided statistical data related to such information (Kim, 2005). Another study focused on North Korean refugees' difficulties in psychological and sociological problems, and the study tried to find factors that would cause such problems through their experiences (Jeon, 2000).

This chapter describes subjective experiences of North Korean refugees' border-crossing process or their life in a third country, and the difficulties and crises they have experienced after they entered South Korea, instead of focusing only on actual statistical data or problems. By describing such experiences, this chapter tries to look into positive factors that helped them to survive and adjust in adverse situations. This chapter corresponds to the qualitative study, which focuses on individual and family resilience that helps North Korean refugees' psychological adaptation. This chapter's content, combined with the quantitative study in later chapters, will help readers to understand North Korean refugees' experiences in depth.

Since our interest is on North Korean refugees who became South Korean citizens, this chapter will cover not only their experiences in North Korea, a third country, or their border-crossing process, but also their entry process, and experiences in South Korea. Thus, the first part of this chapter will briefly describe their border-crossing in actual context. The second part of this chapter will describe their lives in North Korea and their decision to exit. The third part will describe their experience in a third country including China. The fourth part will describe their experience in entering and living in South Korea. Lastly, in the fifth part, resources used in the border-crossing process and adaptation in South Korea will be described.

In the sections "North Korean refugees' life in North Korea" and "Experience in a third country" we focused on internal factors that pushed them out of North Korea to a third country, external factors that pulled them to a third country or South Korea, their decisive opportunities to exit North Korea, and crisis they have experienced. This would help us to focus on the psychological and social experiences and conflicts they encountered during the border-crossing process. Simultaneously, it would also allow us to discover psychological and social implications in regard to North Korean refugees, or perhaps the North and South Koreans after unification.

Rather than illustrating general and objective characteristics of North Korean refugees' experiences during the crossing process, this study will present various experiences that are individual and subjective. This is because we found that refugees' crossing process and experience during the process differs by individual families. Therefore, we focus on the description of factors that maintain and recover individual's and family's psychological and sociological integration, which are processed through resilience of the individual and the family.

We have discovered some matters to consider in understanding and describing North Korean refugees' process of border-crossing, entry to and adaptation in South Korea. We have illustrated these accordingly. First, North Korean refugees not only have their own perception and interpretation, but also report selectively on the same experience according to individual characteristics and views. In some cases, refugees moderate facts to give legitimacy to their crossing or their actions and judgment in the crossing process. For example, in a case where one of the relatives was arrested and executed for trying to contact another relative in South Korea, a husband and a wife reported differently. The husband (Q-1) reported that his close relative had contacted his grandfather simply to find his family, and yet, was questioned and ultimately executed by the North Korean National Security Intelligence Service. On the other hand, his wife (Q-2) reported that the relative was heavily in debt with some financial problems and the reason for contacting the grandfather was to disengage him from debt. Hence, if the relative were able to deal with some economic problems, he probably would not have been executed. In another example, many participants expressed their hardships in their crossing process and life in South Korea. Among them, a small minority even expressed that they wanted to go back to North Korea. Meanwhile, other refugees expressed that although they had difficulties, such experiences have made them "special" and they tried to have a new prospect on their life (H-4). In this way, it is useless for a scholar to verify which are more to the actual fact when different interpretations and meanings exist in the same situation. Thus, even if the descriptions that each person gave were different, all of the contents will be used as valid data. Since this study tries to understand the process of making a decision and adapting to a new environment in times of difficulty, where subjects experienced crises in North Korea, in a third country, and in South Korea, understanding their subjective experience is crucial.

Second, the border-crossing experience, if possible, was analyzed in a family unit. If an individual had exited from North Korea through a different route or had an unusual experience, such an experience was described additionally and the explanation for such differences was described in an additional page when needed. For instance, in the case where participants lived with family at the time of the interview, and yet, their crossing and entry to South Korea were done individually (D-1, D-2), they probably had different experiences. For such cases, each member was put into an analysis unit. As members of the same family, they would have the same experiences in South Korea, but when there are different experiences at different ages and developmental stages, such experiences were dealt with individually.

Third, North Korean refugees' experiences of poverty, political inequality, or school education are experiences from their special circumstances and this should not be generalized in reflecting the North Korean society as a whole. That is, most experiences of North Korean refugees are limited to residents of Northern Hamgyeong province or people who have contacts in South Korea. In other words, they might have had a different experience if they were not residents of Northern Hamgyeong province, or if they were from a higher social class. Therefore, North Korean refugees' experiences described in this chapter must be understood as unique cases experienced differently depending on an individual's residential area, class, developmental stage, and not as the general circumstance of North Koreans as a whole.

Lastly, we did not reveal our participants' names, their border-crossing routes, origins, name of locations, and dates because such information is not critical in this study. Remaining family members in North Korea or perhaps the refugees themselves might be in danger if such information is revealed.

1. Border-crossing process of North Korean refugees

Prior to examining North Korean refugees' crossing and decision making processes, we present background data that are needed to understand our interview contents. These data were obtained from other research and official statistics. The data are as follows.

1) Size of North Korean refugees

For several reasons, it is difficult to estimate the exact number of people who have crossed North Korea. Firstly, border-crossing by North Korean residents happens very secretively. Secondly, refugees living in a third country such as China live in hiding from the Chinese police. Thirdly, the crossings happen in large masses, yet very privately. Lastly, the term "North Korean refugee" is vague, causing disagreements in defining the term the definition of "North Korean refugee" among organizations that compute statistical data (Kim, 2005). And yet, the estimated sizes of North Korean refugees presented by research organizations or NGOs are as shown in <Table III-1>.

<Table III-1> Estimated numbers of North Korean refugees

Organization (year)	Estimated number	Source
The UN Refugee Agency (UNHCR)	30,000	Assumption
US Committee for Refugees and Immigrants (USCR 2003)	100,000–300,000	Assumption
Commission to Help North Korea (CNKR, 2002)	50,000	Increase of forced return, improvement of food supply
Good Friends (1999)	Max. 300,000	Research
North Korean Human Rights (2004)	100,000	Research
The Christian Commission of Korea	Long-term sojourner /100,000–300,000 Short-term sojourner/over 1,000,000	Report from local missionary
Mistry of Foreign Affairs and Trade (1999.6)	10,000–30,000	Assumption
Government of Jilin	4,000–8,000 per year	Informal assumption
Kim, Ha-Joong (the formal Korean ambassador to China) (2002.9)	Tens of thousands	Assumption

Source: Kim (2005)

2) Origins of North Korean refugees

From 1995 to June 2004, North Korean refugees who became citizens of South Korea mostly originated from Northern Hamgyeong province (65.8 %), Southern Hamgyeong province (11.7 %), followed by Pyeongan province (8.1 %), and Pyongyang (4.2 %). Most North Korean refugees who participated in this study were from Hamgyeong province.

3) Motives for border-crossing

When research on North Korean refugees' border-crossing motives was examined, the most significant motive was poverty. According to Yoon (2004), prior to 1999, political motives constituted 83.7 % of the refugee population, whereas economic motives constituted 77.8 % after year 2000, which shows a dramatic change in border-crossing motives before and after 2000. The number of North Korean refugees gradually

<Table III-2> Yearly trend of North Korean refugees' size and exit motivations

Year	Poverty	Fear of punish-ment	Ideo-logical dissatis-faction	Family-accom-panied crossing	Settle in China	Family troubles	Others	Total
1995	0	24	5	7	4	1	0	41 (0.5)
1996	0	21	10	20	3	2	0	56 (0.7)
1997	6	12	16	42	9	1	0	86 (1.1)
1998	11	20	9	18	9	4	0	71 (0.9)
1999	27	32	39	41	4	5	0	148 (1.9)
2000	127	66	52	51	13	2	1	312 (4.0)
2001	293	73	33	171	7	2	4	583 (7.4)
2002	606	93	96	259	37	39	9	1,139 (14.5)
2003	774	80	123	194	46	53	11	1,281 (16.3)
2004	1,125	104	156	401	12	87	9	1,894 (24.1)
2005	849	81	96	308	7	36	6	1,383 (17.6)
2006.6	543	39	19	208	4	24	17	854 (10.9)
Total	4,361 (55.6)	645 (8.2)	654 (8.3)	1,720 (21.9)	155 (1.9)	256 (3.3)	57 (0.7)	7,848 (100.0)

Data: Ministry of Unification's National Assembly inspection on government offices (2006)

increased between 1995 and 1998, and the number doubled almost every year from 1998 to 2002. Then, the number dropped noticeably from 2003 (Table III-2).

This phenomenon, according to L-1's interview, is probably due to the fact that from 1995 to 1998, border-crossing was life-threatening, whereas opportunities for the crossing increased toward the end of 1999.

> Of course, at that time, we took a risk… crossing mainly has two aspects. From 1995 to 1998, North Koreans tried life-threatening crossing. The crossing was upon their lives. But from 1999, North Korean refugees in China sent money to border garrisons, or money came from North Korea directly to them. Anyways, border garrisons started to take money and in return they began to let North Korean refugees out of the country. So, the crossing from 1999 till present can be seen as planned crossing or business crossing. Before that, soldiers didn't allow crossing for the sake of money. (L-1)

4) Border-crossing routes

North Korean refugees mainly use the northern border area (the Tumen Basin, the Yalu Basin, Mount Baekdu valley). For the Tumen, as it is upstream and closer to Mount Baekdu, the river width is narrow and the depth of water is shallow, which allows people to cross the river easily. In the case of the downstream of Tumen, other than flooding season, the wave is relatively gentle and the depth of the water is shallow, making river-crossing possible. In the winter, the frozen river allows river-crossings. Crossing through the Yalu is rare not only because of its deep water depth, wide width, and severe security, but also because of the small number of Chosun-zok (Korean Chinese) living across the Yalu.

Mount Baekdu valley is a mountain region, which makes it difficult for Chinese police to access the area, and allows refugees to easily find a hiding place. Moreover, many Chosun-zok residences near Mount Baekdu valley allows refugees to adapt themselves to a new environment easily after crossing (Kim, M, 2004).

5) The third country and the length of stay

North Korean refugees live in a third country for a while after exiting from North Korea. The length of stay differs from person to person, but it is inevitable to stop at a third country since Korea is divided. The third countries include China, Thailand, the Union of Myanmar, and Lao People's Democratic Republic.

Countries where North Korean refugees stayed and the length of stay are as follows. According to *GOODFRIENDS*[*]' research in 1999, 55 % of the participating refugees lived in Yanbian Korean Autonomous Prefecture and 45 % lived in Liaoning, Jilin, or Heilongjiang three provinces of Dongbei. On the other hand, as for the length of stay of North Korean refugees living in the Northeastern area of China is observed, 74.6 % live in the Yanbian area within the first three months of the crossing and as the stay lengthens, the rate of refugees living in Dongbei increases (Table III-3). This shows that most refugees live in the Yanbian area right after they cross the border, but they return to North Korea or move to different regions as time passes (Kim, 2005).

The shortest route to enter South Korea is through Beijing from Yanji or Dongbei. Other routes that pass through China start from

[*] Translation with note: *GOODFRIENDS* is Korean NGO working for peace, human rights of North Koreans and refugee assistance.

<Table III-3> The refugees' length of stay in Northeastern China

Length of stay	Less that 3 months	3–6 months	More than 6 months
Yanbian	74.6 %	14.0 %	11.4 %
Three provinces of Dongbei	19.4 %	31.0 %	48.8 %
Total	50.3 %	20.9 %	28.8 %

Report on North Korean refugees' status and human rights by *GOODFRIENDS* (3).

Dongbei to various regions in China, to the Union of Myanmar, or to Thailand. Routes rarely pass through Lao People's Democratic Republic or Mongolia. For many refugees, going to South Korea wasnt their first choice. They simply wanted to have a better life in China rather than settling in South Korea. However, they decided to enter South Korea after experiencing push factors that force them out of China and pull factors from Korea.

The place or method of stay were varied: cases in which refugees received financial help from relatives in China while living in a stranger's house; cases in which refugees stayed at a local house until migrating refugees were filled; and cases in which refugees worked at temporary jobs or run business in China.

2. Refugees' lives in North Korea

The refugees' lives in North Korea will be described in the following six stages. First, the lives of refugees when they were in North Korea will be described. This part will help us to understand not only the general life style, but also various financial, social, and psychological resources they used in North Korea. Second, difficulties and conflicts that refugees experienced for long in North Korea before they left the country will be illustrated. This will help us to understand their motives for the crossing. In this part, internal factors that pushed refugees out of North Korea will be discussed. Third, external factors that pulled refugees out of North Korea will be discussed. Fourth, factors that made refugees hesitate to cross the border will be discussed. This study tries to examine conflicts they faced in deciding to cross the border by discussing such factors. Fifth, determinant factors that led North Korean refugees, who faced conflicts between the stimulating factor and the hesitating factor, to decide to escape from North Korea will be discussed. This is because the refugees' wish to leave their adverse lives and carrying out the actual crossing process are completely different. Therefore, this study tries to examine direct causes of crossing, and finally the preparation process and actual crossing process will be briefly described.

1) Life in North Korea

We have to recall that even though life in North Korea was difficult, refugees adapted to that environment in a way or another. By and large, there were two ways in which they had adapted to their society.

One way is to become a party member adopting to the North Korean regime or to become a member of the society by acquiring professional skills and knowledge by their utmost efforts. People who chose to take this way decided to live in the North Korean society as a member of the party. They were also the kind of people who could be a member or professional since they had intellectual and professional abilities. They were financially better off than other classes more or less, and since they were politically stable, they could live in North Korean society unless there was other definite cause.

Among refugees living in South Korea, there were people who had stable jobs without experiencing any financial difficulty. Among manual workers, people working in restaurants were relatively well off. Government officers, soldiers, Public Relations (PR) for politics or writers were better off as well.

> My family was well-off in North Korea. Honestly, people were dying of hunger at that period of time. There were people dying of hunger and people earning money at the same time. My family belonged to the latter group. My family-in-law and my family didn't have any desires to leave the country.
> (Interviewer: What did your father do?)
> He managed in XYZ. Well, he was a government officer and we made a living from my mother's work.
> (Interviewer: How did your mom make money?)
> My mother did business after working at a restaurant. Working at a restaurant is good in North Korea because food they eat are different. It's difficult to get a job at a restaurant, and they are considered to be rich. You know, they don't have any problems eating. Not many people would have left, if they didn't have food shortage. People wouldn't defect. They would just live there. They are naïve. They ate whatever they had, and did whatever they were told, and it was okay. (B-1)

People with professions like doctors had rather decent lives. This was not because they received pay-checks, but rather, they sometimes had additional income from treating patients in China.

> Doctors weren't receiving any pay-checks nor rations since 1996. But, we still had to go to work. If we don't show up at work, we are tracked

> down by the military. We couldn't do anything else… but we started to cross the Tumen after we stopped receiving rations. I was a doctor, so I could make home visits to the local district. Then, I received things they gave me as compensation. I can't ask for it, but if they offered, I took it. (A-1)

Likewise, people with financial stability left sometimes, and their reason was not poverty or adverse livelihoods. Rather, the reasons were because their political status was at stake, they were in danger due to family members' crossings, or they became aware of life conditions of other countries and relative poverty. Details of these causes will be discussed later.

Second, unlike people described earlier, the following is about those with financial risks who could not be members of the party nor become professionals. After food shortages and the worsened economy from mid 1990s, these people had to survive. They dug or gathered anything of some value from neighboring seas and mountains to buy food, or they took risks by taking journeys to China or other regions in North Korea to get some help.

> If your business is too big, they take it away. (…) We barely live day by day. If we go fishing that day… we catch fish in the sea… then we sell them. If we sell fish, we buy some rice with the earnings. We go fishing again when we run out of rice… (I-2)

> I didn't have a job when I was in North Korea, only my husband worked. We did this kind of business. It is hard for five people to live as one family. So, in the spring, we went out and picked edible greens and came home in the evening. We went out at 5 in the morning. Mountains

> were far away. So when we went out in the morning, we arrived there at noon. We ate meals on the way to the mountain. On the way back home, we got hungry so we ate the greens we picked. We had to arrive home by 5 o'clock. When we arrived, my grandmother boiled water to parboil greens to prepare it for selling. We had to sell it to get something to eat at night. In the spring, we picked wild greens, in the summer, we picked berries, and in the fall, we picked hazelnuts, and then we cut wood. (N-1)

People who had relatives in China or Japan were better off. Although there was always a chance of being caught, it was easier to contact people in North Korea from China. As long as they do not contact South Koreans, they will not be punished harshly. So, when they had a major financial crisis, they could ask their relatives in China or Japan for help. The following shows such a case.

> We lost contact with our relative in Japan. My mother heard that it would be easier to make contact from China so (...) Mother made a decision to leave. I think she exited to get help from a relative.
> (Interviewer: You didn't think she would go to South Korea?)
> No. I didn't at all. She didn't even think of going to China. She heard that if she goes to the border of Yanbian, she could make contact easily and that's why she left. So, she didn't think of going to China or even South Korea. (H-4)

2) North Korea's internal factors that pushed North Korean refugees out

There are two main factors that intensify North Koreans' desire to exit. One factor is internal, which pushes people out of North Korea and the other is external, which pulls them out of North Korea from the outside.

North Korea's internal factors that push North Koreans out of North Korea are very complex. In the experiences described by North Korean refugees, serveral factors have worked together in making a decision to exit North Korea. Moreover, there would be more factors that weren't included in North Korean refugees' interviews. Nonetheless, based on North Korean refugees' subjective perspective, push factors that forced them out of North Korea can be summarized as 1) worsened economy, 2) inferior social environment, and 3) political and sociological discrimination. These factors are not decisive factors that triggered the crossing. And yet, these are factors stimulated North Koreans' needs to escape from North Korea and pushed them out of the country.

(1) Worsened economy and food supply problems

North Korean refugees reported that North Korean economy was not so serious until 1990s. The economy was still endurable until the death of Kim, Il-Sung in 1995, but it rapidly got worsened after 1995. That is, the amount of rations decreased from the early to mid 1990s. Until 1993, when the rations were temporarily stopped, missing rations were redistributed as economy got better. From 1994, the rations were discontinued many times and redistribution of missing rations lessened. Amount of ration rapidly dropped as well.

> We didn't think about it until 1995. But we began to think from 1996 because of food. When Kim, Il-Sung died in 1995 and Kim, Jong-Il took over, people started to die from starvation. It became very difficult from 1996 to 1998, so in 1998 (…) People said we could have some food in China… (Q-2)

> The worst times were 1997 and 1998. Rations weren't distributed well before that. About 5 years ago, rations weren't distributed on time. It was, so to speak, for us to starve for a while and if food comes at once, we had to wait in line from dawn to get one ration. If rice was gone, we had to go back home without anything. So, people risked their lives to get some rice. (I-2)

The greatest decrease of rations occurred between 1996 and 1998, which resulted in decreased ration not only for regular citizens, but also for public organizations that were considered to be the first priority. Even the army, who had the best food supply at that time, was affected as well. When food supply got worse, soldiers sometimes plundered food from residents. Yet, residents could not do anything about it because they also knew that soldiers had to supplement what was taken by their superiors. They could not hate the soldiers for taking their food because they sometimes heard their relative or friend's children died of hunger in the army.

> So to speak, when people are searched by the army or a guard or whatever, their belongings are taken away. Even soldiers take away snacks from elders coming from a relative's house. (...)
> In fact, there's no one whose children aren't in the army. All children were sent to the army. (...) People can't do anything about things taken away by the army. (...) When military officials order soldiers to bring food, soldiers have to take whatever they can and give it to them. (...) Soldiers' faces were swollen from malnutrition and were dying. How can they make it home even if they wanted to? There aren't any trains or cars, and it takes at least a few days to a month to get home. So, they die on the way, or if someone dies in the army, they send a notice to the family.

> Since they have to deliver the notice on foot, they send notices when there are about 10 dead soldiers. So, a resident at my place was notified about his son's death in February, when the son died actually in April of the year before. (A-1)

As North Korean economy worsened, North Korean refugees not only experienced severe food shortages and poverty directly, but also experienced psychological shock by witnessing the deaths of their neighbors and corpses lying all over the place. A few of the worst cases heard from North Korean refugees are as follow.

> Everybody died from starvation. My mother-in-law passed away from hunger as well. It's true. Everyday, more corpses piled up. A person I saw the day before was dead next day. Many children and elders died. Anyways, my neighbor's husband dug up arrowroots to provide something to eat for his family. One day he went to dig up arrowroots, and he died in the mountain because he couldn't get down... One father gave a piggyback ride to his son. Then, a Korean-Chinese gave him some food to feed his son. We don't think he fed his child. He ate it all. Because next day, the kid was dead and he was all swollen up. (...) The father was okay. The more people die, the more orphans we have. As more people enter China, the more remaining people die from hunger. (B-1)

> It was okay until 1995. Death from starvation increased in 1996. It was around 1996 and 1997. (...) Let me tell you how bad it was. There were piles of corpses... whether dead or alive, I don't know, in front of a train station. When I went to xx station, there was this guy standing by the wall whose face was covered with orange color fungus because he

> couldn't eat nor wash. It was 1996. As we walked out of school, friends screamed because there was a dead body at the gate of the school, and we saw a crow eating it. (G-4)

The sudden decrease of rations and the worsened economy resulted in plundering by soldiers and death from starvation, which then led individual and social insecurity. Such economic status raised motivations for North Korean refugees to exit North Korea. However, a bad economy was not the sole factor, and surely not a direct factor, that pushed North Koreans out from North Korea. Factors that pushed citizens out from North Korea are degraded living conditions, and political and social discrimination.

(2) Degraded living conditions

One factor that pushed North Korean refugees from North Korea is the inferior social environment. The degraded living conditions they describe include conditions of education, transportation, and electricity.

As the economy worsened, some teachers did not show up at school, and started to work illegally in commerce in order to maintain a living. At the same time, many students did not come to school. According to a former professor (case I-1), student attendance rates were less than 10 % in 1997. There were several reasons for not attending school, such as bad economy, students' engaging in other occupations, or malnutrition.

> We experienced food shortages from the early 1990s while I was still a professor at that school. As life became impoverished, student attendance rates gradually dropped from the mid 1990s. The attendance rate was less than 10 % in 1997. At that time, many professors and student passed away. I was very worried about the future… (I-1)

The transportation situation in North Korea can be understood through case H-2, which describes the experience of a mother and her first-born son who went to China, and cases H-3 and H-4, which describe the stories of a second and a third son who went back and forth to the border near Tumen from Hwanghae province 4 to 5 times to meet their mom and brother. According to these individuals, people need a pass to travel to other provinces. And even with the pass, sometimes trains do not pass by for a few days, which made them run out of prepared food and beg for food.

> My elder brother and I went off after a month. We missed Mother a lot, and she told us to come after a month. Since it was school vacation, we went off to meet Mother by ourselves. We didn't know what was coming. (…) We suffered a lot. We didn't know how long it would take to get there. I think it took us about 2 weeks to get there. We only prepared a week's amount of food, and who knew that it would take so long! We stayed at this one train station for three days. Three days! People were all on board, but a diesel locomotive to pull the train was missing. Some people got off to go on foot. We were about to do that, but decided to wait a while longer. The diesel locomotive came in three days and pulled the train. We starved from then on. Since we ran out of food, we asked people to give some of what they were eating. Mother gave us this address and how this is how we got there. (H-4)

Another significant experience was the limited supply of electricity. Some parts of North Korea only had a few hours of electricity a day. The metropolis like Pyongyang did not have such problems, but the situation got worse in rural areas.

> It was as if the whole country was a prison without the bars. We only had electricity for thirty minutes a day. It came during the daytime. We had dinner very early. You know, people cannot sleep forever. We went to bed around 8 PM in the summer and around 5 PM in the winter. It was dark everywhere, and when I woke up, it was only 10 PM. Then, I tried to go to bed again. When I woke up again, it was still midnight. (...) Candles were expensive. (P-2)

Inferior social circumstances do not directly act as a decision-making factor for the crossing. However, such circumstances provoke desires to exit and act as factors for people to leave North Korea when an opportunity comes around.

(3) Political and social discrimination

Political and social discrimination does not refer to sudden threats to one's political and social status, which will be discussed in *'Determining momentum for crossing'*. It refers to a long-term discrimination that lies within the entire society on people with an insecure political status. Although these factors do not serve as direct reasons for crossing, they provide a background and situation for the crossing.

In the North Korean society, if one does not have a good social status, one has a very insecure political status and faces difficulties in climbing the social and political ladder. People treated as "harmful" refers to people who had been engaged in an organization formed by the South Korean army during the Korean War, people who worked for Japanese institutions during the Japanese colonial era, former land owners, or political offenders and their families. People in bad background strata suffered greatly from political and social discrimination.

> Yes. They strictly discriminated one group from another. People with bad background strata cannot get married nor join the army. Well, nowadays, they can join the army since there is a shortage. But, they still cannot attend college. If they are from the bad strata.
> (Interviewer: Is background strata something like people from South Korea?)
> No. It's something like... well... there were people who joined the organization that was established by the South Korean army during the Korean War. Also, there were some people who fled to South Korea during the war. (...) These are people of bad basic element. There were people who worked for the Japanese during the colonial era and those who worked for former land owners. They couldn't do anything. They were treated as "harmful". Discrimination is severe in North Korea. Anyways, I suffered a lot there because of my father, but I have no regrets now. On top of that, my daughter sent me some money, and the North Korea National Security Intelligence Service watched me all the time because of my status. It wasn't easy living there. That's why I left. (P-1)

Some people tried to overcome the political and social discrimination through education or marriage. Yet, those efforts did not change anything. The following case explicitly shows this reality.

> I wanted my one and only daughter to go to college. It is impossible to get a college education in North Korea. Even though I was a doctor... What really happened there is more like a fictional story. That's how she went through college. My daughter was doing well at school. So, they transferred her to sophomore without an examination. I didn't want my daughter to marry my son-in-law because I didn't like him. I wanted her to marry someone from a well-off family who is a member of the party,

> a "good element" so that we could survive. (...) The difference between people in the good element and the bad element is like a feudal lord and a slave. (A-1)

One discrimination against people with bad elements was to send them to live further north of the country. This policy was to make them live in the farthest place from South Korea, but it actually led them to encounter news about South Korea as China became more capitalized.

Political and social discrimination, along with the worsened economy, led North Korean residents to have interest in world outside North Korea. It acted as a societal factor that strengthened the desire to flee from North Korea.

3) External factors that pulled North Korean refugees out

A second type of potential factor that compelled North Korean refugees to flee is the external factor that pulled them out from North Korea. There are several external factors. The first is positive information regarding South Korea from the media or people who come and go between China and North Korea. The second is financial support from outside. The third is strong persuasion by relatives in China or people who had already exited. The fourth is direct persuasion from South Korea (not China), which happens though very rarely. In fact, most North Korean refugees did not think of settling in South Korea before they crossed to China or to a third country. At the time of border-crossing, their top priority was to settle in China. Settling in South Korea was something they did not want nor thought of. It was very rare, special case if one decided to go and settle in South Korea from the beginning.

(1) Positive information on China and South Korea

North Korean residents heard information that China is economically superior to North Korea, which is suffering from its worsened economy. In the past, such information was gained through direct traveling by oneself or by families and relatives who had foreign experiences. However, recently, such information was more often heard from radio or TV media that they brought in. More directly, people could access information about South Korea through letters or phone calls from South Korea. Especially, elites could access such information about South Korea or China through books or scholarly journals. Through this information, North Korean residents began to have a more realistic view on their internal circumstances, foreign countries, and even South Korea.

> I had visited Russia before the crossing. Before I went to Russia, I believed that there wouldn't be much of a difference even if other countries lived better than us. But, when I visited Russia, I couldn't believe what I saw. Only then, I realized that we have all been fooled by the government. I thought Kim, Il-Sung was the greatest man alive (...) I went to Russia in 1988 and Soviet Union interfered in 1990. (...) From then on, I had a radio. It is called a "recorder" in North Korea, while it is called a "cassette" here. Radios sold in North Korea do not have frequency meters so that people couldn't listen to it. Mine was directly brought from a foreign country, so I had to go to the National Security to register and set the frequency. But before I registered, I disassembled the frequency meters so that I could listen to South Korean radio stations such as the KBS Social Education broadcasting channel.* (G-1)

* Translation with note: The Social Education Service reflected the South Korean government's peace and prosperity policy in its programming, by taking part in the reconciliation

> When I was in college, there was the people's library in Kim, Il-Sung Square. We read many books during the weekends there. In the library, there were some Japanese books, which people from Jochongnyeon* read. In those books, anything related to South Korea was censored by cutting the pages off or covering the contents with a black marker. And yet, among those books, we found some Russian books. Some books were written in English that had materials on South Korea. Moreover, we realized that other countries' scientific technology was much more superior to that of ours by reading the Japanese science technology journals. I can say that 100 % of all college graduates in Pyongyang know about South Korea and other western countries. We all know that North Korea is going in the wrong direction.
> (Interviewer: You knew about South Korea since the 1970s?)
> Yes. I knew it well. The higher they were in their social class, the more they knew about South Korea. (I-1)

Still, people who had encountered such information did not decided to go to South Korea right away. Even if they decided to exit from North Korea, they desired to live in China rather than in South Korea.

(2) Financial support from outside

Relatives or family members in China became the major human resource for getting help when the economy deteriorated in North Korea.

The depth of the river near the northern border was shallow enough to cross. Receiving financial support from China was permitted, as long

---

and cooperation of the two Koreas, and fulfilling its role of connecting Koreans around the world.

* Translation with note: The pro-North Korean residents' league in Japan.

as they did not contact South Koreans. So, North Korea refugees could get by using the money sent from China. As they travelled to and from China, they realized that the country was economically affluent, and they expected to have economically better lives in China.

> It was 1998, and we heard that my mom used to live in China and Korea during the Japanese colonial era. I worked at a service organization in North Korea. The lives of people who worked at restaurants are better off than the rest. One leader came to our restaurant and told me to visit China if I had any relatives there. He said, "China is so much better off than North Korea". I asked him for a certificate and he gave me one... (M-1)

(3) Persuasion from relatives in China or other North Korean refugees

Relatives in China and North Korean refugees who already lived in China changed people's minds. Sometimes, people fled to China because their relatives in China promised to give them some money. But, in fact, there were some cases where families in South Korea made that story up in order to bring them from North Korea. This is because most refugees would not flee from North Korea if they knew they would be settling in South Korea. Families had to use such incentives in order to lure them out. As a result, refugees cannot return to North Korea and their status becomes very insecure to continue living in China. At this moment, they hear positive information about South Korea from relatives or acquaintances, and they become aware that they have the option of going to go to South Korea.

> (Interviewer: Would you tell me about things that happened in 2001?)

> Yes. Well, North Korean residents go back and forth to China because people are engaged in commerce. This guy came to my house and said my relative in China is looking for me. He said he will give me money when I go to China. We didn't have anything to eat, so I was going to cross the border with my son just to get the money. I asked my father to stay home, so he said good-bye. That's why I crossed the border and never returned.
> (Interviewer: Did you really have a relative in China?)
> No. My sister was in South Korea. She defected first. She had her settlement fund, and she planned to take out my son and me first. I spent a night in China, and she took us directly to Yanji. We took some pictures and somehow managed to get passports. That same night, we went to Shenyang. The next day, we were on the plane to South Korea. (…)
> I didn't have a clue that my sister would be in South Korea. I thought she was in China and I didn't think of coming here at all.
> (Interviewer: When you sister sent someone to you, did you think that you were just going to China?)
> Yes. I heard her real plan when I was in China. I was fooled by her lies. (N-1)

Sometimes there was human traffciking by taking advantage of people who wanted to go to China for financial support. North Korean refugees were often taken advantage of. Case D-2 describes a North Korean refugee woman in such a situation. She joined the army because it was one way to earn social status. After she completed her services in the army, she was qualified to join the party. Yet, she was stimulated to earn some money as she witnessed her friends becoming financially stable by working. At that time, she fled from North Korea after hearing news that she could earn some money in China. Unfortunately, she was deceived and became a victim of human trafficking instead.

(4) Direct persuasion from South Korea

Most North Korean refugees flee to China in hopes of living an economically well-off life. For them, China was their top priority destination, and South Korea was rarely taken into consideration. Nonetheless, there were a few cases that considered South Korea as the final destination. In a case, one was advised to help a specific indivisual to defect North Korea (he remembers the indivisual as a captive from the Korean War, but it could not be confirmed) in return for a big cash reward. He reported that he had helped the individual for a monetary reward and participated in some meaningful work of bringing back a captive of war simultaneously.

4) Factors that made North Korean refugees hesitate to exit

There were push factors such as North Korea's economic poverty and insecure status, and pull factors such as information on economically affluent China and South Korea or financial support, but there still were strong factors that made people hesitant before making the final decision for the crossing. There are several factors that stopped them from crossing. The first is their familiar life style in North Korea, the second is the consequence they would face if they were caught, and the third is possible the harm that remaining family members would face.

(1) Familiar life style in North Korea

Although life in North Korea is difficult, people become accustomed to it. Particularly, people with occupations like soldiers, managers of historical places, hospital directors, professors, or writers did not face political, social and economical problems in North Korea. Economic poverty had become their burden, and yet, they still had political and social power, which made it difficult for them to leave North Korea. In this circumstance, it was hard to think about the crossing only because of their poverty. Moreover, living a new life in a strange place is not easy for them if their children were attending college, a foreign language school or the army, which gave them something to hope for in North Korea.

(2) Consequences they would face when arrested during the crossing

One of the factors that make people hesitant in crossing is the fear of punishment. Because of this factor, North Korean residents hesitate to flee the country. However, there were times when people were not severely punished, even when they were arrested during the crossing. In this situation, the government authorities acknowledged that they were trying to get financial help from China on the condition that they did not get in touch with South Koreans. Moreover, there were cases where people were released during the Inter-Korea Summit Talks. However, North Korean refugees could not get rid of the fears of getting arrested. They felt even extreme fear when someone merely glanced at them, assuming that someone was there to arrest them. Based on others' experiences, they knew about the punishments they would receive if they were arrested. Direct and indirect experiences and stories played a great role in stopping North Korean residents from crossing.

> ...People have been caught by the police there. I was arrested again in two months. (...) So, I was forced back to North Korea. (...) The

labor camp in Onsung was a place where prisoners are punished, so the work load was very heavy. I began to feel sick from X month X date, and I couldn't eat from that day on. I was living on just water and some popped rice for one or two months. I was about to die, and it was hard for me to move at all. Everyone was beaten up there. I cried and cried while praying to God. I prayed that I could stay alive until I go back to my hometown to meet my son. I was arrested in two months and got punished in the labor camp for a month. It is only a 15-minute walk from the police station to my house. And yet, it took me one hour to get home, because I couldn't walk after being released from the camp. (…) Afterward, I was in bed for about a month. In two months, I was brought in to do forced labor. I remember it happened on my birthday. Even in severe poverty, my family made me a cake out of hulled millet. On that morning, a police came to take me to the forced labor camp. I was in forced labor for the following six months. I had to pick the ears of potatoes for obtaining my three months of food. Then, I was put into forced labor. The ears of potatoes were very small, which was not enough to fill our stomachs. I couldn't even go to sleep because I was very hungry. When I was released, China or South Korea never came across my mind ever again. I was determined never to go to China without saving my son. (S-1)

(3) Harm to the remaining family members in North Korea

Harm to the remaining family members in North Korea is another factor that stopped people from the crossing despite the economic poverty and the political and social insecurity. Especially when a family member is in the army or is a party elite, the crossing would harm the remaining members. For this reason, the crossing is a difficult decision to make. For instance, a remaining daughter in North Korea was harassed at school by friends because of her mother's crossing, and a man whose family members fled decided to stay in North Korea because he had an old mother.

> Her first child will be in first grade at school. He is beaten up at school because his mother had fled to China. A teacher hit him with a belt. One time, like in the movies, the teacher told other students to hit him with the belt. So, she had to bring her child with her, and left her second child in the care of her close friend whom she can trust. (A-1)

There are cases also that people carefully arranged to let themselves be registered as missing or deceased so that their remaining families wouldn't be harmed. These days, such an arrangement is difficult to plan, but during the time of the case, there were many missing people in North Korea, which made easy for them to be registered as missing.

> At that time, I didn't think about South Korea. Because during that period of time, if someone defects to South Korea, there was a huge media coverage with real names appearing all over the place. Then, family members in North Korea were executed or sent off to prison. Then, there was no afterlife. At that moment, if any North Korean refugee appeared in the South Korean media, every family member, even distant relatives, were arrested. That's why no one dares to think about going to South Korea. So people went to China, instead. (I-1)

5) Determining momentum for crossing

North Korean refugees suffered in North Korea's society and expected to have better lives economically and socially, in China. There were rare occasions where they had positive expectations about South Korea, but most wanted to live in China. These thoughts have acted as push or pull factors. However, as described earlier, there were strong factors that stopped them from crossing. When there is an equilibrium between internal or external factors triggering the crossing and factors that stop them from crossing, people do not leave. When the equilibrium breaks, people decide to leave, and such determining force includes rapid personal changes and threatening factors beside chronic economic poverty and political inequality.

The determining forces for crossing are as follows: death of a family member from poverty or disease; insecurity and threats after being accused as a political offender; insecure social status and increased surveillance; sudden political or social event that threatens a family's survival; direct contact from a parent who was believed to be dead; desires to know family members' existence; and concurrence of pressured conditions. These determining forces differ according to each individual's circumstances, family member's political status, relational problems in family, age, and developmental stage. That is, it is hard to generalize the determining factors for individual crossings as a consequence from North Korea's economic and social circumstances. Previously discussed determining forces and psychology behind the decision-making process are described below.

(1) Death of a family member from poverty or disease

Food crisis, poverty, or political social inequality, as discussed in Chapter 1, are situational factors rather than direct factors. However, it seems that some North Korean refugees decided to cross the border when their child or a family member died from poverty or disease. In case L-1, he did not decide to leave despite the severe food shortage since 1995.

He did not decide until his wife's death from illness. In case R-1 as well, he had difficulty deciding the crossing because his family was a member of the party. He made a decision to leave when his family died from starvation.

> The motive was food shortage... it was during 1995 to 1998. My wife came down with a disease during the food shortage period. I was shocked when she died, and that's why I came here, to look for food. I didn't have any political motives. (L-1)

Case H-1 (a mother) and case H-4 (a son) lived far from the northern border. When the economy declined, they went to the border area to find out whether they could get help from relatives in China or if they were able to cross. Then, the mother came down with typhoid fever, which was life threatening. They figured there was no hope left in North Korea. With this event, the equilibrium between the factors that triggered and stopped the crossing broke, which led him to immediately decide to leave. For the mother, besides her illness and inferior economic social circumstances, worries about her child's future gave validity to her crossing.

> When I came down with fever while trying to get to a different province by train, I was furious. In fact, I was going to go back home after getting money from a relative. But, what would a "promise" do good for me when I am dying? (...) At that moment, my only thought was to survive. That's why I crossed the Tumen. Otherwise, I wouldn't dare to cross the border. (H-1)

Children's chronic illnesses had also been a determining force for crossing. In case K-1, two daughters were diagnosed with diseases that cannot be cured in North Korea (one of daughter had leukemia and the other had pulmonary tuberculosis). It was difficult to keep them well nourished as the doctors prescribed. On top of that, persuasion from her sister in China (in fact, her sister was in South Korea, but at that moment, she believed that her sister was in China) was a major factor. An interesting point in this case is that she said she would not have chosen to flee to South Korea although she had known her sister resided in South Korea before. This shows that North Korean refugees did not consider coming to South Korea, even if they defected from North Korea. That is, children's illnesses or other factors can be a determining force for the crossing, but this implies that it does not serve as a triggering factor for settling in South Korea. It shows that North Korean refugees felt South Korea as a faraway and alienated place, whereas China as a very close place.

> Frankly speaking, if I had known that my sister was in South Korea, I wouldn't have come to China. I came to China because I heard my sister was here. But when I came here, my sister and brother had already fled. (...) I came to China on January, 2002, and my brother left China on December, 2001.
> I didn't know. I wouldn't have come if I had known. (...) Yes, yes. Both of my children were sick. I brought them with me. My second daughter was diagnosed with leukemia in 2001, and she was hospitalized for a month. And my first daughter was diagnosed with tuberculosis and was in the hospital for two months. As you know, there aren't any drugs in North Korea. (...) In North Korea, if someone is diagnosed with leukemia, there is no chance of survival. Doctors told me to feed her well, but we had no money because we lived in the farming area. (K-1)

Economic poverty plays a role of a push factor, but the crossing is actually carried out by factors that arouse a sense of urgency and fear, such as their own illness or death of close relatives. Yet, factors that induce fear to North Korean refugees may differ by their age or developmental stages. Children and adolescent refugees feared that they might turn into a Kotjaebi* rather than they were worried about political inequality or economic poverty. In case G-4, he was 14 years old when his parents discussed with him about the crossing. He describes how he decided to go along with his parents.

> My father told me that our lives will become worsen and we actually didn't do well. I thought about becoming a Kotjaebi if we went bankrupt. I saw many of them wandering off. I thought I would be better off listening to my father than living a life of a Kotjaebi. (G-4)

(2) Insecurity and threats after being accused as a political offender

Besides economic factors, political and social insecurity played a major stimulus for crossing. Case Q-1 describes a relative who has been bugged while making a phone call in an attempt to find his grandfather in South Korea. The relative was connected to South Korea, and the existence of his grandfather who was reported to be dead was confirmed to be alive in South Korea. The relative died in a concentration camp for political prisoners. Because North Korean National Securities were fearful of being called by their superiors to account for the death of political prisoners, they temporarily released the Q-1. At that moment, he

* Translation with note: Kotjaebi refers to North Korean homeless children. While there are several explanations on the origin of 'Kotjaebi', the most plausible explanation is that it is originated from Russian word 'Koyeвbe' which means wandering people.

decided to flee North Korea.

> One of my relatives' phone had been bugged when he called South Korea from China. Chinese pubic security requested an investigation to North Korean National Securities. He died in six months during his preliminary hearing. He was beaten to death. We were treated as offenders in North Korea. They took all of my family members. He was just calling in an attempt to find a family member in South Korea. That was it. In the past, he had said although his original hometown was South Korea, he didn't have any relatives there. But later, it turned out that he had relatives in South Korea. He was caught lying. We can become offenders for lying. (...) Whatever and however I tried, I figured I had no chance of survival. So, I decided to defect from North Korea. (Q-1)

(3) Insecure social status and increased surveillance

Surveillance by North Korean Securities on people with bad strata was strengthened as number of North Korean refugees increased. This led more people to leave from North Korea because people couldn't handle the fear and constant surveillance. Case P-1, a person with bad strata, decided to defect as North Korean National Securities' surveillance on money sent from his daughter in South Korea worsened.

> Yes. They were strictly distinguished. People in a negative stratum of society cannot get married nor join the army. Well, nowadays they can join the army since there is a shortage. But, they still cannot attend college. If they are from bad strata. (P-1)

(4) Sudden political or social event that threatens a family's survival

In case M-1, a man always considered the option of crossing, but when his son was in danger from breaking out of the barracks, he finally decided to leave. If his son was arrested by the Chinese Public Security and was forced back to North Korea, his son had a high chance of facing execution. For this reason, he decided to settle in South Korea.

> I was trying to figure out how to live in China. My youngest son rescued his son from the army, which would cause a huge problem. If we are with him, every family member would be arrested.
> Runaway soldiers who were arrested in China were all sent back to North Korea and publicly executed by a firing squad. It was very scary. (M-1)

(5) Direct contact from a parent who was believed to be dead

In case J-2, a North Korean female refugee, then only 13 years old, had a missing parent. Her father was missing a few years back, and her mother left home without saying anything two years ago. She believed that her mother was dead. Her mother contacted her through a broker to let her know that she was alive in South Korea. After she talked to her mother on the phone, she decided to leave North Korea with the broker.

> People went back to their houses when I told them I won't leave. Then, they came back.
> (Interviewer: The same day? That late at night?)
> Yes. There were no cellular phones in North Korea, but he had one. He said I can talk to my mother. (J-2)

(6) Desires to know family members' existence

In this case, a factor unrelated to politics or economics became the determining force. Case J-1's husband left North Korea to get help from relatives in China two years ago, but never returned. She heard rumors that her husband was with another woman, and they had children together. She decided to leave just to find out about her husband's existence and to confirm this fact. In this case, her desire to find her husband, in addition to economic poverty, became the determinant.

> It was very hard for six of us to survive in North Korea. My husband left to get some help from relatives in China, and he never came back. I still remember it. There was no one.
> (Interviewer: What exactly happened?)
> I don't know. He just couldn't come back, I guess. As soon as I came to China, I asked relatives whether he had come by. People like to talk about others. I heard so many things in North Korea about him. They said he is living with another woman, they have children together, and he sent food in amounts of tens of cars to Pyongyang. (…) I begged on my knees to relatives to tell me the truth about my husband. I even said I will be fine even if he is now living with another woman. My relatives said they would have told me if he had come by, but he never did. They cried while saying that. So, I realized that he never came here. He disappeared. He's not in China, and he left North Korea. So, I guess I have to believe that something went wrong while he was crossing the Tumen. (J-1)

(7) Concurrence of circumstances

In cases C-1, 2, 3, people decided to leave due to a concurrence of several complex factors. In case C-1, the mother of a family had a husband who desired to cross despite his politically safe job. He attempted the crossing while she was on a business trip. Since then, case C-1, who had previously lived a politically safe life, was under surveillance over six times, and her status became politically insecure. After several years, she hesitated when she got a notice from her husband to send their son, mother-in-law, and sister-in-law to the border area. At that time, her son, whom she had wanted to become the party elite by serving the military and attending a military school, was rejected from the military school. Moreover, after he accidentally killed and ate sheep while the army was grazing, he broke out of the barracks. Besides his father's persuasion, he decided to leave in order to protect himself. The mother came back to see her son for the last time. Suddenly, she was persuaded by her son, and she decided to defect with him.

> Everyone disappeared on yyyy-mm-dd. We weren't so poor in North Korea. I was in X and my husband was in Z city, Y province. (…) My son was serving the military, and my daughter went to school. She was living in a dormitory. (…) My husband took two daughters with him when they came for winter break. I knew later on that they went all the way to China.
>
> (…) My son could have been successful only if his father was there. A year later, he was out of the military and wanted to attend a military school. Since his father and two sisters were missing, he received a clearance verification about six times. He was rejected from the school (C-1)

In another case, the father (M-1), a party secretary at a hospital, was entrapped and the hospital was taken over by the party. When the first son (M-3) found out what had happened to his father, he was furious and broke out of the barracks. Due to his insecure status and fear of his son getting punished, he decided to defect.

> During the conversation, my brother said he couldn't live in North Korea like this, and that he wanted to go to South Korea. I cursed at him, so he suggested running away to China since we could no longer live in North Korea. After what I heard from my brother, I realized what our family might have. Before I got out of the army, my father worked at a hospital and our life was just fine. I even served in the military for this country. And yet, they destroyed our family completely. It's a long story. My father was a good doctor and treated patients very well. For this reason, they set up my father because party elites were jealous of him. They took over the hospital. (M-3)

6) The crossing preparation process and the actual crossing

After carefully examining the decision-making process for crossing, we found that some left alone without discussing this matter to anyone while others discussed the issue. People who made decisions by themselves were people without family or simple-minded people who served the military for a long time (D-1). In case D-1, he not only made an impulsive decision to leave, but also made rash decisions regarding matters after exiting North Korea.

> When I came home for a vacation from the military, I just didn't want to live there. My house was near the border to China. So, I figured why not go and see China. That's how I came to China. (D-1)

People with families discussed the issue of making the decision of crossing together. Some people spent a long time making a decision due to conflicting opinions with their spouse.

> I couldn't tell my wife about my desire to leave until 1998. I was scared because she kept overhearing when I was listening to the radio. Afterward, I talked to her about things I heard from the radio, and my wife became curious. Life was becoming worse in North Korea. There were no more rations for us. She said she would farm anything she could in her sister's house. It is easy to say that but what she was suggesting was a very difficult thing to do. (…) I had lived in Russia, and I was a cultivator there. I told my wife that we could sell it and live off of it for a while. She said I should go by myself if I really insisted on going. She never lived outside North Korea before. I gave her some time to think about this. She said we will get some rations in six months, but it didn't happen. I waited for a few years, then I asked what we should do. She couldn't say anything. (G-1)

There were some cases where a man left only with the children because his wife was opposed to the idea, and he invited her into China later (C-1). Some people were persuaded to cross by relatives in China. In case B-1, a husband was caught while contacting with people in China. He asked his wife to move to China, but she was extremely against the idea. She then decided to follow him because relatives told them that they wouldn't be able to meet again. Even then, they decided to go to China, not South Korea.

> As soon as my husband came home from China, he asked me to go to China with him, but I said "No". My husband kept insisting on going and he said he will take the baby. He said we will live together or die

> together. My parents told me to go with him even if we would die together. That's how I left home. (B-1)

Some people's decision making was based on their children's opinions. In this case, their children were in the army, or they were adults whose future would be affected by the crossing. Sometimes children's opinions were needed to persuade a spouse.

> We could get caught on the way. It's not like someone is inviting us to come. We are trying so hard to survive here. When we get arrested, we could be killed. This is what I told my children. But my sons, then 14 and 12, insisted going. My wife couldn't say anything. We left reluctantly the next day because my children were insisting. (G-1)

Sometimes, people made the decision to leave without any prior preparation. Case C-1 decided to leave without any preparation because she was just going to see her son's departure. At that moment, she decided to leave with him. Moreover, there was a case of people who made the decision in only one day after hearing that they could earn some money in China.

> (Interviewer: Who invited you to come to China?)
> People I don't know. I didn't know them, but they asked me if I want to earn some money in China. I was doing my laundry at a riverside, and they came to me. They said if I work as a maid, I can make some money. So, I accepted because I wasn't doing so well there.
> (Interviewer: You sneaked out of the country without telling anyone, right?)
> Yes, of course. Nobody knew it, even my family. (D-2)

On the other hand, some people had thoroughly prepared by checking the border areas several times and selling their property one at a time (G-1). In case I-1, prior to his crossing, he examined situations in China, and he asked his friend to report him as missing or dead so that remaining family members wouldn't be harmed after his crossing.

> I realized that I should leave North Korea after hearing the KBS Social Education broadcasting channel. I planned the crossing since 1998. I discussed it with my brother. We went to XX, a place near the border, disguised as people who were trying to get food. In order to get to that place, we had to go around the Tumen. So, we took a look around the border area, and I had confidence that I could cross the Tumen. (...) Some parts of the Tumen had a water depth that only came up to my knee, so I figured I should cross here.
> We sold everything we had to have some cash. I told my neighbors that I would be moving to my brother's farm. It took me several months to sell everything. I bought a house in China where we could stay. (G-1)

Some people did not just look around the route or sell off their property. They thought there was a high risk of getting killed if they were arrested, so they even prepared to commit a suicide. (A-1, C-1, G-1, G-4)

> I had rat poison inside of my pocket. If I was caught, I would be dead in North Korea anyway. (A-1)

3. Experiences in the third country

North Korean refugees live in a third country for some period of time after exiting North Korea. It was very rare and special for refugees to come directly to South Korea without passing a third country. The third country includes China, Thailand, the Union of Myanmar, Lao People's Democratic Republic, and Mongolia. China is the country where most North Korean refugees pass by not only because it is the nearest to North Korea, but also because it is the most preferred country to go to, even over South Korea, by refugees.

North Korean refugees' experiences in a third country will be discussed in four parts. First is the third country internal factors that pushed refugees out of a third country. Second is South Korean factors that pulled them out from the third country. Third are factors that stopped them from reentering North Korea, and fourth is their crossing process and crisis in a third country.

1) Third country's internal factors that pushed refugees out

Most North Korean refugees' first target destination was China. Among the refugees, only a few wanted to come to South Korea from the beginning. Most dreamed of living in China without any financial struggle. Nonetheless, they faced unexpected circumstances in China. That is, although the financial situation improved, and the fears of death from starvation or threats from North Korean National Security were lessened, they had very unstable lives constantly hiding from the Chinese Public Security and status insecurity. The following is summaries of their experiences in China or a third country in relation to their entry process to South Korea.

(1) Pursuit by the Chinese Public Securities

North Korean refugees in China were tracked down by Chinese Public Security, because they stayed illegally. In the early days, the Chinese Public Security's pursuit was not severe, but as the size of North Korean refugee population increased and they became a global issue, it became severe. When refugees were arrested by the Chinese police, they were forced back to North Korea, and captives would be punished harshly. Refugees lived in fear of the Chinese police even though they were financially stable in China.

> What I suffered from the most in China was that I couldn't do anything and had to live in hiding. But the most fear was the idea of being sent off to North Korea when I was caught by the Chinese police. (I-1)

> I was living fine when I came to China. Food and drinks were everywhere, but as the number of refugees like me increased rapidly in China, the police chased us. When refugees got caught, they were sent off to North Korea... Yes, it was very hard in China. I had to figure out how to survive, and if I were sent back to North Korea, I knew what would happen. I found a house to hide in, but there was this thing called a census. When people came to take a census, I locked the door and hid. I didn't even breathe. It was so difficult to live in China. (I-2)

(2) Insecure status and discrimination

North Korean refugees in China experienced status insecurity and discrimination. In case T-1, a woman who came to China as part of human trafficking, complained that her name could not be entered in the family register.

> I was 27 years old. I came in 1997. I was very shocked to learn that people were able to commit acts of human trafficking of the same race! I mean, we are all Koreans. (...) I came to think that I wouldn't have lived a life if I stayed in North Korea. (...) So, I ended up living with this man. Since he was Korean Chinese, we could communicate. My son and I couldn't be registered in family registry because we are North Koreans. I was married to this man but I didn't have a family registry. Since I didn't have citizenship, I lived in insecurity. (T-1)

North Korean refugees were discriminated against in China due to their insecure status. People took advantage of them by giving much lower wages than the average or no wage at all.

> We worked. Well, I wasn't treated that way. I was being paid well. But my sons weren't getting paid. Let's say, if they worked for a year, they only got paid 3 or 4 months' worth of wage. They, so to speak, were treating us as if we should be thankful for just letting us hiding there. (H-1)

(3) Children's unstable identity

Case L-1 decided to go to South Korea despite the financially and socially stable life because of his child's unstable identity.

> It may differ from person to person, but I earned some money as a writer in China. I earned what would be twenty years worth of salary for a regular Chinese public official in just two years. I bought an apartment and saved lots of money. So, I didn't think about coming to South Korea. I could live like an upper class in China. Nonetheless, I was worried

> about my children's identity. They should have a definite citizenship and belong to a country.
> (Interviewer: Was your status still insecure back then?)
> I had a fake Chinese citizenship. I had money. In China, if you have money, you can do whatever you wish. But, I wanted to give my children their country back. So, I got a fake passport and entered South Korea first. (L-1)

2) External factors that pulled refugees out of the third country

North Korean refugees determine to depart to South Korea when factors that stop them from reentering North Korea and factors that pull them from South Korea are combined. Reentering North Korea is a difficult decision to make, since first of all, they had fled for a reason and they were afraid of the consequences they would face if they returned. And yet, settling in another third country would not be much different from living in China. Thus, the next destination they could choose after China had to be South Korea. Positive information they had heard regarding the country had triggered their consideration of going to South Korea. Factors that pull North Korean refugees to South Korea are as follows.

(1) Factors that stopping North Korean refugees

Despite status insecurity, threat of arrest in China, and positive information on South Korea, there were factors that made North Korean refugees hesitant about entering South Korea.

Punishment for refugees who did not make an attempt to enter to South Korea was different from the punishment for refugees who contacted people in South Korea or tried to enter South Korea. Thus, when refugees were arrested in China, whether or not they tried to contact or enter South Korea determined the gravity of the punishment. Refugees live in an extremely unstable condition due to the pursuit by Chinese police, threat of arrest, and discrimination. In such conditions, they face a choice of reentering North Korea or going to South Korea. Since only death awaited them in North Korea, they chose to go to South Korea where they were guaranteed financial and social stability.

> (Interviewee 1) We watched Korean television programs and heard Korean radio channels, and we found out how well Korea is developed.
> (Interviewer: Did things you watched motivate you to go to South Korea?)
> (Interviewee 1) I watched and listened about South Korea. We knew we couldn't go back to North Korea, and we had to leave China in a hurry...
> (Interviewee 2) We had to live in hiding in China. We realized that we needed to go to South Korea. China was heaven compared to North Korea. There were lots to eat and wear... But the Chinese told us that South Korea was ten years ahead of them. (M-1)

(2) Factors attracting refugees to South Korea

North Korean refugees came across information about South Korea while they were suffering from their insecure status and fear of getting arrested. Some knew about South Korea when they were still in North Korea, but in most cases, they gained information on South Korea after they entered China. Even if they knew about South Korea, their top priority was to settle in China. They looked for another escape route as their status became unstable and threats of forced repatriation increased in China. One of the escape routes was South Korea, which guaranteed them not just a status, but also the financial stability. The followings are factors attracting refugees to South Korea, content of information they received, and the process of passing the information.

Positive information on South Korea includes how wealthy South Korea is, how South Korean government accepts refugees, and how the settlement fund is given to refugees. Such information was passed on to refugees in China by radio, television, relatives in South Korea, South Korean students, and their Chinese neighbors.

> Yes. I listened to "People We Miss", a radio program offered by KBS for Koreans living abroad. When the program was on, I listened to it even when I was busy doing something. That's how I heard about things. Sometimes, there was a discussion about current issues in North Korea. That's when I realized why the dictatorship is bad and how bad North Korea had become. I thought North Korea was the best when I was there. I decided to go to South Korea after hearing the discussion on the radio. (H-1)

Yet, refugees hesitated to go to South Korea because they were worried about their remaining family members who could be harmed (B-1). In some cases, refugees reentered North Korea to bring their remaining family members to South Korea (F-1).

> At first, we said we would not go to South Korea. At that time we thought that our family in North Korea would be harmed if we go to South Korea. (B-1)

> My second child was four years old. I left him in the care of childcare

> before I exited North Korea. (...) I missed my baby so much, and I just couldn't live without him. I felt so guilty because I knew my baby would be starving there. (...) I was determined to go back to get him and I wasn't sacred of anything. (...) I thought I was the only person who can save my child. (F-1)

News, which claimed that the South Korean government does not reveal refugees' identity, made refugees think that they could save their remaining family members. As the fear that they might endangering their family in North Korea lessened, more people decided to go to South Korea.

> ...I wasn't able to send my child through middle school or high school. At that point in time, the South Korean government decided not to reveal refugees' history, and that led me to decide to go to South Korea. (I-1)

4. Crisis during the border-crossing process

North Korean refugees experienced several crises during the border-crossing process. Such crises arose in times of exiting North Korea and settling in a third country. This part will discuss the crises that refugees faced during the entire border-crossing process. Crises reported by refugees include arrest by North Korean National Security, false information, betrayal by a broker, and tracking and arrest by the Chinese Public Security.

1) Arrest by North Korean National Security

Arrest by the North Korean National Security and Chinese police was the major crisis of the North Korea refugees. Crises of an arrest played an important factor, hindering them from crossing. The risk of getting arrested can be the biggest factor that holds the refugees from border-crossing. Case P-2 describes her situation when she was arrested.

> ...I got arrested and all of my money was taken away. I suffered a lot at the detention room. People don't call the detention room as it is called in North Korea. They call it a toilet. It is much smaller than this room, maybe the size of a place to store shoes. It's a prison. It's a room made of concrete without any heat. There are no doors and there are only bars and a doorway and windows. Windows were covered with vinyl and even that was torn apart. Wind blew directly into the room. There were about 10 people in the room. We had to be physically attached to each other or otherwise, we couldn't sleep because of the cold. We would have died from the cold. They just gave us a very thin blanket. At night, they would give us rotten corn... they cooked the corn with its husks and hulls. The soup was very salty, and we became very thirsty. So, we drank water from the toilet, and we had diarrhea. Some died from it. There was a toilet inside the room, and it didn't even have a door. So, the room was filled with the stink of urine and dung. It felt like we were sitting in a fertilizer room. I have been in that room. (...)
> At first, I was there for nine days. Then, it became three months or a year depending on the seriousness of crime. (...) I thought I would get killed if I was caught. I think I got heart disease from the fear of getting caught. It is better now, but just 5–6 months ago, I couldn't sleep at night because my heart beat so fast. (P-2)

2) False information and betrayal by a broker

In case G-1, a refugee believed that it would be easy to go to South Korea, just by going to the Korean embassy or the Korean consulate in China. He found out that it was extremely difficult to go to South Korea when he arrived in China. He looked for the location of the embassy. But someone had misinformed him that the embassy was located in Shenyang, when in fact, it was located in Qingdao. As a result, he spent money for nothing. He finally entered South Korea through the help of a church.

Another crisis is the betrayal by a broker. A refugee's attempt to meet his mother and brother at a certain point failed because a broker deliberately gave wrong information solely to gain profit. For this, he had to make a trip to the Tumen area from Hwanghae province four times.

> My mother and the owner of the house (where interviewees would stay at the frontier) owner made an arrangement, but they called it off. They didn't keep their promise. When we were at the frontier, we rarely had contacts from my mother. She usually sent us some money, but the house owner told us to go back to our hometown because it's too dangerous. Maybe the house owner lied to us because he wanted to steal the money. Well, that, I don't know. We had to listen to what they said because we knew nothing about the situation there. The second time we came, we couldn't get in contact with them for a month! (H-3)

In case E-1, a refugee was promised to be taken to South Korea if he helped the specific personnel exit North Korea. However, when he heard that such promises are not usually kept in China, he was very upset and nervous. Similar to this case, there were cases where the trusted person betrayed a refugee by leaving him behind in China or turning him over to the Chinese police or the North Korean National Security. The following case is rather lengthy, and yet, it well describes the actual facts.

> I followed him to XY. (…) But he was a changed person since the time of departure. He told us, "Stay apart in XY. Both of you stay apart in XY." So, I said, "I came all the way here and waited for so long. And now you tell me to go away? I can't go back. I don't know anyone there. How can I go?" Then, he said he would come and pick us up in a week. I disagreed with him. I made a life-threatening decision to come to South Korea. He couldn't do anything but take us to XY. (…) I tried to understand even if he showed his bad temper. I thought it would be hard for him to evacuate three refugees. (…) We waited. On the third day, he told us we would get our passports in two days, and we could finally go to South Korea. I was delighted for the first time. (…) On the night of the third day, he said he couldn't take us. When I asked him the reason why, he said there's a problem with that old person's security and the South Korean government denied us to enter. (…) He said he figured out some other way, and told us to go to this place until he calls us. (…) He said to follow this man, and we said goodbye to him. (…) It was a house of a Chinese. We stayed there for about 20 days. (…) Another five days had passed, and the Chinese man called us. (…) I lived in that house with hope, but he told me to get out of the house. He said it would take more than six months to go to South Korea if I stayed there. He said he would help me to enter South Korea through Mongolia. (…) He said that the Chinese man would be harmed if the house was exposed. (…) I didn't know where to go. (…) I received a call again. (It was about) "Your friend, ABC, is coming here tomorrow morning to pick you up. You should go back to North Korea." I was heartbroken. What's that

> supposed to mean? I came all the way here and stayed for almost 20 days. What would happen to me if I go back now! I said I could not go back to North Korea. I begged him to let my wife go to South Korea, because she followed me all the way here. But he said "No". At that moment, I was so furious and confronted him by saying "Why shouldn't I be allowed to go to South Korea?". I cursed him for being so irresponsible. He brought me here, and he was now saying I should go back to be killed? Then, he said he would kill my children and brothers. (E-1)

3) Pursuit and arrest by Chinese Public Security

Case G-1 describes a situation where a refugee was in danger of getting arrested by the Chinese Public Security, but luckily, he got away.

> That was a time when inspection was extremely severe. We thought we would be caught. Everyone was very nervous because it was the day of the census taking. (…) When there was a knock on the door, we didn't open the door. (G-1)

Many refugees were arrested while living in China. They were arrested when exiting North Korea, living in China, or coming to South Korea. In case M-1, North Korean refugees were arrested by North Korean National Security while living in China, but as North Korean National Security officers were arrested for entering China without permission by the Chinese police, they were under supervision of the Chinese police. They were about to be forced into repatriation, but the Chinese police released them in the XX area.

In case H-1, two sons and their parents were separated due to the Chinese police's inspection. The youngest son was able to enter South

Korea became a pastor adopted him. After he settled in South Korea, he brought his remaining family members to South Korea with his settlement fund. In this case, a crisis worked as an opportunity.

> ...The Chinese police came after me again. So, we were on the run again. My relatives told us we should separate to avoid arrestment. I ended up being a housemaid, and he worked at a restaurant. My two sons were put into a church. We were very lucky, because my youngest son, who was 14 at that time, made entry to South Korea only after six months. It was 1999.
>
> This is how it happened. The church minister, a single woman, was involved in welfare of caring for handicapped children. She decided to adopt my son as her own. But she didn't know the regulations regarding how a refugee should be treated in making entry to South Korea. So, she just forged a passport for my son and brought him to South Korea. (...) She was in trouble with the Immigration Bureau. (H-1)

5. Entry process and experiences in South Korea

1) Entry process

(1) First entry

Entry to South Korea is reported as one of the most overwhelming emotional experiences expressed by the refugees. The following cases well describe their feelings of relief, feelings of being in their hometown unlike a third country, gratitude for people who helped, and feelings of achievement.

> It was early morning of New Year's holiday. The sun didn't rise. The sky was clear without fog. North Koreans had many dreams about South Korea. I was the same. When my foot landed South Korean soil, I couldn't even describe it. I was very relieved and excited. I held my wife's hand, and all of a sudden I burst into tears. (...) I don't know how to describe it. It could have never happened without many thankful people. (E-1)

> When I landed in Incheon International Airport, I felt relieved. I couldn't relax when I was in Cambodia. (...) I was at ease just by thinking that I am alive and there's no one to arrest me here. The air was so fresh. When I got on the bus, I felt that I survived. When I come to think about it, the air is so polluted in South Korea, and yet, the air felt so fresh back then. (J-1)

North Korean refugees were shocked by the size of Kimpo International Airport and Incheon International Airport (D-1), clean cities (D-1, G-1), many foreigners (F-1), and numerous cars (G-1). Some were charmed by the numerous neon signs on the roads. Yet, other important experiences were confusion and embarrassment. Refugees were confused when seeing that South Korea was so much different from what they were taught in North Korea.

> I was surprised by lots of buildings. It was so different from what I had heard. I thought there were only slums. I was taught in the army. But, I was so confused to see fancy skyscrapers. I couldn't see any slums. (D-1)

For certain refugees who lived a high-class life, the life of South Korea wasn't a new experience. However, the cleanliness of the country and the polite, and lively people came as a new experience.

Some refugees who haven't had positive experiences in their entry to South Korea still were concerned about their future and being photographed.

> I was living in severe tense. I didn't feel anything when I entered South Korea. (…) I just thought we were out of danger. However, on my way to South Korea, I heard that we should be careful because there are many North Koreans living here. Anyways, North Korea obtains information about refugees through various routes after they make entry to South Korea. I figured we should be careful… I knew we escaped danger, but there were still many worries. I was anxious about people taking pictures of me when I entered South Korea. (…) When I arrived, I looked for ways to hide my identity. (E-2)

(2) Daesung Public Affairs

Daesung Public Affairs is a government organization that performs inspection on North Korean refugees' history and their crossing routes in order to verify them as refugees and not Chosun-zok (Korean Chinese) or Chinese. First impressions of Daesung Public Affairs by North Korean refugees vary from very positive to negative. That is, people who reported positive emotional experiences such as gratitude and happiness, showed similar emotions toward Daesung Public Affairs regardless of the situation. Likewise, people who reported negative emotional experiences, such as insecurity and criticism, showed similar responses toward Daesung Public Affairs regardless of the situation. On the other hand, one North Korean refugee was being accused as a North Korean spy at Daesung Public Affairs. Despite tensions he experienced at Daesung Public Affairs, he tried to understand it in a positive way.

Some experiences on Daesung Public Affairs were extremely negative for a few refugees. Case E-2 illustrates a negative experience such as insecurity, fear, and discrimination.

> After I arrived at the National Intelligence Service (hereafter NIS), there were only police officers who welcome us. You know how police officers have a sharp image. They don't talk to us nicely. They treat us as criminals. I was very disappointed at how I was treated after going through so many hardships. (E-2)

Inspection was focused on one's North Korean life in general and the crossing experience if a refugee was a civilian, whereas soldiers were inspected on reasons for serving the military, the place of their military service, and their assigned work. During the verification process, a refugee was put into a single room for as short as a few days to as long as few weeks. Even after they were verified, refugees had to wait in Daesung Public Affairs until a group is filled. Then, they were sent off to Hanawon During the inspection, refugees were asked to write their lifelong experiences on paper that usually fills up to tens of pages. Sometimes, a lie detector was used. Some refugees understood their conduct, but some could not.

Refugees who understood such conducts accepted the process as part of a mandatory procedure (A-1, F-1). On the other hand, refugees who could not accept such procedures were disappointed at the situation where they were treated like criminals (E-2), acted sensitively on instructions to write their lifelong experiences (D-2, H-1), prohibition of smoking (D-1), and on the surveillance hole (D-1). Some even had a fight with police officers.

> Yes. I was very frustrated there. I tried to forget everything and tried to live day by day in fear of the past couple of years. When they told me to remember everything that happened during those years, I couldn't remember them well. I was very sensitive during the inspection. That was difficult. (H-1)

> I felt really bad when I went to NIS. I was put in solitary confinement for making trouble at the NIS.
> Yes… I have been there after the inspection. There was a desk, a bed, a refrigerator, and nothing else. (…) Then, I found the surveillance hole in the door. Who would feel good about it? No one does. I screened off the hole with a paper. They took it off. I screened it off three times, and they took it off every time. I told them I wouldn't do any harm to South Korea. I moved the bed to a different place. (…) So, they couldn't see me sleeping. The police saw me smoking on my desk… they were only in their early twenties at most. They came into my room and said, "That bastard is smoking!" I was furious and had a fight with them. (D-1)

In extreme cases, there was a refugee who wanted to go back to North Korea while being investigated. Case N-3 believed that since he entered South Korea directly from North Korea, not through China, he was suffering more than others because he didn't have an adaptation period in China like others. He thought that if he had more time in China before hye entered South Korea, he would have better adjusted to the different ideologies.

> People told us we had the shortest period of entry to South Korea from North Korea. I think I would have known things better if I had more time in China… Things were wasted too much here. (…)

> When I was investigated in Daesung Public Affairs, I was very scared, so I told that I would go back to North Korea.
> If you were in my shoes, you would understand me. I was being educated in North Korea, so it is obvious that my psychology still belonged to that world. (...) Back then, I was very used to the communist country... I told them I want to go back. My father and relatives are still in North Korea. I didn't know I was coming to South Korea.
> I came here without knowing anything, and people told me I'm now in South Korea. When I told them I would go back the NIS, they said they can send me there. But I heard that I would be executed when I reentered North Korea. Afterwards, I decided to stay. (N-3)

(3) Hanawon

Educational experiences at Hanawon reported by North Korean refugees had both positive and negative aspects. Case H-1 showed a strong negative response to education at Hanawon. The refugee pointed out that educational program at Hanawon did not take into consideration their unstable psychology from the experiences in the third country. Moreover, terms and dialects used by teachers were difficult to understand. The refugee also suggested that it would be efficient to provide adolescent refugees who experienced special circumstances in their life with some psychological therapy before starting the education program.

Case L-1 reported that education offered at Hanawon was not practical and suggested that it would be rather helpful if they could hear the settling experiences in South Korea by refugees who came earlier. Case M-3 expressed that lectures and actual training related to everyday life, such as going to a bank, helped them, whereas sexual education or cultivation activities did not help much. Case M-2, who attends the college of oriental medicine in South Korea, suggested that education programs at Hanawon should give more confidence to refugees by exchanging their own successful experiences, even a little one, rather than just discouraging them by telling them not to have high hopes because adaptation to South Korea is difficult. In addition, programs should move their focus from textbook lectures to vocational education that shows ways to success in adapting to the real world.

2) Experience in South Korea

North Korea, whether it is good or not, the most familiar place for North Korean refugees. Nonetheless, they made a decision to leave with the hope to live better lives in China. Although China provided a financially better lives life for refugees, they constantly had to fear the Chinese police and forced repatriation to North Korea. Thus, they had decided to make an entry to South Korea, a place where they did not think of settling. Unfortunately, South Korea was a challenging place to adjust. Needless to say, they didn't have to fear starvation nor the pursuit of the Chinese police. However, South Korea had turned into a new challenge for them. The followings illustrate refugees' experiences in South Korea.

(1) Pride as a Korean

North Korean refugees were proud to be citizens of South Korea. Their life circumstances have not changed dramatically, and yet, being treated as a South Korean citizen gives them a sense of pride and confidence.

> Thinking about China, even at this point, gives me bad memories. That's

> because I was caught in a prison when I was in China. (...) There was one thing I realized when I spent time in prison (...) People should be born in a good country. Regardless of one's own fortune, Chinese people despised us because we were from North Korea and we were poor. But now, I am in South Korea. I am so grateful to be here, and I promised to myself to work hard. There was one time when I went to China after I became a South Korean citizen. People who treated me badly back then, now treated me with totally opposite attitudes. Why did they change their attitudes toward me? I am who I was before. But they treated me differently. At that moment, I felt so proud to be a South Korean citizen. They treated me nicely only because I am from South Korea, and they want to come to Korea to find jobs. Chinese people are like that. (...) Even with a smaller country, South Korea has developed far greater than China in a short period of time. In that respect, Chinese people respect South Koreans. I am so thankful that I am now a citizen of the Republic of Korea. (M-2)

(2) Efforts to bring remaining family members to South Korea

The biggest effort refugees make while settling in South Korea is to bring their remaining family members in China or North Korea to South Korea. These days, the entry of remaining family members is done through a professional broker, and such expenses differ by the means of transportation they take. Crossing expenses through church organizations or cheap brokers is relatively low, but there is usually a longer duration of stay in China or a third country. Case B-1 tried to bring her husband to South Korea. She heard that if things go bad, people might die or get hurt during the crossing process, and this led her to choose a rather expensive but safer route for her husband. As a result, her husband could enter

South Korea in just a week after he exited North Korea. Many refugees including case E-1 reported their need for hard work in order to bring their remaining family members to South Korea. Case N-1 who still has remaining members in North Korea, felt bad on holidays. Refugees, who have family members in North Korea but are unable to bring them to South Korea, experience guilt, and try to provide financial support.

> What's my stress? The biggest stress is to adapt to the South Korean society and yet it is very challenging. The other is my remaining family members in North Korea. I feel so bad for them. I know how they would be starving. I always wanted to live with them here, and always think of them, especially on holidays or days of celebration. (N-1)

(3) Language problems

One of the main difficulties refugees undergo is the language problem. Despite similarities between the Korean spoken in the South and the North, there are several reasons for difficulties faced by refugees. First, there are too many foreign words adopted in the Korean spoken in the South. For instances, if they don't understand the meaning of words like "mart" or "outlet", there is some difficulty in their daily lives (M-1). Second, meanings of the same phrase may refer to different things (S-2). For example, a phrase "*il upda*" means "It is okay" in the North, whereas it means "Don't mind on other people's businesses" in the South, creating a big difference in the meaning. Third, intonation can be a problem for both children and adults. Refugees report that their different speech intonations create discomfort to the listeners.

In the case of children or adolescents, it is difficult to understand foreign words adopted in the language (F-2) or to build relationships with friends in South Korea (H-2). For adults, language problems are not only problems in misunderstanding from language differences, but also greater problems such as not being able to find a job, facing prejudice and discrimination, and raising excessive interest. Thus, problems created by language differences are not just language-related issues, but they lead to prejudice and discrimination. Case D-1 had to quit his job because people found out about his identity as a North Korean refugee. Case E-1 describes his awkward experience from his language.

> Yes. I felt discrimination in places other than work as well. (...) When I am on the subway, people ask me for directions sometimes. When I speak to tell them that I don't know the way, one person even turned his head away even before I finished speaking, after figuring out that I am not from the area. A nice person once asked me if I am a Chosun-zok. In that case, I couldn't tell them that I am from North Korea. When I say that, people just walk away and that breaks my heart. I should just act as if I am deaf, and people won't notice where I am from. (E-1).

(4) Difficulty in employment

North Korean refugees attempt to find a job to support themselves as soon as they get out of Hanawon. However, getting employed is very challenging for refugees. It is inevitable to reveal their identity due to their speech intonations, and they are rejected during job interviews because of their origin.

> I am very stressed out to wander around with temporary jobs from doing one thing today and doing another thing tomorrow. I cannot get a permanent job. People have a bad impression on North Koreans. Even when I had an interview, I was not hired because of my age and intonation of speech. So, I worked as a janitor and still they were

> concerned about how I spoke. When they first hear me saying things, they ask me if I came from China. At the interview, the interviewers asked me if I am from China and I told them I am North Korean. Then, they didn't hire me. At the end, I became an alien, and that's very stressful. (E-2)

If the intonation of speech becomes a problem at work, refugees usually make up a story that they are Chosun-zok or from the Gangwon province.* However, it seems to be hard to keep their identity a secret at the workplace, although sometimes, their origin didn't matter at the work place.

The followings are jobs or occupations that refugees had: sewing factory worker (B-1), insurance salesman (B-1, H-1), supermarket worker (C-3, N-3), student (C-3, C-2, F-1, G-4, H-3, L-1, L-2, M-3), body-scrubber at a public bathhouse (D-2), gas delivery (D-1), electronics delivery (D-1), driver (D-1, G-2, I-1), home delivery service (E-1, I-1), moving company (E-1), glass factory (E-1), restaurant (E-2), resource center (E-2), cleaning service (G-1), car wash (H-4), house maid (H-1), trading company focusing on China (H-2), freelance writer (L-1), medical volunteer at a church (M-1), parking lot employee (O-1), international trading (P-1), security guard (P-1), and telecommunications company (Q-1)

(5) Differences in food

South Korean food, along with its language, was the most difficult thing to adjust to. Adults experience more difficulties adjusting to the food than children do. Food of South is relatively sweeter and less bland

* Translation with note: Gangwon province is a northern area of South Korea and its dialect sounds similar to that of North Korea.

compared to that of the North. In addition, there are too many western foods in the South. For these reasons, most refugees eat North Korean style food at home.

> Children didn't have any problems adjusting. Food in North Korea is more spicy and salty, whereas it is sweeter and greasier in the South. I didn't fully adjust to food here yet. But it's getting better. (L-1)

(6) Frauds

Some North Korean refugees became victims of pyramid selling (K-1). Despite warnings and education about the pyramid selling at Hanawon, they were deceived by the people of the pyramid selling. Case K-1 argues that although South Koreans had monetary damage from the scheme of pyramid selling as well, they were partially compensated, whereas he couldn't get any compensation at all.

> My close friend from my homeland told me she worked at the pyramid selling. I truly believed her. People shouldn't go to that place in the first place. You are taken in once you listen to their lecture. I realized that there are many South Koreans who were cheated as well.
> (Interviewer: You mean, the pyramid selling?)
> They had such bad intentions. The instructor of the company explained to us that it worked very systematically, and it did not have a pyramid structure. The instructor was a person of high social status in North Korea. (...)
> (Interviewer: Didn't South Koreans also lose their money?)
> Yes, they did. But they got some money back last Saturday. (...) We relied only on the settlement fund, and when we spend it all, then we have nothing left. Although South Koreans say they have also been deceived,

> they didn't go through things that we've gone through. They don't truly understand how we feel. (K-1)

Pyramid selling was not the only fraud that refugees experienced. Some got swindled by brokers.

> (Interviewer: Have you ever been swindled by anyone?)
> (Interviewee 1) Yes, I have. My son sent three million Korean won to bring his wife here. He was deceived. Brokers didn't bring his wife to South Korea. (R-1)

(7) Changes in family relations

Due to characteristics of South Korean society structure, there is less time to meet or communicate with family members. At the time of difficulty, the spouse is the first person to discuss matters with, and for adolescents, friends can be good advisors. In the case of North Korean refugee adolescents, they turn to friends who are also North Korean refugees rather than South Korean friends. They have more empathy with each other and for that reason they can share more.

There were changes in family relationships after entry to South Korea. Case L-1 testified that he yelled less at his children and he thought much more of his wife.

> (Interviewer: Was there any difference in your child rearing style or how you treat your children?)
> Yes. What's different is that life is so hard in North Korea, and it is a very paternalistic society. North Korean parents are very conservative in handling children. In North Korea, parents force their children to be educated. On the other hand, in the South, parents give more autonomy

> to children. I liked the South Korean style.
> (Interviewer: Wasn't it uncomfortable or hard to change your style?)
> It was difficult. I was so used to the old style and I had been changed against my will. However I had to change in order to change the attitudes of my children. I felt my children and I were being educated at the same time.
> (Interviewer: Do your children say their father has changed? Do they like the new you?)
> They do like it. When I ask them the reason they like me better, they say I don't yell anymore. That implies many things. I don't have to yell at them as much as I did in North Korea. And my first child also tries to show some effort for himself. (L-1)

(8) Change in rage of the community

Whether it is voluntarily or not voluntarily, people were included and lived in a bigger community in the North than in the South. Contrarily, in South Korea, some people say it is hard to expand the community beyond their own family.

> We don't know anything about people next door. Such a thing is not possible in North Korea. We live together, have meetings, and naturally hang out with each other. It's not like that here. There is a neighborhood meeting which is not obligatory. We have to be part of every meeting and do things for the community together in North Korea. The only time I see my neighbors is when I am in the elevator on the way to work. Here, only family matters. (G-2)

In some cases, the atmosphere of urban cities in North Korea is similar to that of Seoul. This shows that change in the community is reflected differently depending on their origins.

> (Interviewer: Do you have anyone close here?)
> No, I don't. In South Korea, people don't know about where people live. Neighbors don't know each other. That's similar to North Korea.
> (Interviewer: So, neighbors do not know each other in North Korea as well?)
> No. In the urban city, people don't know each other. Maybe in rural areas, people are close to their neighbors. But that's not the case in the city. (P-1)

(9) Experiences of children and adolescents

Experiences of children or adolescents differ from those of adults. Their testimony is rather very direct and honest.

> (Interviewer: How is South Korea different from what you have seen though TV dramas when you were in North Korea?)
> There are only wealthy people in most TV dramas. I was actually disappointed after I got here. There are definitely good points, but one of the bad things is that we have to study in order to get into a college. My friends and I just played in North Korea. We did jump rope and played some games. That was fun, but in the South, I only get to go to all these academic institutions without any time for play. (F-2)

Adolescents were very sensitive about their experiences on how people neglected them.

> When people know I came from North Korea, they see me differently. There was this troublemaker who also came from North Korea. One day

> at school, he bullied me for staring at him. I ran away with my friend. When we told my friend's mother about what had happened, she said "Why does he make trouble at school when he should be laying low for coming from North Korea!" It was difficult hearing that because she didn't know I came from North Korea as well. That's how she feels about people like us in general. (F-2)

One of the different aspects of culture adolescents experience in South is the material culture. Some adolescents have a hard time resisting their desire to have material consumption.

> There was so much to do in South Korea since everything was a new experience. There are motorcycles and fancy cars. They want to spend all their settlement fund to buy that stuff. But that should be understood, because we have been so oppressed in the North. Frankly speaking, I want to try some of that, but I am suppressing my desires. I realized that I can't achieve my goals of becoming who I want to be if I get involved in such pleasures. Some adolescents from refugee families established some kind of a motorcycle gang. They are only 17 or 18, and they go around at night making noises. (H-3)

(10) Differences in the education system and the environment

One of the first difficulties faced by children of North Korean refugees is that they cannot get formal schooling due to differences in school age systems. For example, when a child quits school in the first grade of middle school (Since elementary school is a four-year program in the North, a middle school first grades in the North is a fifth grader at elementary school in the South. Thus, although the child graduated from elementary school in the North, the graduation diploma cannot be acknowledged in the South), the child has to register for school as a fifth grader. However, since the child could not get any education during their stay in China or a third country, the child is, at the least one or two years to at most three to four years, older than his classmates. Such students attempt to have a qualification examination for elementary school (or middle school) rather than to enter the regular school. Thus, they do not get to have an opportunity from the beginning, to spend time with regular school students.

Case G-4 graduated from elementary school in North Korea. Yet, he had to take a qualification examination. The student entered South Korea in September of 2001. In order to enter school in accordance to his age, he planned to take a qualification examination for middle school in April of 2002. When he found out that his elementary school diploma was not acknowledged in the South, he was very discouraged. He then passed a qualification examination for elementary school in May of 2002, and middle school in August of 2002. He took a comparative evaluation on December of the same year, and he was able to enter a regular high school in 2003. Since he entered high school with other Korean students, no one knew that he came from the North. Case G-3 quit in his second year of middle school in the North, which is equivalent to the sixth grade of elementary school in the South. This led him to take a qualification examination for elementary school. Later then, he entered college by passing the examination for both middle school and high school without attending any regular schools.

> I studied really hard until then. But not now. Back then, there was a clear goal, which was to pass the qualification examination. I do my best only if there is a realistic goal. I am the type of person who can concentrate on studying even when others make noise. My elementary school diploma from North Korea was not certified in South Korea. That is, I

> dropped out of school when I was a first grader of middle school, which means that I only had five years of elementary education. That caused a problem. That's why I couldn't take the exam for middle school. I had to take the elementary school qualification exam first. It was held in May. I hated studying elementary stuff because the exam included music like reading a music score. I got my elementary school diploma in May. I passed the exam for middle school in August. (G-3)

In addition, parents want to give their children some extra help in their education, and yet, they cannot provide such education due to financial reasons. Case D-2 reported, "I don't spend that much on my child, since mine is still young. But later on, I would have to send her to several educational institutions like others do." Case L-2 expressed the desire to get some extra education, but due to financial reasons, it's difficult to get any.

(11) Anxiety about future

One of the difficulties that refugees undergo after getting out of Hanawon is tedium from having nothing much to do (G-4). Anxiety about their future is another factor that makes refugees nervous. Case G-4, a student, is anxious about the future and described himself as a burning candle.

> I should work harder. I should have developed a skill that I can do well and prepared myself for the future, but I don't think I fulfilled any of those goals.
>
> (Interviewer: Do you feel anxious about your future?)
>
> I think I still have a bit more time to figure things out. But I don't know how much time left for me. It gives me a headache just by thinking about

> these things. (...) I have to be in charge of my life but I am too passive and still have insecurities. I feel like there's less and less opportunities left for me. I feel as if I am a burning candle...
> (Interviewer: What do you want to do after graduation?)
> I focused on experiencing school life and understanding the campus atmosphere. As I am about to graduate, I don't feel like I am ready to go out and sacrifice everything for the job. I am very depressed now. (G-4)

3) Psychological conflicts and the overcoming process

Amid psychological experiences that North Korean refugees go through in South Korea, prejudice, lack of understanding, and loneliness occupied a majority of these experiences.

(1) Prejudice and the lack of understanding

One of the psychological conflicts faced by North Korean refugees is a feeling that South Koreans have prejudices against them. Refugees were hurt the most when Koreans believed that they would fall behind in education or in abilities only because they were from the North. For example, case B-1's husband tried to get a job as a tofu delivery man. He was rejected at the second interview, because the store owner could not allow money-handling work to a North Korean. Case B-1 and her husband believed this is because Koreans have a prejudice against North Korean refugees that they lack abilities and have a tendency of stealing money. North Korean refugees are deeply hurt when refugees face such prejudices.

Another perspective by South Koreans is that all refugees have suffered from severe poverty in North Korea. In fact, although they have undergone difficulties from poverty, they get hurt when people sympathize or ignore them. For instance, prejudices such as, "People are all beggars in North Korea" (E-2) or "North Korean female refugees are women without any feminine virtue" (E-2) are hard to accept by refugees. Koreans' responses like "Are people really dying in North Korea?" or "They should eat ramen if they don't have any rice" reflect the lack of understanding about North Korea by Koreans in the South.

Another prejudice they experience is that people automatically judge them as Chosun-zok (Korean Chinese) without even asking. Refugees thought they could be acknowledged as Korean citizens, but people judged them as a foreigner from their speaking style. Refugees experienced psychological conflict when South Koreans discriminated and undervalued them.

> The store posted a notice of an opening for a part time worker. I lacked confidence and was scared at first, because I didn't know what kind of work I would be doing. I went to the store and asked them if they are looking for a part time worker. Back then, I used a North Korean dialect. They believed that I was a Korean Chinese without asking. Afterward, I could feel the hidden discrimination and belittlement. I didn't notice it in the beginning, but I do now as I live in Korea. I am desperate to change my way of speaking. (M-2)

In such a case, there are two different responses. Like case B-1, one can devote oneself to work by restraining one's feelings. On the other hand, case B-1's husband had fights with others by releasing his anger. As a result, case B-1 expresses her fondness toward South Korea, whereas her husband expresses his desire to go back to North Korea.

(2) Belittlement

Belittlement by South Koreans is another psychological factor faced by refugees. In case B-1, when a refugee was quarreling with a neighbor in regard to a problem between their children, the neighbor looked down on her by saying "You are just a bunch of beggars living on government funds."

> When she said, "You are just a bunch of beggars living on government funds," I was furious. She mentioned something like "beggars" and "foreign country" in her statement. She was implying that how dare we, who are on government funds living in a foreign country, take out our anger on them. So, I went back at her and said she needed to realize her situation too, that she was also very poor living in a low-income apartment. South Koreans still don't have an awareness of North Koreans. For this, we were hurt many times. (B-1)

North Korean refugees feel they are being belittled when doctors respond carelessly to their inquiries (K-1), or they are left out in the process of receiving compensation for losses as victims of a pyramid business. In fact, these could be general responses to anyone, and yet, some refugees suspect that people have belittlement attitudes because they are from North Korea.

(3) Loneliness

Some refugees perceive South Koreans as people of only words, who say they would help, but do not put their words into action when help is really needed (H-3). Refugees feel that South Koreans are too family- oriented without much relationships with neighbors.

> Refugees who came alone tend to be easily indulged in a relationship with South Koreans in thinking that they are nice people. These are the kind of people who are taken advantage of easily by South Koreans. For this, many refugees closed their hearts to people in the South, and only spent time with people like us. When we need help, we never ask our South Korean friends, even if we have close friends. We only turn to refugees like us. South Koreans always say that they are always here for us, but that's it. But, refugees are not like them. That's because maybe we were taught to help each other in our community when our friend is in need. By doing so, we have a strong integrity toward each other. But in South Korea, everyone is very self-centered and this may be because they are suffering a lot in the market economy. People do not build a relationship even between neighbors. In North Korea, when we move to a new place, we get to know each other the very day. Contrarily, people in the South don't know about their neighbors even if they live there for decades. Frankly, I don't like it. I even tried to be close to them at school, but they just come and go to school quietly, or they just participate in their club activities. In the beginning, I signed up for several clubs, but it became tiresome. I couldn't do anything else but to be there. So, I withdrew from all the clubs except one, and I don't even go there during school break. When clubmates call me to come, I just tell them I am busy. (H-3)

(4) Overcoming process

Despite the difficulties of psychological conflicts such as prejudice, belittlement, and loneliness, some refugees overcame such difficulties in their own ways. When such a conflict arises, family can offer help, but it doesn't always resolve the conflict. Rather, case H-3 reports that friends from North Korea can be a greater help than family members.

> Although family can help, but there are only a few people within the family. So, it's just you at the end. It's a matter of how you think of yourself, make a decision, and keep your principles. Many students who came alone do well. I know people who came alone graduated school and have nice jobs. Initially, I thought refugees who came with parents would do better, but that wasn't necessarily the case. I am so proud of students at my age who work really hard even if they are all alone in South Korea. We learn from each other. Even though we get along with Korean friends, I think it's fifty-fifty. We get along better with our group of North Korean refugees. If my North Korean friend asks for help while I have a prior arrangement with my Korean friend, I would cancel the prior arrangement and help out my North Korean friend instead. (H-3)

Case H-4 has undergone hardships and loneliness from not having any close friends in the South due to a lack of commonalities. He then realized that such psychological difficulties and conflicts arose due to his lack of understanding, because he had come from a different culture, and a lack of consensus needs time to be resolved. In addition, by acknowledging that his "loneliness" itself can also be experienced by other friends in different circumstances, he could have something to share with friends in South Korea.

> (Interviewer: Did you have any difficulties at school?)
> Well, I had difficulties from the lack of knowledge. It was easy to be intimidated because I didn't know the culture here, but I thought to myself that it is natural, that I don't know because I came from the North Korean society. I became very lonely from not being able to get along with friends. I suffered tremendously psychologically, because I was a loner at school. I regretted coming to South Korea. Then, I realized that

the root of my problems was my lack of knowledge about this culture. It's not a surprise that I don't know the culture, and it is not something to be ashamed of. Once I realized this, I tell other refugees that they only need to learn the culture. It might be hard to make a good relationship with friends because of this, and yet, they shouldn't suffer from it. (...) In many cases, refugees fall because of such problem. I was about to fall, but then I stood up.
(Interviewer: What was difficult?)
It's the same. I felt I was all alone among my classmates at school. I was lonely. That's the real pain. At first, my classmates paid attention to me because of the fact that I came from North Korea. And for that, I thought at first I was very close to them. Then, I realized that we had nothing in common. There was nothing to talk about because we lacked common ground. That period of silence itself became the consensus between classmates and me after going through the overcoming process. We still talk about that time when I see them now. (H-4)

6. Border-crossing process and resources used in adapting to South Korea

1) Personal traits

(1) Individuation

Individuation refers to an attitude of acknowledging individual as independent, and each individual in society is different from one another. Such attitudes can be characterized as an attitude of positively evaluating oneself who is different from others, and an attitude of not being influenced by others' judgment or prejudice on oneself. In the course of human development, this kind of attitude is the ideal feature of healthy humans. Refugees, who established individuation relatively better than others, could well manage to bear the agony and anger.

In case of B-1 and her husband, when there were problems with neighbors, or quitting the job due to the boss's prejudice, B-1 overcame the situation by expressing her thoughts clearly to her neighbor or repressing her feelings toward people with prejudice. Contrarily, her husband showed anger or fought when he was faced with prejudice. In the question of asking their satisfaction to South Korean life, the former responded that life is good in the South, whereas the latter revealed his desire to go back to North Korea.

Many refugees attempt to hide their identity as North Korean. On the other hand, case H-4, a 21-year-old young adult, is very confident about his identity as a North Korean refugee and puts great value to his unique experiences which make him more mature than others of his age. Such attitude is helpful in building a firm identity and confidence, which plays as a critical role as a resource in overcoming difficulties.

> It has been five years since I settled in South Korea. I lived long enough here that people even ask me whether I am really from North Korea. Yet, I am still a North Korean. I had different experiences in North Korea, which I would never want to forget. I tell them I am different from them. That is based on my real experiences. Nowadays, I study and tell college students why the unification has to be achieved, and why we have to save the North Korean society. (H-4)

(2) Self-confidence

Self-confidence refers to a belief and attitude that one can do something in times of difficulty. Self-confidence is strongly related to the belief of refugees that they can overcome current difficulties whether they are in the North or they are adjusting to a new life in the South.

Self-confidence, in many cases, is acquired in their work place, regardless of where they are. For example, confidence of case L-1, who once was a writer in North Korea and now works as a freelance writer in China and South Korea, can be shown through the description of her experiences during the interview. Moreover, A-1 and M-1, who once were doctors in North Korea, believe that they are people with abilities, even when they cannot work as a doctor in South Korea. Such thoughts help refugees to overcome crises such as the crossing process or difficulties faced in South Korea. The following passage is a description of a self-evaluation of case M-1.

> (Interviewer: We found many refugees who are suffering from adjusting to South Korea during the interviews. First of all, they have a hard time finding a job.)
> Yes. I heard things. Someone got a job, and the co-workers had a prejudiced perspective toward him for being a North Korean refugee. The refugee was stressed out again, and as a result, he quit the job. This process is repeated over and over.
> (Interviewer: Have you ever had that kind of stress?)
> Of course! I was even stressed out by the church.
> (Interviewer: How did you react to that situation?)
> People were looking down on me because I came from North Korea. You know, I am a man of temper.
> (Interviewer: Were they your co-workers?)
> Yes, some were my people at my office and my co-workers. They were discriminating against me, so I brought it up to my boss. Haha, I even got an apology from the boss. (M-1)

Besides people having confidence at their jobs, regardless of where they are, refugees who had successful experiences in accomplishing school admissions and certificates of qualification showed positive attitudes and strong confidence in their abilities. Case F-1, who is attending a college of pharmacy, had confidence in believing that he could become successful as he accomplished things that were once thought impossible.

> My strength is that I never gave up my dreams, which seemed impossible in real life. After I graduated from high school in North Korea, I wasn't able to get an admission to a university because I came from a family of bad element. I was very disappointed. When people told me that I could go to college after working for a few years, I worked hard to fulfill my dream. I finally got an admission to a college. I wanted to pursue further academic achievements in South Korea because I achieved it with great effort. Even the Hanawon staff told me that I have to give up what I studied in the North. (Case F-1 was advised to throw away everything he had learned in North Korea as a pharmacist, and start over.) Frankly speaking, since South Korea is a society in which wage is always paid for labor, people can earn money by doing anything. It's not like North Korea where no wage is paid for work. However, I thought I could do anything if I have a strong will, because this is a country of free will. I didn't want to give up my dream, and I achieved my dream. Among six thousand refugees, I am the only person who attends a college of pharmacy. Everyone I know tells me I am amazing for doing this with two kids. But I pursued what I desired until I finally got it. At first, some people told me I will lose everything due to my stubbornness, but I think I am who I am now because of my stubbornness. (F-1)

(3) Strong goals

Strong goals play the role of a critical resource in overcoming difficulties. North Korean refugees' goals had different aspects in North Korea, a third country including China, and South Korea. Their goals in North Korea were survival, escape from starvation, economic prosperity, status stability, and reunion with husband (case J-1), whereas the primary goal in China was status stability. Their goals in South Korea were stable jobs, accomplishments at work and school, and fulfilling future dreams.

In case H-1, when her husband died from electric shock while working as an electrician in the North Korean army, she did not send her son to the military and revealed her hopes, and her goal of sending and goal of sending her son to college.

> No, no, he was an electrician and was electrocuted... So, I didn't want my son to join the army. I thought I was going to faint, if I sent even my son away.
> So, I sent him off to college. He was in his sophomore year and the first year somehow went by. There is this awareness for enduring difficulties. That is, people tend to think more positively to overcome hardships. I thought positively and decided to educate my son. One of my relatives told me what the point of getting an education is when everyone is dying from hunger. But I wanted my son to gain better knowledge from education. I feel bad when I see him, because I think he would have grown more if he had decided not to go to college. He didn't have enough nutrition when studying. I sold everything to prepare for college tuition. (H-1)

According to reports by North Korean refugees, they behaved more actively and did not fall into confusion or boredom when their goal was definite. Although they were fearful facing difficulties in North Korea or China, they had then a strong goal of survival or status stability. Ironically, one of the difficulties they experienced in South Korea is losing their goal or losing heart for accomplishing their goal.

(4) Positive outlook

Positive outlook also plays as a critical role in overcoming a crisis. Case C-2, in spite of his difficult life in South Korea, had a positive outlook on his current circumstance. For instance, C-2 responded with a light attitude that he learned the language because he didn't want to go back and forth to make any transaction from miscommunications in his work. He described "I had to go to places at least three times to get things done when normal people can finish it at once. (...) When they ask me for something, I don't know what it is. (...) I learned the language because I didn't want to go through all the hassle. Learning the language is fun. It's fun to live". In addition, on the question about his life in South Korea, he reported, "I think life is harder in the South. (...) But I think it's a matter of how you look at it. If you think it's hard, then it will come to you as hard. If you look at it from the other side, it may be easy. (...) People tell me it's hard to adjust, but I think I will be fine". Furthermore, for the question of difficult job finding, he responded, "Some companies have bad impressions on North Korean refugees, but some companies give them a job because they are interested in them since they never had refugees in their company." Due to his attitude, he was regarded as one of the hardest working students by his teachers at an academic institution.

(5) Giving meaning to one's situation and work

Finding meaning in one's work, other than economic value, and making oneself valuable may be a critical resource in overcoming the difficulties. Examples are case A-1, who found meaning in giving medical treatment to others although she had financial difficulty in North Korea, and case E-1, who found great meaning in saving people's lives by taking P.O.W.s with him when he escaped from North Korea. Such examples show that adding meaning to what they do help them to endure hardships.

> (...) In any way I could, I saved a person's life. Anybody would have done the same if one saw the old man lying there. He was actually dying. It was so hard to carry him on my back through the journey. Although I was financially rewarded, my thoughts of wanting him to meet his brothers in the homeland were greater. I risked my life for this... (E-1)

(6) Perspective-taking ability

Perspective-taking ability is defined as an ability to understand a situation in the other's perspective beyond their own, and have empathy with others. This ability allows North Korean refugees to have an attitude of "I can understand their attitudes (South Korean) when I am in their shoes" instead of making negative evaluations on South Koreans for not understanding them.

> I am not meaning that the South Koreans were bad, because I would have done the same if I were born here. I can understand them if I take their perspective. In this respect, people cannot understand others without knowledge. That's probably why South Koreans are unwelcoming toward us. I think I would have felt the same if I were them. People have to figure out a way to handle it. That's the reality.
> ...No. I do not get hurt anymore. It hurt me at first. But now, I believe that I would have done the same if I were them. I, too, looked down on

> people who were less fortunate than me when I was in North Korea. (G-4)

(7) Transcendence of spirituality

One of the essential resources for North Korean refugees is transcendence of spirituality. It refers to the recognition and expectation on a transcendental being, and an attitude of relying on the power of the transcendental being for things beyond human control. Evidently, North Koreans did not have the freedom of religion. Thus, they do not know the principles of religion. Yet, they acknowledged a transcendental being and depended on it in times of adversity. By doing this, refugees could endure the unbearable fear and insecurity they faced in reality.

In case A-1, she could not let go of her fears because her daughter had been imprisoned for reentering North Korea in search of her granddaughter. However, she could continue to the hope for her daughter's well-being after taking a religious perspective.

Case M-1 has three children. Two are studying oriental medicine and one is studying nursing at a university. She believes that she has been looked after by God.

> I think I have been looked after by God... I was able to settle in South Korea with the help of God.
>
> (Interviewer: Did all of your family members make the entry?)
>
> Yes. Everyone came. God led all of us here without any damages despite all the difficulties.
>
> (Interviewer: Initially, you probably didn't believe in a religion, right?)
>
> No, I didn't have any. As I think about it after I came here, it was all God's help that made it possible for us to settle in South Korea. (M-1).

2) Family support

(1) Close relationship within family members

Close family relationship is undoubtedly a supporting resource in the course of adaptation to South Korea. The following is the case M-2's description.

> Characteristics of my family? Speaking of family, I believe I have been blessed in many ways, but was most especially blessed to have parents like my mother and father. My parents are very nice people. I am thankful for that. There aren't many refugees who come along with their parents here. I think it is so great that I can live with my parents. One of the characteristics of my family is that everyone tries to contribute. The fact that everyone tries to do something on his own gives me strength to resist many temptations. There exist so many temptations. There are a total of eight people in our family, and none of them try to depend on others. I think this helps my family to maintain itself. I am the oldest daughter and people obey me well. I am very grateful for this. (M-2)

(2) Expectation and attachment on children

Expectation and attachment on their children have given North Korean refugees courage to overcome fears in the moment of difficult decision-making. For instance, case C-1 could endure difficulties in North Korea by the expectations for her son to grow up as a member of the party after graduating from military school. When her son was in a situation where he was unable to enter a military school (they had a runaway soldier in the family), she decided to leave. Likewise, the expectation on her offspring helped them to endure adversity in North Korea.

In case F-1, a mother, who had left behind her second daughter in

North Korea due to circumstances beyond her control, tried to reenter North Korea in search of her daughter. The fear of getting arrested and punished by the North Korean government could be overcome by her love for her daughter.

(3) Holding environment

Attachment to offspring as "holding environment" given by their parents, plays a great part in children's development. For example, case C-3's report of her 17 days of prison life and about things her father had done for her shows the positive experience with the father, and positive views she has for the experience in prison. Although the causal relationship does not exist between these two experiences, considering the fact that the attachment relationship with her father is often mentioned in her report of South Korean life, it might be a crucial resource in her adaptation process.

> Every father loves and takes care of their children, but I think my father is relatively better in taking care of us than other fathers. Unlike sons, we daughters have menstruation periods, and most fathers don't know how to deal with it. However, when I started menstruation in China, my father took good care of me on things that mothers would do. He told me about physical changes that girls go through in the process of becoming women. Some people told him that a father cannot take care of daughters, so he should leave us behind and try to bring us back later. But my father told them he can never leave us behind. I never once was apart from my father even in severe difficulties. (C-3)

One interesting phenomenon is that some refugee children, unlike adults, remember the North Korean society as a very happy place. They do not recognize the crossing process as negative as adults do. Such phenomenon can be explained by the following reasons: children have internalized functions that make it easy to recover from an external shock for their psychological survival; they are not mature enough to understand surrounding circumstances beyond their family community; or parents or family members eased external shocks preventing them from being affected by the shock. Case I-3, then six or seven-year old, illustrated North Korean life as follows.

> (Interviewer: How was it when you were in North Korea?)
> Well, it was good.
> (Interviewer: What was good about it?)
> I had friends there. Little ones… I lived in a tile-roofed house, I mean, in the rural area. I remember playing with my cousin there. Then, I moved to a five story house, and I remember playing with children in my neighborhood. There was a crane next to the house.
> (Interviewer: Was there? So you played near it?)
> There also was a bakery in front of the crane. There was a kind of pancake that is not sold in South Korea. That pancake had red bean paste inside, which made it more delicious than the ones in China. In my house, there was a big room and a small room next to it. There was also a dining room. I remember visits from my grandfather and many relatives.
> (…)
> (Interviewer: So, do you have good memories of North Korea?)
> Yes.
> (Interviewer: Do you remember any hard thing about North Korea?)
> None.
> (Interviewer: None? Can't you remember anything?)
> I remember hiking to a mountain when I lived in a roof-topped house.

(I-3)

3) Social resources

For their crossing process and their adaptation to new society, refugees need not only individual resources but also social resources and support. The crossing process and experiences in a third country undergone by refugees are experiences during a crisis rather than typical everyday experiences. When surrounding support is not available at the right moment, refugees instantly face a crises such as arrest, starvation, or illness. Thus, support from others plays a critical role in their survival during the process of crossing.

On the other hand, aid from the government or public organizations help refugees in their psychological and social adaptation rather than in their survival. Social resources, which helped the refugees fir their survival and adaptation, are as follows.

(1) Social resources in the crossing process and the third country

In general, resources from surrounding people, rather than from a specific group, helped North Korean refugees for their survival before they entered to South Korea. For instance, for one having relatives in China, a Chinese police officer released refugees before sending them in custody to North Korea, Chinese and Korean, provided food to them and helped them in a ship to South Korea. Case B-1 testifies how she was helped in the boat on the way to South Korea.

> I thought I was going to die on a ship on the way to South Korea. I was very weak, and I had to hide in the bottom of the ship. It was December

> and I was all wet because the water leaked into the bottom of the ship. There were about sixty people in this place that was barely larger than a bed. (...) We only had one meal per day for 16 days before getting on board the South Korean ship. I got sick as soon as I got on board. The place when we hid was very cold. It's somewhat disgusting to talk about, but I couldn't take care of my own body waste. I couldn't even lift a finger and I thought I would die. (...) It was a smuggling vessel, so it just anchored in the open sea until a Korean boat arrived.
> (Interviewer: Did you transfer to a South Korean boat in the open sea from a Chinese boat?)
> That's how it was done. We transfered again to a smaller boat in South Korea. In the smaller boat, people started to give me some medicine, and I got better afterwards. Then, they put me in the captain's cabin where it's warm. That's how I am still alive. I heard that they just throw dead bodies into the sea if someone dies in the boat. (B-1)

In addition, there were family members or relatives who entered the South before the refugees, crossing brokers, an American missionary (O-2), a churchman who provided shelter and food for four months, and a gang who helped the refugee from getting arrested in China.

In a unique case, D-2 got help from her mother-in-law who had tried to get a bride for her son through human trafficking but later when her son did not like her, the mother-in-law helped her to enter South Korea.

Not only were there people who helped North Korean refugees by directly providing financial support or by guiding them in the process of the crossing, but there were also those who encouraged them so that they would not lose hope. Case G-4 remembers and appreciates a person (she remembers as an owner of a Korean restaurant) who encouraged her by treating her as a human being.

> I have never been treated like that at a restaurant before nor afterwards. The owner gave me everything that was on the menu, and asked me my age. Then, he gave me 100 Chinese Yuan.* In fact, I could get more money even from others. However, for me, the value of money didn't matter. What mattered to me was that how he treated me. I can never forget that moment. He taught me how to eat certain foods and told waiters to bring more food. There was no belittlement. I was very thankful. (G-4)

(2) Social resources in South Korea

Social resources that can be acquired during the entry process and for life in South Korean include Hanawon and its staffs, welfare center staffs, and church volunteers. One police detective introduced several jobs.

> (Interviewer: How did you get a job as soon as you left Hanawon?)
> When we left Hanawon, every person is assigned to a police detective. In most cases, detectives find us jobs. That was true in my case, too.
> (Interviewer: When you quit working at the pipe factory within a month, what kind of job did he find for you?)
> I was jobless for about two weeks after working for one month. I asked the detective to find me a job and he found me one at XYZ. I started working there since last July. (R-2)

* Translation with note: Chinese currency. 100 Chinese Yuan (CNY) is equivalent to approximately 15 USD.

Other refugees became a great resource for them in times of difficulty and loneliness.

7. Summary of the border-crossing process of North Korean refugees

Despite difficulties of life in North Korea, refugees generally lived a life in their own way. In fact, people with high political and social status did not have many difficulties. However, as the economy worsened, as the social environment became inferior, and as people experienced more severe discrimination, North Koreans began to think about the possibility of escaping from North Korea. In addition, they thought about crossing when they received positive information regarding China and South Korea, when they realized that North Korea was economically inferior to other countries, when they had relatives in China or South Korea, or when they were persuaded by people in South Korea. However, they hesitated to leave North Korea because they were accustomed to the life in North Korea, the punishment when caught during the crossing process was harsh, and they were afraid of the danger that remaining family members in North Korea might face. Despite their reasons for hesitation, they decided to leave when family members died from poverty or illness, became politically disadvantaged, their social status was degraded, got in touch with a parent once thought to be dead, were in pursuit to find family members, or if these factors took effect concurrently. The crossing process varied by individual families.

Most refugees' primary goal was to settle in China. Yet, life in China was not as easy as they thought. That is, they had to endure their fears of being chased by the Chinese police, face status insecurity, and cope with discrimination. In addition, they were worried about their children's unstable identity. At the same time, some wanted to go back to North Korea, but could not act upon their will because of the harsh punishment they would face when they reentered the North. Moreover, news that the South Korean government would not reveal their identity led them to consider settling in the South.

Refugees experience several crises during the crossing process. The biggest crisis among external crises reported by refugees in this study was getting arrested by the North Korean government. Other crises included the arrest by the Chinese police, and false information.

After entry to South Korea, North Korean refugees settled in the South Korean society after going through the Daesung Public Affairs and Hanawon. Refugees are proud to be South Korean citizens while trying to bring their remaining family members in China or North Korea to the South. Yet, their adaptation process was complicated. They had difficulties in language, especially with words from foreign languages, North Korean dialects, employment, food differences, and fraud targeting refugees. Family relationships and the community models were different from those of North Korea. Adolescents suffered from adjusting to the new culture, the education system, and the school environment, which was especially hard to adapt to. They had undergone psychological challenges due to prejudice, a lack of understanding, and belittlement by South Koreans, which led them to loneliness. They used several resources to recover from psychological and social anguish.

North Korean refugees utilized psychological and social resources such as individuation, self-confidence, strong goal, positive outlook, giving meaning to one's work, perspective-taking ability, and transcendence of spirituality during the crossing process. The higher the use of resources, the better they adapted to the South Korean society.

In addition, close relationships within family members, expectations and attachments to offspring, and the holding environment provided significant support in the crossing and adaptation processes to South Korea.

IV

Border-Crossing Experience and Personal Changes of North Korean Refugees

The adaptation process of North Korean refugees in the South Korean society can be explained with the process of cultural adaptation. The early studies on cultural adaptation process of individual and family in a new society describe the process of accepting a new culture by immigrants with the concept of assimilation. The early theory on assimilation by Gordon (1964) described several processes that the immigrants have undergone in order to assimilate to the main stream society; cultural assimilation, structural assimilation, identity assimilation, attitude acceptance assimilation, behavior acceptance assimilation, civil acceptance, and social value and cultural assimilation. This means that in the long run, immigrants or minorities lose their unique characteristics and eventually melt into the mainstream society. In fact, in the case of the United States, during the first immigration rush from Europe, Europeans started to lose their national traits and completely assimilate to the American society in terms of education, occupation, language, and marriage over generations.

Since the 1960s, immigrants from Latin America, Asia, and many of non-European countries started to enter the United States creating the second immigration rush. With the second immigration rush, the assimilation theory was challenged since the new group of immigrants' adaptation process to the mainstream society, unlike the European immigrants, could not be explained with the existing theory. Contrary to the expectation that various cultural backgrounds of immigrants would be incorporated into the American culture, the immigrants' unique identity and culture were maintained and even enhanced over time and generation (Chun, 2002).

In attempt to describe this process of cultural adaptation, scholars introduced a new concept of 'acculturation' instead of the assimilation process. Acculturation means integrative process of selection and modification of both cultures instead of absorbing everything about the new culture or replacing the old values with new values of the new society (Buriel, 1993; Patel, Power, & Bhavnagri, 1996). Acculturation is a multidimensional process rather than a single dimensional event, which takes place in each area of life (Jain & Belsky, 1997). The changes occur in a faster rate in some aspects of life, slower in other areas, and sometimes changes never take place. For example, change in clothing may take place more quickly than in food, and changes may occur faster in behavioral lifestyle in a materialistic aspect than in lifestyle related to thoughts such as value and belief (Park, Kim, & Doh, 2000). In this chapter, the course of adaptation for the North Korean refugees in the South Korean society is seen as an acculturation process, and their value, identity, and psychological characteristics were examined during the process. By analyzing the changes they experience, their way of selectively accepting and interpreting a new culture as a newly settled immigrants can be understood

1. Changes in values

The North Koreans in South Korea after the crossing responded about the differences in the values of the North and the South to be as follows. The difference between the refugees' average score for the materialistic orientation value was 3.93 in the North Korean society and 2.99 in the South Korean society. The scores for the materialistic orientation value in the North and the South were significantly different. What is the implication of the result of stronger materialistic value orientation found in a communist society than in a capitalistic society? It may be related to the fact that the North Koreans who experienced the lack of necessities for survival in the North Korean society are more obsessed with material. Once they enter the South Korean society, with the financial aid and housing provided by the government, their obsession and desire in materials may have decreased.

Their average scores for the collectivist values between the North and the South were significantly different with 3.27 in North and 2.84 in South Korea. The strong collectivist value orientation found in the communist society of North Korea is well known. Therefore, it is convincing that the respondents are highly aware of their collectivist value orientation in the North Korean society.

> It is not the case for us North Koreans. Well, I don't know if that's because we are trained that the comrades have to help each other when one of the co-workers is sick in an organization. We have that sincere integrity. When we move to a new neighborhood, we get very close the very day. (H-3)

An interesting fact is the report on the individualistic value

<Table IV-1> The refugees' different value orientations in North Korea and South Korea

Classification	North Korean society			South Korean society			t
	N	M	SD	N	M	SD	
Materialism	190	3.93	.64	189	2.99	.63	13.27***
Collectivism	192	3.27	.61	190	2.84	.70	7.02***
Individualism	192	3.32	.85	186	3.27	.71	.49
Familism	194	3.76	.69	188	3.09	.61	12.38***
Gender-role	195	3.58	.81	188	2.49	.65	15.17***

*** $p < .001$

orientation. There was no significant difference between the individualistic value orientation in the North (3.32) and the South (3.27). We have predicted the individualistic value orientation in the South to be much higher than that of the North. Yet, the actual score distribution was found to be otherwise. The individualism did not seem to increase despite the greater freedom and competition in the South due to lack of social experience in the South Korean society along with the government subsidy program preventing the North Korean refugees from being exposed to the competition and struggle for survival.

The familism value orientation score was significantly different between the North (3.76) and the South (3.09). The North Korean refugees perceive far more familism value orientation in North Korea than in the South. Familism can be interpreted in the same context with paternalism. The patriarchal gender role scores in the North and the South were significantly different with the score 3.58 in the North and 2.49 in the South, which indicates that the awareness of patriarchal gender role is more evident in the North than in the South (Table IV-1).

1) Materialistic values

We compare the materialistic value of the refugees when they were in the North and when they are now in the South. These values reflect their subjective assessment on the North and the South with respect to materialism. The refugees think that the tendency to think that 'trying to get close to managers at work would help their career' is stronger in the North than in the South, and the tendency to 'express gratitude and apology with materials' is much stronger in the North than in the South as well. In addition, the North Koreans tend to think that 'in order to care for others, one has to be well off himself first' more strongly than the South Koreans (Table IV-2). These results indicate that the value of materials is found to be considered more important in the North than in the South in above three questions measuring the materialistic values. In a communist society, uniform distribution of property and goods is ideologically considered the principle of social function. With

<Table IV-2> Differences in materialistic value of the refugees

	Items	North Korean society			South Korean society			t
		N	M	SD	N	M	SD	
Materi-alism	1. The reason to get close to managers at work is to help their career.	192	4.05	.82	191	2.76	.83	14.66***
	2. It is right to express gratitude and apology with materials.	195	3.81	.83	189	2.95	.87	9.67***
	3. In order to care for others, one should have high income.	192	3.89	.91	191	3.27	.97	7.01***
	Mean	190	3.93	.64	189	2.99	.63	13.27***

*** p < .001

the communist ideology, the North Koreans must be familiar with the communist system where food is distributed equally. On the contrary, focus on the value of materials is exhibited less in the capitalistic society of South Korea than in the communist society of North Korea. The strong recognition in materialistic values displayed in the North may be attributed to the lack of materials in the North Korean society. In addition, the inequality of resource distribution from the hierarchy of status in the communist society may have caused the maldistribution of wealth. This maldistribution may have caused the North Koreans to internalize stronger materialistic values as can be seen from the below case.

> To be honest, the rich managerial officers get richer and richer and the poor ones like us can never get rich. If you have the authority, you live well, but if you don't have the power, you can never get wealthy. (H-1)

In order to explore on the variables associated with the materialistic reasoning in North Korea, various demographic variables related to the materialism were analyzed by regression analysis. The regression analysis used gender, age, education level, family-accompanied crossing, marital status, period after the crossing, and period after the entry to the South as the independent variables, and materialism in the North as the dependent variable. According to the regression result, family-accompanied crossing (β=0.29, $p<.05$) and marital status (β=0.53, $p<.001$) were found to have significant influence on the materialistic value in the North. This means that the refugees who were accompanied by a family or married perceived the materialism of North Korea stronger. This may because they felt more responsibility and burden to support their family than those who did not have a family to support.

<Table IV-3> Regression analysis of the refugees' materialistic value

Variables	Materialism			
	North Korea		South Korea	
	b	β	b	β
Sex (male=1)	-.08	-.10	.04	.04
Age	-.07	-.50	-.12	-.09
Education level	.02	.03	-.02	-.02
Family-accompanied entry	.24	.29*	-.13	-.15
Marital status (married=1)	-.44	.53***	.04	.05
Time after the crossing	-.17	-.09	.27	.15*
Time after the entry	.10	.07	-.20	-.14
Constant	4.33		3.08	
F	3.22**		1.52	
R^2	.18		.09	

* p < .05, *** p < .001; β is a standardized coefficient.

However, the regression model for materialism in South Korea was not significant with the independent variables such as the refugees' gender, age, education level, entry status, marital status, period since the crossing, and period since the entry to the South (Table IV-3). Among the above independent variables, period since the crossing (β=0.15, $p<.05$) was the only variable that explained the materialism in South Korea. The materialistic reasoning of the North Korean refugees increases over the period after the crossing, which implies that the longer the stay in a third country after the crossing, the stronger the materialistic orientation. However, the longer the settlement period after the entry to South Korea, the lower the materialistic orientation gets. This result could mean that the materialistic values tend to diminish after the entry to South Korea in the short term since the urgent needs were met by the government subsidies on goods and housing that were required for survival in the South Korean society. In addition, in a long run, the North Korean refugees may come to understand that the wealth and goods do not come along easily by just desiring them, and they learn to realize that by having too much desire to possess materials could raise many issues in South Korea.

2) Collectivist values

Among the two items in measuring the collectivist value orientation, there was a significant difference between the scores for the North (M=3.17) and scores for the South (M=2.70) on the question 'My own interests should be sacrificed for the benefit of the group.' As far as the question 'I feel comfortable when I have the same opinion with the other people of the group that I belong to, and not comfortable when I have different opinion' is concerned, the score for the North Korean society was 3.37 points significantly differing from 2.99 points for the South Korean society. The two questions demonstrate that the refugees' collectivistic awareness in the North Korean society is somewhat weakened when they are in the South Korean society. Considering the underlying collectivistic system in a communist society of North Korea, it is a meaningful fact that someone from a communist society realizes the easement of the collectivist awareness he or she used to have with the settlement in South Korea. This evidently indicates that one's reasoning is formed and influenced within the social ideological system, possibly leading the pattern of the ideological orientation to a new direction.

Contrary to the collectivist values, the individualistic values emphasize individual freedom. Two items were used to measure the individualistic value orientation, which were 'I should handle my own

<Table IV-4> Differences in the refugees' collectivist and individualistic value

	Items	North Korean society			South Korean society			t
		N	M	SD	N	M	SD	
Collectivism	5. My own interests should be sacrificed for the benefit of the group.	194	3.17	.86	190	2.70	.82	5.57***
	6. I feel comfortable when I have the same opinion with other people from the group.	193	3.37	.73	191	2.99	.83	5.81***
Mean		192	3.27	.61	190	2.84	.70	7.02***
Individualism	7. I should handle my own matter as I wish.	193	3.46	.90	188	3.40	.85	.70
	8. If I believe something is right I would do it even if my boss opposes.	194	3.18	1.05	187	3.14	.83	.24
Mean		192	3.32	.85	186	3.27	.71	.49

*** $p < .001$

matter as I wish' and 'If I believe something is right I would do it even if my boss opposes'. The scores on these items relating to free will showed no significant differences between the South and the North (Table IV-4). The result shows that their degree of individualistic values is similar in both societies. How can these results be interpreted?

The difference found in the North Korean refugees' evaluation on the collectivist values between the South and North Korea society is attributed to the characteristic of the North Korean society. The collectivism policy is internalized for North Korean children from the early age. As can be noted from the slogan 'One for all and all for one,' the North Korean society impose collectivistic human qualities on both the children and adults. In fact, everyone is a member of an organization in North Korea. As soon as a child reaches age of seven, he/she automatically becomes a member of *Youth Group*. A leader is elected from the organization and the *Youth Group* official trains the group. The disengagement from such organization is possible only when they reach age of 65 for men and 60 for women (Park, 1995; Lee et al., 2001).

In North Korea, all social activities are structured and run as a group. Most children are raised at the day care centers from the early age. They learn to say the name of the generalissimo even before their parents' names. They spend the whole day at the center with teacher and peers. With this collective training of children as a group, North Koreans are able to control the parenting variables of each family and internalized the human qualities that the North Korean society requires from the early age (Yi, 1999).

North Koreans grow consciousness about the monitoring by officials and peers and become familiar with self-criticism, criticizing fellow colleagues, or being criticised in the assembly. Individual behavior and independent thinking are forbidden. They are forced to think and act as they are told by the party and school. Since every child is soaked into the similar thoughts and life, they grow up without thinking otherwise. In other words, they form collectivistic human nature without any resistance to the collectivistic settings. In addition to the school setting, group activities such as Red Youth Guard install the collectivistic ideology to the youth group in order to increase the work efficiency and prevent any deviation from the group. As can be seen from the below case, the community life is used to suppress individual needs and desires, and to promote the interest of the group.

> The idea of mine cannot be considered in a collectivistic community life. Because I cannot be wanting for myself. I think the communist principle of sharing is good but… (H-1)

<Table IV-5> Regression analysis of the refugees' collectivist value

Variables	Collectivism			
	North Korea		South Korea	
	b	β	b	β
Sex (Male=1)	-.11	-.14	-.02	-.03
Age	-.06	-.05	.02	.02
Education level	.16	.21	.13	.20
Family-accompanied entry	-.21	-.26*	.01	.01
Marital status (married=1)	.09	.12	.10	.15
Time after the crossing	.13	.07	.15	.10
Time after the entry	-.17	-.12	-.17	-.15
Constant	3.50		2.68	
F	1.41		.72	
R^2	.09		.05	

* p < .05; β is a standardized coefficient.

In search for the variables associated with the collectivist values, a regression analysis was conducted using various demographic variables. A set of independent variables of the North Korean refugees such as gender, age, education level, family-accompanied crossing, marital status, and period after the crossing were used for the regression analysis of collectivist tendency in the North and the South. The regression analysis showed that both models were in significant. However, the collectivism in the North and family-accompanied crossing (β=-0.26, p<.05) showed a significant negative relationship. That is, the perceived collectivist reasoning appeared to be higher for the refugees who escaped alone than the family-accompanied refugees (Table IV-5).

3) Individualistic values

In analysis of variables associated with the individualistic values, a set of variables such as gender, age, education level, family-accompanied crossing, marital status, period after crossing, and period after entry to the South were put into regression analysis. The analysis result showed no significance of the model and none of the variables was significantly related.

4) Familism values

The familism values were measured with three items. First, the score for the item 'My success is important because it is the honor of my family rather than for myself' was significantly higher in the North (M=3.94) than in the South (M=3.71). The second item relating to succession, 'Discontinuity of a blood line due to lack of a son is an adversity for the family and clan', scored significant higher in the North Korean society (M=3.70) than in the South (M=2.66). Lastly, the item 'Divorce is never a choice in any circumstances' received significantly higher score in the North (M=3.70) than in the South (M=2.66) (Table IV-6). This result indicates the stronger emphasis on the sense of family, succession, and taboo on family disorganization when in the North than when in the South. It is evident that one's perceived values in the North can be very different from that of the South. The similar tendency of values among the refugees may be attributed to the distinct value differences on familism between the North and the South. The familism value is stronger in the North than the South, which means that the North Korean society puts more emphasis on the familism values. The case study also affirms the stronger familism value shown in the refugees. The

<Table IV-6> Differences in familism and patriarchal gender-role values

Items		North Korean society			South Korean society			t
		N	M	SD	N	M	SD	
Familism	10. My success is important because it is the honor of my family rather than for myself.	195	3.94	.85	188	3.71	.92	3.44**
	11. Discontinuity of a blood line due to lack of son is an adversity for the family and clan.	195	3.62	1.05	189	2.92	.95	7.91***
	13. Divorce is never a choice in any circumstances.	194	3.70	.96	189	2.66	1.15	11.38***
Total		194	3.76	.69	188	3.09	.61	12.38***
Patriarchal gender-role	12. Housekeeping is a work of a wife even if both man and woman have a job.	195	3.85	1.04	188	2.42	.90	14.91***
	14. In a society, there is a separate job for man and woman.	195	3.32	.90	189	2.57	.74	9.16***
Total		195	3.58	.81	188	2.49	.65	15.17***

** $p < .01$, *** $p < .001$

emphasis on familism value strengthens the bonds between the parents and children and helps to maintain a close family relationship.

> Family is important in life... Of course, I would risk my life to spare my children's life. I do not mind dying if I can save my child. (E-1)

In a society with such strong familism values, dissolution of a family is unacceptable. The dissolution of the family is strongly forbidden in North Korea. Despite worldwide increase in the divorce rate, the perception of divorce as taboo is still intact within the people and the government of North Korea as can be found in the below case.

> (Interviewer: Is the divorce rate high in the North?)
> It is very difficult to divorce in the North. Maybe one case out of ten? It is even less than that. Perhaps one out of hundred... But divorce is not admitted in the North. So once you become a family, you have to stay with what you have... It is the principle. You are not to break it. (F-1)

The same set of independents variables were used in a regression analysis in order to find the variables associated with the familism values in the North but no significant variable was found.

5) Patriarchal values in gender roles

A typical patriarchal value with dominating husband and obedient wife is widespread in the North Korean society. The patriarchal values lead to distinct gender roles in the North. Yet the patriarchal gender roles of refugees go through changes with their entry to the South with the new socio-cultural setting. They first come across the sway of patriarchy in China before the entry to South Korea, and then they experience a strong change once they enter into the South. The gradual weakening of perceived patriarchal values is witnessed as belows. The refugee seems to be displeased with the weakened patriarchy, complaining that it is a bad manner they have learned.

> They acquired bad habits early. When we were in the North, the wives obeyed their husbands. But when we went to China, the women were more stubborn than men, and when we came to the South, women were

stubborn as well. And men seem to gain a little awareness about that. (V-1)

The patriarchal gender roles may be associated with familism. On an item to measure the patriarchal gender roles for the refugees such as 'Housekeeping is a work of a wife even when both man and woman have a job', the score for the North Korean society was 3.85 and 2.42 for the South. The score for the refugees' perception for the North for an item 'In a society, there is a separate job for man and woman' was 3.32, which is significantly higher than the score of 2.57 for that of the South. The reasoning of work distinction for man and woman is a baseline for the gender labor division and gender discrimination. It indicates a stronger patriarchal value in the North Korean society than in the South. In addition, it is an interesting fact that the same person, who once lived in a communist society, and then moved to the capitalist society, is self-conscious about his/her change in values in accordance to the social ideology that he/she is exposed to.

What is the cause of the strong patriarchal values for the North Korean society? The root cause is the North Korea's socio-cultural environment. The patriarchal values are imposed upon people through socialization. The last principle of ten oaths of allegiance that the North Korean people commit to is to study the household of Kim, Il-Sung. They are obligated to memorize the year of birth, place of birth, family lineage of Kim, Il-Sung and his son (Yi, 1999). Stories about his parents, grandparents, mother of Kim, Jong-Il are introduced in the textbook and they are worshiped. Hypothetical stories about his family lineage are depicted as fictional characters in a novel and used as a textbook material. This is possible because of the remaining patriarchal political system in the North Korean society. This patriarchal political system in the North is attributed to the distorted Korean Confucian elements that remain underneath the mind of North Koreans including the politicians. When Kim, Il-Sung succeeded his authority to his son, their father-son relationship was reflected in their titles as well.

2. Change of identity

1) Self-identity

Self-identity formation of the North Korean refugees were investigated here. The three aspects of self-identity of the North Korean refugees examined are continuity, constancy, and uniqueness. The continuity of an identity refers to the belief that one maintains the same identity regardless of elapsed time. The constancy of identity is defined as recognition of an unchanged self-identity within many different circumstances. The uniqueness of self-identity means that one acknowledges one's distinctiveness from the others. The two questions to measure the self-continuity are 'I sometimes feel like I am not the same person as I was' and 'I sometimes feel like somebody else in a new society'. The scores on these items were higher than the three out of five points indicating the continuity of their self-identity. In addition, the two items to measure the self-constancy which are 'I sometimes feel like a different person when I meet with many people' or 'I sometimes questioned myself about who I am when I was with many people', scored higher than the three. The item that measures the uniqueness of self-identity, 'I am living a life of my own', received higher score than the three showing a positive result. However, among the two items that measure the uniqueness of self-identity, the item, 'There is no one else like me' scored lower than the three. In other words, the refugees may

<Table IV-7> North Korean refugees' identity

	Items	Composition	N	M	SD
Self-identity	1. I sometimes feel like I am not the same person as I was.	Continuity	193	3.08	.86
	2. I sometimes feel like a different person when I met with many people.	Constancy	194	3.12	.80
	3. There is no one else like me.	Uniqueness	194	2.72	.75
	5. I am living a life of my own.	Uniqueness	193	3.56	.92
	6. I am who I am before even after I settled in a new society.	Continuity	193	3.06	.87
	7. I sometimes questioned myself about who I am when I was with many people.	Constancy	190	3.14	.72
Family identity	9. I am confused whom my family is from moving to many places and living with many different people.	Family identity confusion	191	3.79	.91
Ethnic identity	8. I questioned myself which ethnic group I belong to after meeting with Chinese in China.	Ethnic identity confusion	189	3.54	.95
Total			175	25.94	2.58

Items 1, 2, 7, 8, and 9 were inversely coded.

have experienced the confusion of identity living in two societies with distinctively different ideologies, yet it is evident that the refugees do not experience the confusion of identity anymore (Table IV-7).

What would be the identity-related variables? A set of independent variables which are gender, age, education level, family-accompanied crossing, marital status, and period after the crossing, period after entry to the South, were taken into a regression analysis. The result indicate that the model explained 9 % of the variance. Yet none of the demographic variables was significantly associated with the self-identity.

2) Family identity

The formation of family for the North Korean refugees tends to be rather complicated. A new family is formed while moving around different countries including China, but sometimes the families split, or reunite with previous family members from the North. While undergoing such a complex family structure, the North Korean refugees may have experienced the weakening of family cohesion or a blurring concept of family. Thus, possible family confusion of the North Korean refugees was further investigated. However, for the most respondents, the scores were higher than the median score of three. It is an indication of the North Korean refugees' stable family identity. This result can be attributed to the growing affection, trust, and stronger bond within the family members through relying on each other while going through a crisis.

> (Interviewer: Did your family relationship improve when you came to South Korea than when you were in the North?)
> Of course, it got better. It's obvious. Our family went through a life or death crisis together. How can our relationship get worse after all those crisis? We shouldn't be. (M-1)

3) Ethnic identity

Ethnic identity can be threatened while wandering around many different countries for a long time. Many of the North Korean refugees who entered the South, wander off in a third country such as China, after the crossing from the North. Thus the ethnic identity of the North Korean refugees was examined. As a result, most of the respondents scored higher than the median score of three. This indicates that the North Korean refugees have formed a stable ethnic identity.

What are the demographic variables that are related to the ethnic identity? A regression analysis was conducted with the independent variables namely gender, age, education level, family-accompanied crossing, marital status, period after the crossing, and period after the entry to the South. According to the result, the regression model of ethnic identity explains 10 % of the variance. However, none of the demographic variables predicted the ethnic identity.

4) National identity

A stable ethnic identity of the North Korean refugees has been confirmed, however the change in the national identity has not been examined yet. In order to investigate their national identity, the following item about whether one considers oneself as both a citizen of North and South Korea was asked. Surprisingly, the score did not exceed the median score of three. It means that the refugees have an identity of one national citizenship. That is, the North Korean refugees consider themselves to be either South Korean or North Korean but not both. In order to indirectly confirm the national identity, the refugees were asked to choose one team to cheer for during a sports game between the South and the North. The result shows higher score than the median score of three, which means their cheering for North Korea. In other words, the North Korean refugees still recognize themselves as the citizens of North Korea.

> (Interviewer: Which team would you cheer for if there is a soccer game between North and South Korea?)
> Is there a need for cheering? It is a matter of their own strategies and

> techniques... whichever team wins... But in my heart, I want the North team to win. Maybe that's because I have my brothers and children in the North... It must be the same for the South Korean people. They will cheer for the South team to win. (E-1)

In order to examine the refugees' national identity as North Korean citizens more in depth, we asked this question to North Korean refugee-related personnel who have dealt with the refugees for many years. Most of the personnel pointed out that the North Koreans defected from the North not because of ideological and political conflicts but simply because they could not handle the hunger. According to them, since the North Korean refugees have been brainwashed with the idea of Democratic People's Republic of Korea, Monolithic ideology, and Juche ideology for decades ever since they could speak, disturbance or change in their national ideology may be negligible. Thus, little change in ideology caused by undergoing rapid crisis with the hunger can be historically and socio-culturally evident.

Nevertheless, how can this exaggerated national self-esteem be maintained so strongly? It can be attributed to their educational curriculum that brainwashes the idea of Juche nationalism against imperialism. A nation and revolution history of Kim, Il-Sung which has received recognition on its legitimacy by the Juche ideology, is taught to students from kindergarten through college. The Juche ideology enhanced the idea of closed-society, strengthened awareness of unitary nation, and boosted the worship of Kim, Il-Sung and his son. The national identity weaved together with cult of Kim, Il-Sung and his son is implanted into the people thus causing the North Koreans to maintain very strong national identity.

3. Changes in psychological characteristics

1) Attribution

Attribution can be divided into two types which are internal and external attribution. Internal attribution assigns one's causalities to factors within oneself such as one's effort or ability, whereas external attribution assigns one's causalities to outside factors such as luck, coincidence, someone else's fault, or social pressure. Typically, one who uses internal attribution is expected to overcome any crisis or problems they face by trying for themselves since they seek the cause for the problem within themselves.

As for the North Korean refugees, it takes some time for them to gain internal attribution attitude. The refugees once expected to be provided with everything they wanted by the South Korean society. They attributed their difficulties in adaptation to the South Korean government or South Korean people rather than to themselves. However, as the difficulties continued, they gradually started to change in the mode of attrition.

> All of sudden, I just realized… I need the skills that the society needs, otherwise, I will not have any chance to do work other than what I am doing now for the rest of my life. I need to have skills or earn qualifications. Then I will be treated appropriately. By just working hard as I am told, I will never have any improvement. I felt the strong need for learning. I felt I needed to pioneer my fate by myself. (M-2)

A unilateral approach that provides everything the refugees need is not the right way to help them to adjust well in the South Korean

<Table IV-8> Internal attributions of North Korean refugees

Items	N	M	SD
1. My future success is up to help from other people.	195	3.69	1.03
2. A large portion of life event is not determined by coincidences.	194	3.26	.94
3. Sometimes I come across misfortune that I cannot avoid even if I try.	193	3.03	.79
4. I got what I wished for because I was lucky.	193	3.00	.82
5. Whether I make many friends is up to me.	194	3.76	.76
6. My life was primarily affected by other people's decisions.	194	3.61	.96
7. I can protect my own interest by myself.	192	3.61	.91
8. If I get into a car accident, it is not my fault but other's.	194	3.55	.84
9. My life is determined by my own effort.	195	3.61	1.01
Total	185	31.20	3.85

Items 1, 2, 3, 4, 6, and 8 were inversely coded.

society. They need to support and encourage themselves to overcome the difficulties in a new environment. Rather than blaming the bad environment or difficult situation, the refugees need to become an autonomous person who realizes the responsibilities for themselves.

> If everyone pitied me and offered everything I needed from the beginning, I would not have learned so quickly. I don't think I would have realized so fast that I was to be responsible for my own life. At first, I cried a lot and tried really hard to make a living. Now that I think about it, it really helped me. (M-2)

In this study, the North Korean refugees' attribution attitude was conducted with nine items. The respondents' answers were positive with the mean value of 3.69. In other words, they showed internal attribution attitude which assigns their success to one's effort rather than others' help.

As can be seen from the nine items determining the refugees' attribution style, consistent internal attribution was shown in all of the questions asked (Table IV-8).

A regression analysis was conducted taking the internal attribution attitude as the dependent variable and a set of demographic variables as the independent variables including gender, age, education level, family-accompanied crossing, marital status, period after the crossing, and period after entry to the South. None of the variance predicted the refugees' internal attribution attitude.

2) Depression

Since the North Korean refugees encounter various difficulties and crisis in a third country away from their homeland before the entry to South Korea, we predicted the refugees' emotional state to be very depressive and pessimistic. In order to examine the refugees' emotional state, eleven questions from a personality test (MMPI) were asked. Out of eleven items, only one item, 'I worry all the time,' showed a higher score than the median value of three. For the rest of ten items, the respondents showed light disagreement. The ten items are as follows; feeling fatigue and tired; having no interest in anything; feeling of difficulties about everything and feeling of helplessness that there is no hope for the future; feeling of guilt that everything is my fault; loneliness and sense of emptiness; feeling of depression that cause to break into tear and desire to commit suicide. The result showed that the North Korean refugees showed weak signals related to helplessness, feeling of guilt, and feeling of depression. According to the survey result, the refugees are found to be in a healthy and optimistic emotional state (Table IV-9).

As mentioned previously, the North Korean refugees have tendency

<Table IV-9> Depression of North Korean refugees

Items	N	M	SD
1. I feel fatigue and tired.	195	2.68	.89
2. I want to die.	195	2.19	.88
3. I burst into tears for no reason.	194	2.55	.88
4. I feel guilty that everything is my fault.	193	2.71	.97
5. I feel loneliness.	194	2.85	.89
6. I am depressed.	193	2.73	.85
7. I worry all the time.	191	3.23	.83
8. I feel emptiness.	192	2.69	.78
9. I have no interest in anything.	191	2.62	.82
10. I feel like there's no future.	195	2.64	.87
11. Everything seems difficult.	191	2.97	.83
Total	179	29.94	5.62

of trying to answer what seems to be the correct answer. In the North Korean society, they have been trained to respond appropriately in the formal questions as they are told. Therefore, the refugees tend not to reveal their honest feelings automatically. However, in an one-to-one interview, they seemed to let down their guard and open up to tell their honest feelings. The following case expresses the sense of isolation, loneliness, and abandonment that one interviewee experienced.

> I... felt I was abandoned. It got me really thinking about it. Maybe it is the new system... perhaps everyone would feel like me at first... hmm... Everyone suffers from the psychological pain. I think everyone does. But since our family came here together... aren't we better off when compared to others? It is very painful for people who came alone. It is really lonely. (M-2)

A regression analysis was conducted on depression with a set of demographic variables as the independent variables including gender, age, education level, family-accompanied crossing, period after the crossing from the North, and period after entry to the South. Interestingly, none of the independent variables was significant.

3) Self-esteem

A survey was conducted to examine the North Korean refugees' self-esteem. The result indicated that the respondents did not show negative answers about themselves in all of the nine items. The refugees assess themselves to be not less than others, a person with good personality, a person who can do the job well, an useful person who can contribute to the society, and a valuable person. In another word, the North Korean refugees are satisfied with themselves (Table IV-10).

<Table IV-10> Self-esteem of North Korean refugees

Items	N	M	SD
1. I feel like I am less than others.	193	3.45	.96
2. I think I am a valuable person.	194	3.22	.92
3. I have a good personality.	194	3.36	.87
4. I feel like I am a failure.	193	3.38	.97
5. I can do my job well.	193	3.63	.75
6. I don't have much to showoff.	193	3.01	.73
7. I am satisfied with myself.	192	3.33	.81
8. I sometimes feel like I am worthless.	190	3.53	.79
9. I sometimes think I am not a good person.	193	3.54	.80
Total	177	30.65	4.11

Items 1, 4, 6, 8, and 9 were inversely coded.

The origin of such positive sense of self or self-esteem has not yet been exactly defined. It may be seen as unsubstantial or overly generous in self-evaluation. However, it is very likely that the confidence and success gained throughout the crossing and the entry process from the North to the South may have led to recognize and evaluate themselves very highly. A person with self-worth and self-satisfaction can be evaluated as one who possesses a healthy ego. In fact, the refugees' positive self-awareness and self-confidence were evident in the qualitative research result. The case below provides a glimpse of their healthy confidence and competency.

> (Interviewer: Am I capable person?)
> I have the capability but I don't really act on it. So I give 6 points. (N-3)
> I just want to work hard. I have no other thoughts than to just work hard. I have some people skills. I have no trouble getting along with people I meet for the first time. (E-1)

In order to examine the variables related to self-esteem, a regression analysis was carried out. The dependent variable was self-esteem, whereas a set of variables such as gender, age, education level, family-accompanied crossing, marital status, period after the crossing from the North, and period after the entry to the South, was used as the independent variables. None of the independents was significant.

4) Falsehood

Falsehood was tested for the North Korean refugees. The following items used were taken from the Minnesota Multiphasic Personality Inventory (MMPI). For an item 'I sometimes have thoughts that is too bad even to let out of my mouth,' the respondents answered somewhat unlikely. As for an item 'I sometimes want to throw insulting words', the answers were somewhat negative. An item, 'I don't always say the truth', received somewhat negative answers. Respondents showed somewhat negative answers in an item, 'I don't read newspaper editorials everyday,' as well. For item 'I sometimes get angry', the refugees showed somewhat negative answers. An item, 'I sometimes procrastinate my work to the next day', also received weak denial from the respondents. As can be inferred from the North Korean refugees' responses to above items, it seems likely that their answers may be false.

Yet, for an item 'I sometimes get bad tempered when I am not in a good mood', the refugees actually showed positive answers. As for an item 'My table manners at home is not as good as when I am eating out with others,' they somewhat denied. A statement that states 'If I don't get caught, I would enter the movie theatre without paying for the ticket', also received weak denial from the respondents.

Yet, the North Korean refugees showed a positive agreement on a statement 'I want to rather win than lose in a play or a game', with a mean score of 3.66. For statements 'I want to get to know people with authority' and 'I don't like everyone just because they are my acquaintances', they also agreed. However, they denied on statements 'I sometimes talk ill about others', 'I sometimes cast vote to someone I don't even know well', and 'I occasionally enjoy and laugh at listening to obscene jokes'. In fact, most people do talk ill about others' misdeeds or cast a vote for someone they don't really know well without serious intentions. Occasional talks on obscene jokes and laughing at them are considered practical. These are behaviors that may pass without any deep guilty feelings for committing. However, the refugees showed denial on these statements causing doubt for the truthfulness answers (Table IV-11).

<Table IV-11> MMPI of North Korean refugees

Items	N	M	SD
1. I sometimes have thoughts that is too bad even to let out of my mouth.	194	2.29	.95
2. I sometimes want to throw insulting words.	194	2.60	1.00
3. I don't always say the truth.	194	2.81	.82
4. I don't read newspaper editorials everyday.	191	2.81	1.07
5. I sometimes get angry.	193	2.84	.81
6. I sometimes procrastinate my work to the next day.	194	2.91	.70
7. I sometimes get bad tempered when I am not in a good mood.	194	3.20	.75
8. My table manners at home is not as good as when I am eating out with others.	193	2.80	.64
9. If I don't get caught, I would enter the movie theatre without paying for the ticket.	193	2.26	.91
10. I want to rather win than lose in a play or a game.	191	3.66	.90
11. I want to get to know people with authority.	192	3.27	.84
12. I don't like everyone just because they are my acquaintances.	192	3.13	.70
13. I sometimes talk ill about others.	192	2.78	.68
14. I sometimes vote for someone I don't even know well.	189	2.50	.85
15. I occasionally enjoy and laugh at listening to obscene jokes.	194	2.70	1.00
Total	178	42.39	5.80

On average, the respondents showed positive answers to only four out of the fifteen items and slightly negative answers to the rest of eleven items. The number of items that are considered to receive negative or positive answers are determined based on the mean scores, thus it does not describe the individual distribution of the answers for each item. Therefore, the frequency of positive and negative answers on each item

<Table IV-12> Frequency of the refugees' mental health analysis

Number of negative response ('No')	Frequency (N)	Percent (%)
0	19	9.7
1	34	17.4
2	28	14.4
3	30	15.4
4	27	13.8
5	14	7.2
6	6	3.1
7	10	5.1
8	3	1.5
10	2	1.0
11	2	1.0
13	2	1.0
15	1	.5
Sub-total	178	91.3
Missing	17	8.7
Total	195	100.0

was examined individually.

The frequency of total respondents for each item is as seen in <Table IV-12>. In general, people are sensitive about their moral behavior and it may lead to false report for the sake of their dignity. The statements may portray a person as one who engages in a fraud and ill-natured activities, yet at the same time, they can be considered and accepted lightly. However, the North Korean refugees showed denial on most of the statements. One of the respondents denied all fifteen items, and seven respondents showed denial on up to ten items. Twenty-six respondents denied on more than six items, which is two third of the total

<Table IV-13> 10 items of the refugees' mental abnormality, T>70

Classification	Frequency (N)	Percent (%)
Normal range (Number of 'No' < 10)	171	87.7
Abnormal range (10 ≤ Number of 'No')	7	3.6
Sub-total	178	91.3
Missing	17	8.7
Total	195	100.0

items.

As for the frequency of positive answers on each item, 19 respondents showed no positive answers, 34 respondents had one positive answer, 28 respondents showed agreement on 2 items, 30 of them agreed on 3 statements, 27 respondents agreed on 4 items, and 14 of them agreed on 5 items (Table IV-13). Total of 111 respondents, which is 62.4 % of the total sample, answered less than 3 agreements out of the total items. Positive answers on less than 5 items were found in 152 respondents which is 85.4 % of the total sample. The scale categorizes respondents who denied more than 10 items to be off the standard range, and 7 of the refugees, 3.6 % of the total sample, who participated in this survey, fit into this category.

4. Recognition on South and North Korean society

Social consciousness is formed living in a particular society. Moving from one society to another may lead to changes in the social consciousness. In particular, if the two societies have very different ideologies and

<Table IV-14> Differences in the refugees' awareness of North and South Korean society

Classification	North Korean society			South Korean society			t
	N	M	SD	N	M	SD	
Personality	191	2.82	.44	183	2.75	.40	1.21
Compliance with rules	190	3.04	.62	191	3.85	.63	-12.29***
Free competition	188	2.29	.65	186	4.33	.67	-25.48***
Respect for authority	188	3.16	.52	189	3.38	.57	-3.87***

*** p < .001

political systems with different development rate, the change in social consciousness is inevitable. In this section, the North Korean refugees' ideas on the North Korean society and that of the South were compared. The research result indicates that the North Korean refugees evidenced no significant personality differences between the people they met in the South and the North.

The refugees' perspective on compliance with rules in a society was compared for the South and the North as well. The refugees witnessed that rules are observed well in the South Korean society but not as well in the North. Unlike the communist society in the North, the degree of freedom and competition is comparably high in a democratic society. The degree of free competition in both societies was evaluated by the North Korean refugees. As a result, the refugees recognized significantly higher competition in the South than the North. In addition, the degree of respect for the authority in a society was compared between the South and the North. The refugees also evidenced higher degree of respect for authority in the South Korean society than that of North (Table IV-14).

1) Personality

The refugees view personality of residents in both the South Korean and North Korean society to be nice and generous in overall. The survey result showed no significant differences in the participants' overall view on the personalities of people from both societies. However, significant difference was found for an item about their perspective on the value of money between the South and the North Korean societies. The participated refugees reported that people in the North Korean society put more value on money than in South Korean society. Contrary to an assumption that people from a communist society would have weak sense of money, the survey result reflects the North Korean citizens' stronger regard on materials and money in a society where supply of food and goods has been discontinued and everyone is responsible for one's own life. That is, in a communist society without food rationing where one has to purchase food and goods from the black market for survival, the desire and importance for money may grow very strong. This finding can be explained by the refugees' experience with the comfortable and prosperous life in the South Korean society compared to the poverty in the North, which has allowed the refugees to value money less in the South than they did in the North.

Another reason for the refugees' strong value on money is closely related to the North Koreans' strong desire to purchase goods, which is formed in a communist society. In a capitalist society, self-control for financial temptation is formed. As citizens of the capitalist society, South Koreans realize the importance of money, yet they learn to manage their financial temptation and recognize the fact that money cannot do everything. They also learn to understand the disastrous consequences that may follow with avarice for money. However, the temptation of money to purchase goods is overwhelming in a communist society. The commercial transactions and strong urge for consumption of goods in China displays the power that goods and materials have on people in a communist society.

The North Korean refugees' evaluation on honesty is interesting to look at. They believe that people in North Korea are good and generous, yet their honesty is not rated high. Honesty is considered the basis of morality, and as can be seen in developed countries, individual and social sensitivity about honesty set the moral standard of a society. For example, lying is regarded as the most immoral conduct in America. Lying, false report, false testimony, and tax evasion are treated as a serious crime. In the North Korean society, untruthfulness bosses, false reporting, false testimony, and tax evasion are seen rather frequently, weakening the moral sensitivity.

> Every year, the government promised to provide for us. At first, we believed our lives would be the best to live in the North, but after three years, we then realized that we were all being deceived by the government. (G-2)

However, in the case of North Korea, they cannot afford to evaluate such conducts to be immoral. According to one refugee's testimony, throughout several food crisis, people who were honest, and did not steal other's food, died of hunger. Lying was a necessary act of evil for survival. North Koreans had to earn money in order to buy food, and paradoxically, the desire and obsession for money grew very strong in the communist society (Table IV-15).

> Just a little bit of change in everyday lifestyle... because the harder it

<Table IV-15> Differences in the refugees' awareness of personality

Items	North Korean society			South Korean society			t
	N	M	SD	N	M	SD	
1. People are nice and warm-hearted.	193	3.25	.74	191	3.26	.76	-.07
9. People value money.	192	2.06	.80	189	1.53	.81	8.06***
10. People value honesty.	192	3.14	.64	185	3.50	.74	-5.68***
Mean	191	2.82	.44	183	2.75	.40	1.21

*** $p < .001$; Item 9 was inversely coded.

got for people to sustain their lives, they started to realize that money is precious. Because of food shortage, money was valued more. In that sense, they are getting little closer toward the market economy even though there isn't any big reform taking place… (L-1)

2) Compliance with rules

The lack of material goods is expected to reduce the concept of morality and moral behaviors. In fact, the refugees reported that the North Koreans are less observant with the rules or laws in contrast to the South Koreans who follow the rules and laws well.

Establishment of the rules or laws is used as means to set up the social discipline and social order. Members belonging to a particular society have their own concept of abiding rules or laws, and law consciousness. The social atmosphere and culture are reflected in the content and level of law consciousness. What would be the perspective of the refugees on the South and North Korean's law consciousness? As the refugees indicate, the residents in the South are better with valuing punctuality, promises, and following the laws and rules than

<Table IV-16> Differences in the refugees' awareness of compliance with rules

Items	North Korean society			South Korean society			t
	N	M	SD	N	M	SD	
8. People abide rules and regulations.	192	2.98	.73	191	3.49	.70	-7.14***
11. People value promises.	193	3.08	.81	191	3.94	.78	-10.18***
12. People value punctuality.	191	3.05	.84	191	4.12	.91	-11.63***
Mean	190	3.04	.62	191	3.85	.63	-12.29***

*** $p < .001$

the people in the North (Table IV-16). Considering the uniform and strict social atmosphere of a communist society, it is a surprising fact that the South Koreans are better at abiding laws than the North Koreans. Then, does that mean the concept of law or law-abiding consciousness is in accordance with the socio-economic conditions? This raises a question 'Would a country with lower living standard cause the law-abiding consciousness to weaken?' Taking into account that the North Korean residents are witnessed to be good natured and lived in a controlling society for half a century, it is surprising to find that they don't follow the laws well.

An interview with one refugee has provided us with the answer to our question. 'In North Korea, any crime may be tolerated as long as one does not commit a murder or the *Crime number 7*.' The *Crime number 7* refers to making political remarks of the unitary system such as insult about Kim, Jong-Il. The denial of political system and complaint about Kim, Jong-Il is regarded as a political rebellion and severe punishment is followed. Public trial and public execution are still being conducted in North Korea. The lack of government's legitimate process in law enforcement has influenced the residents to overlook the importance of law consciousness or legitimacy.

> When I was in North Korea… I mean… When there is a difficulties like financial difficulty… It is faster to just go after him than going by the law… (H-1)

The expression of dissatisfaction about the national leader is considered as a matter of national security and punished severely, whereas any crime other than murder is penalized lightly. In the same respect, sexual harassment and sexual abuse are regarded as misdemeanor as well. On the other hand, while the North Korean politicians practice strong enforcement in regards to the political rebels, they use sexual matters as means of alleviating the social tension that may arise from the oppressive government. The frequent rate of sexual abuse in North Korea can be understood by such political reasons. To alleviate the pressure from the political restriction, the North Korean law enforcement is somewhat lenient on other unethical misconducts. The refugees are surprised by the fairness that everyone, whether a person with authority or not, is under the same legal restrictions when they came to South Korea. It is shocking for them to learn that the law is enforced in a society with freedom.

> When I actually came, it wasn't as I expected. About the law… you know? I saw it in the TV. The law enforcement and the way the National Intelligence Service investigates. They were all fair. You know? The capitalist society was far from what we used to imagine in the North. The system has orders. I would have never expected. (P-2)

In addition, the refugees are amazed by the guaranteed freedom beyond all bounds. For example, they would never even dreamed of a

<Table IV-17> Regression analysis of the refugees' compliance with rules

Variables	Compliance with rules			
	North Korea		South Korea	
	b	β	b	β
Sex (male=1)	.02	.03	-.01	-.01
Age	-.26	-.21	.10	.07
Education level	.24	.31*	.22	.25*
Family-accompanied entry	-.20	-.25	-.03	-.04
Marital status (married=1)	-.02	-.03	-.01	-.01
Time after the crossing	-.01	-.00	.06	.03
Time after the entry	.01	.01	-.17	-.11
Constant	3.44		3.92	
F	1.40		1.69	
R^2	.09		.11	

* p < .05; β is a standardized coefficient.

labor strike in the North Korean society

> Because there is so much freedom... workers in North Korea cannot complain even if we do not get paid with wage or any rationing... But here... you know? The workers go on strikes for wage raise. (P-2)

What are the variables related to the compliance with rules? A same set of demographic variables from the previous sections of this chapter was used for regression analysis in terms of compliance of the rules. The six independent variables used are as follows: gender, age, education level, entry status, marital status, period after the crossing from the North, and period after entry to the South. The compliance with rules was used as the dependent variable for the analysis. The analyzed model has

9 % of explanation power for the total distribution with $R^2 = .09$. Among various variables, only the education level ($\beta = 0.31$, $p < .05$) predicted the compliance with rules. In other word, the higher the education level, the better the refuges evaluate themselves to follow the rule in the North Korean society. The result was likewise in their evaluation of rule compliance in the South. The refugees' perception of the rule compliance in the South Korean society was taken into a regression analysis with the same demographic variables. The model showed 11 % of explanation power for the total distribution. The result indicate that among many variables, only the education level ($\beta = 0.25$, $p < .05$) predicts the compliance with rules. That is, the refugees who have higher education also recognized themselves as a better law-abiding person. The education level has a significant close relationship with rule compliance and law consciousness (Table IV-17).

3) Free competition

One of the most remarkable things that the North Korean refugees felt when they entered into the South Korean society was that the South Koreans work too hard (M=4.19). In evaluation of hard working workers, the refugees indicated that South Koreans work much harder than the North Koreans. They also added a comment that the North Koreans don't actually work hard (M=2.98). In an item about freedom of speech and behavior, the participants replied that there is much freedom in the South (M=4.44) but not in the North (M=1.70).

The openness for personal accomplishment in a particular society is critical in providing hopes for the people. Entry to an university may be generally classified as an initial personal accomplishment. In an item about the openness of university entrance that states that anyone can

<Table IV-18> Differences in the refugees' awareness of free competition

Items	North Korean society			South Korean society			t
	N	M	SD	N	M	SD	
2. People work hard.	193	2.98	.79	191	4.19	.79	-15.14***
4. There's freedom in speaking and behavior.	190	1.70	.95	188	4.44	.89	-22.90***
5. Anyone can go to college if they study well.	192	2.05	1.01	191	4.42	.88	-20.07***
6. Hard working people are successful.	192	2.49	1.09	189	4.24	.84	-17.71***
Mean	188	2.29	.65	186	4.33	.67	-25.48***

*** $p < .001$

enter an university if one meets the academic qualification, the refugees responded that it is not likely (M=2.05) in the North Korean society and very likely (M=4.42) in the South Korean society. In the North Korean society, in order for one to enter a prestigious university such as Kim Il-Sung University or Kim Chaek Institute of Technology, one has to be from a good family with parents working as the authorized political party (Lee et al., 2001). Students from a landowner class may not enter a prestigious university regardless of their effort and outstanding academic accomplishment.

For a statement, hard working people are the ones who succeed, the refuges replied that it is somewhat not likely (M=2.49) in the North, whereas it is very likely (M=4.24) in the South. In an open society with opportunities available for personal accomplishments, an individual is willing to work hard to obtain his/her success because one has a hope. However, in a society with social constraints in fulfillment of individual's accomplishment, an individual suffers from psychological and practical difficulties. The North Korean refugees recognize the

South Korean society as a society that provides openness for a personal accomplishment and believe that accomplishment can be obtained with enthusiasm for work and effort. In addition, with the perception of principle of competition, the refugees judge their own competitiveness. By then, the refugees are ready to compete in the free competition of a capitalist society (Table IV-18).

> The North Korea's socialist ranks are fixed. So everyone settles for one's given status because one can only get better to certain point. My effort does not count, you know? Thus, one just has to live as one's given rank. It's easy. Just as I am told… (M-2)

What are the variables associated with the perception of free competition in the North Korean society? A regression analysis was conducted using a number of demographic variables, which are gender, age, education level, entry status, marital status, period after crossing from the North, and period after entry to the South, as independent variables, whereas the concept of free competition was used as the dependent variable. The analyzed model has 9 % of explanation power for the total distribution with $R^2=.09$. Among various variables, only the age ($\beta=-0.24$, $p<.05$) predicted the free competition in the North Korean society. That is, the younger their age, the more they perceived the free competition in the North Korean society.

On the other hand, the regression analysis was conducted for the concept of free competition in the South Korean society with the same dependent and independent variables. The analyzed data indicate that the regression model has 16 % of explanation power for the total distribution with $R^2=.16$. There was no variable that predicted the free competition in the South Korean society (Table IV-19).

<Table IV-19> Regression analysis of the refugees' free competition

Variable	Free competition			
	North Korea		South Korea	
	b	β	b	β
Sex (male=1)	-.04	-.05	-.11	-.09
Age	-.30	-.24*	-.14	-.08
Education level	.16	.21	-.12	-.11
Family-accompanied entry	-.19	-.23	.29	.24
Marital status (married=1)	-.12	-.14	-.29	-.24
Time after the crossing	-.08	-.04	-.18	-.07
Time after the entry	.14	.10	.18	.09
Constant	2.69		4.76	
F	1.47		2.74	
R^2	.09		.16	

* $p < .05$; β is a standardized coefficient.

4) Respect for authority

The North Korean refugees were asked to compare and contrast the perception of authority figures in the North Korean society and the South Korean society. In a statement about parental sacrifice, the refugees reported 'very likely so' (M=3.73) for the North Korean society, however, the participants answered that the South Korean parents are more sacrificing (M=3.88) than the North. The score difference for parental sacrifice is found to be statistically significant. For an item that asks about parents' respect for children's teachers, the refugees replied that the North Korean parents (M=3.57) are likely to respect the teachers as well as the South Korean parents (M=3.45). However, the difference between the two groups is not statistically significant.

<Table IV-20> Differences in the refugees' awareness of respect for authority

Items	North Korean society			South Korean society			t
	N	M	SD	N	M	SD	
3. Parents sacrifice for their children.	191	3.73	.79	189	3.88	.83	-2.04*
7. Leader's concern for citizens' lives.	191	2.37	.96	191	3.34	.80	-9.84***
13. People respect leaders.	193	2.97	1.02	191	2.87	.85	1.02
14. Parents respect their children's teachers.	192	3.57	.85	191	3.45	1.05	1.71
Mean	188	3.16	.52	189	3.38	.57	-3.87***

* $p < .05$, *** $p < .001$

In an item about the leader's concern for the citizens' lives, the refugees responded that the North Korean leader is somewhat unlikely (M = 2.97) to have concern for their lives, whereas the South Korean leader is thought to be likely (M = 2.87). The difference in scores is statistically significant.

When the respondents were asked to reflect on the respect for the leader the citizens have, they answered the North Koreans (M = 2.97) to be slightly not likely as well as the South Koreans (M = 2.87), yet the difference between the two groups was not statistically significant (Table IV-20).

What are the variables associated with the sense of respect for the authority in the South and North Korean society? A regression analysis was carried out in terms of respect for the authority using the same set of demographic variables as the previous analysis. The demographic variables such as gender, age, education level, border-crossing status, marital status, period after the crossing from the North, and period after the entry to the South were used as independent variables, whereas

<Table IV-21> Regression analysis of the refugees' respect for authority

Variables	Respect for authority			
	North Korea		South Korea	
	b	β	b	β
Sex (male=1)	.16	.16	-.05	-.05
Age	-.14	-.09	-.25	-.17
Education level	.25	.27*	-.15	-.16
Family-accompanied entry	-.16	-.16	.14	.14
Marital status (married=1)	.25	.26	-.30	-.32*
Time after the crossing	.20	.09	-.15	-.07
Time after the entry	.02	.01	.17	.11
Constant	2.90		3.97	
F	3.01**		1.86	
R^2	.17		.11	

* p < .05, ** p < .01; β is a standardized coefficient.

the respect for the authority in North Korea was used as the dependent variable. The model is found to have explanation power of 17 % from the total distribution. Among number of variables, the education level (β=0.27, p<.05) was the only variable that had prediction power for the dependent variable. That is, the refugees believed that the higher the education level, the more respect the people have for the authority in the North.

On the other hand, the same analysis was conducted for the refugees' perspectives for the South Koreans. The regression analysis has 11 % of explanation power. Among various variables, the marital status (β=-0.32, p<.05) only predicted for the dependent variable, respect for the authority, in the South Korean society. This refers to the fact that the North Korean refugees recognize married person to have more sense of respect for the authority than singles in the South Korean society (Table

IV-21).

These results reflect the nature of authoritarian society of North Korea. There are a couple of reasons for characterizing the North Korean society to be authoritarian. The North Korean society has a clear hierarchical structure, and the leaders of the party with high position in the hierarchy exercise their authority and power. The detailed structure of the North Korean society is set based on the hierarchical foundation. The elite class that sustains the North Korean society refers to all the Party officials including the Communist Party officials. All the officials including the classroom officials in the 'People's School' to the officials in the 'Central Party', have been selected with the same principle. The first condition of official selection principle is that one has to have a foundation of class. One's foundation of class has to meet the qualification in order to be considered for the senior position of the Party in North Korea. The qualified foundation of class is determined by whether the parents and oneself come from the exploiting class or exploited class. The exploiting class refers to parents who are landlords, capitalists, merchants, usury, business owners, large enterprise owners, ethnic rebels, comprador capitalists, etc. The exploited class means parents who are farm laborers, farmers employed by the Japanese colonial period, farm servant, landed farmers, craftsmen, soldiers, or clerks etc. In order for one to be considered for the senior ranks in the Party, the parents have to be from the exploited class.

Such hierarchical social structure of the North Korean society is established based on the Unitarian ideology. According to the Unitarian ideology, Kim, Il-Sung is the one and only leader. The Unitarian ideology is taught during the subjects, 'The childhood of the great Father 'Suryung' class' and 'The childhood of Kim, Jong-Il class', in the school curriculum throughout preschool to the 'People's School' (Park, 1995). In addition, the learning of Unitarian ideology and cult of Kim, Il-Sung and his son begins from infancy. The teachers tell stories about Kim, Il-Sung and his son and teach songs to praise them to children of 3 and 4 year olds. The praising phrases for Kim, Il-Sung are found in all of the songs taught in the kindergarten. Through such idealization, the North Korean government intends to maintain the current hierarchical society and dominant ruling force within their society.

V

North Korean Refugee's Socio-Cultural Adaptation in South Korea

1. North Korean refugee's settlement in South Korea

Prior to discussion about the North Korean refugee's status of settlement and adaptation in the South Korean society, we examined their self-assessment about the changes. The North Korean refugees' changes do not solely rely on accepting the differences. Rather they accept the differences partly and re-interpret the new circumstances at the same time. Typically, the life threatening process of escape from North Korea and settlement in a new society are considered as a psychologically traumatic experience. Yet even aside from the exchange theory, since experiences accompany cost and benefit, we explored both positive and negative aspects of the North Korean refugees' subjective assessments. In order to understand the actual conditions of settlement, we initially examined their current conditions such as the things they did in South Korea, current job, and family structure. Then we geared to more specific difficulties and problems from the adaptation process and took an indirect approach to grasp how they are dealing with the difficulties by examining their life satisfaction.

1) Actual settlement conditions

The personal backgrounds of the North Korean refugees have already been covered with the socio-demographic information previously. Thus we now focus in three aspects of settlement conditions in the South Korean society by examining the personal educational training received other than from Hanawon, current job, and current family structure.

Their personal training can be viewed as their effort for quick adaptation and settlement in the South Korean society. It also reflects which aspects they feel necessary to retrain themselves. Approximately 64 % of the respondents received computer lessons, 37 % received employment-related training, and about 10 % received English lessons. About 54 % of the total respondents replied that they had obtained a driver's license.

In terms of age, respondents in their 30s had the highest rate in acquisition of a driver's license and computer lessons. In contrast, group of 20s showed the highest rate of English lessons, and the rate of employment-related training was the highest in group of 40s. The fact that more than 50 % of the total respondents have received computer lessons regardless of age shows that the North Korean refugees realize the necessity of computer related training the most. In the case of English lessons, the younger the age group the higher the rate of attendance in private English institutions. On the other hand, higher age groups had more experience of obtaining employment-related education or training than the younger age groups. These results show that the North Korean refugees' choice of training or education for their settlement is somewhat different depending on their age. The implication of above results can be that different social expectations and requirements in education are expected for different age groups or it may be that the different type of

<Table V-1> The refugees' received educational training after the entry by their age

Types of lessons	Total (%)	20s	30s	over 40s
Obtained driver's license	53.6	44.9	59.5	55.3
Took computer lessons	63.7	61.2	64.7	55.3
Took English lessons	9.7	16.3	7.1	0.0
Took employment related training	36.6	28.6	35.3	39.5
N	172	85	38	38

<Table V-2> Purchased goods by the refugees after the entry

Items	Percent (%)
Private insurance	51.0
Mobile phone	93.2
Motorcycle	4.1
Automobile	12.0
Computer	69.7

training is needed depending on the individual's stage of life cycle (Table V-1).

The consumption pattern of the North Korean refugees in South Korea was also examined. More than 90 % of the respondents purchased mobile phone, and about 70 % of the total respondents purchased computer which show that majority of the North Korean refugees recognize computer and mobile phone to be the necessities of life. Other than that, about 12 % of the respondents answered that they purchased automobile and 4 % purchased motorcycle. As for insurance, 51 % of the respondents purchased private insurances (Table V-2).

The employment status of the North Korean refugees examined was as follows. The number of regular and contingent worker was the

<Table V-3> Current occupation of the refugees

Occupation	Frequency (%)	Male (%)	Female (%)
Office/factory worker	39 (23.1)	27 (34.2)	12 (13.3)
Contingent labor	31 (18.3)	11 (13.9)	20 (22.2)
Student	29 (17.2)	10 (12.7)	19 (21.1)
Institution/ Preparation of qualification exam	36 (21.3)	17 (21.5)	19 (21.1)
Housekeeping	6 (3.6)	0 (0)	6 (6.7)
Others	7 (4.1)	6 (7.6)	1 (1.1)
Seeking for employment	21 (12.4)	8 (10.1)	13 (14.4)
N	169	79	90

<Table V-4> Current family structure of the refugees

Family structure	Frequency (%)
Married couple	11 (14.5)
Married couple + Children	21 (27.6)
Single-parent + Children	27 (35.5)
Sibling	6 (8)
Married couple + Old parents	2 (3)
Others	1 (1.3)
No response	7 (9.3)
N	75

highest with 70 respondents (41 %) and 65 of the respondents (38 %) were schooling, training for employment, or attending institution for qualification examination. That is, only 45 % of the total respondents reported that they are currently employed, and the rest were unemployed looking for jobs and attending school or institution preparing for employment. In regard to gender, males had higher rate of employment

(48 %) than the rate of current training (34 %), on the other hand, females had lower rate of employment (36 %) than the rate of current training (42 %) preparing for employment. Accordingly, job search rate was higher in the female group than in the male group. The gender difference of employment in the South Korean society was evident in the case of employment as well. Females had higher rate of employment as contingent labor than as white collar or factory workers, whereas males had higher rate of being employed as white collar or factory workers than as contingent workers (Table V-3).

As far as the family structure is concerned, 109 respondents reported that they live by themselves, 75 reported that they live with their family, and 11 respondents did not answer. In cases of living together with a family, only 68 cases were included in the analysis of family structure excluding the missing cases. Among the total of 68 cases, 28 % of the family consisted of both parents and children, 36 % were single parent and children family, 15 % consisted of only couples, and 8 % were formed only by siblings. Taking into account the considerable number of missing cases in analyzing the family structure, these results may not be reliable in describing the family structure of the North Korean refugees (Table V-4).

2) Positive and negative changes after the crossing

What changes do the North Korean refugees recognize in themselves through the crossing process from North Korea to South Korea? Do they consider those changes to be positive or negative? The crossing process is typically known to be very dangerous and extremely difficult. The crossing experience may bring about intense stress and tension along with psychological trauma, thus negatively affecting the psychological welfare.

However, previous studies about stress and life events indicate that stress does not always have negative impacts. From an existentialist perspective, human beings pursue meaning and growth even in unexpected and difficult situations that these life events may provide a chance for better growth and to find a meaning in life (Farran, 1997). The fact that the negative experience in life provides a chance for self-reflection on the self-identity of the refugees has been shown with testimonies during the in-depth interviews

> We started the computer lesson late. There was a qualifying examination for Word. The level 3 is the lowest and level 1 is the highest level you can achieve. At first I wanted to take level 1 and 2 both, but the teacher advised me to take the test just as a trial to see how the test is like because he was pretty sure I would not pass the test. So he advised me to study for another year to take the test. I took his advice and studied very hard. But when I took the test for the very first time, I passed the level 1 and 2 at the same time. I guess I found my potential in me by myself. (M-2)

In order to confirm the positive effect shown in the interview, we compared the life before and after the crossing experience. For assessment of the positive experience, 6 questions such as 'I became confident about myself to do anything', 'I got to think about the important things in life', 'I felt I have grown as a human being', 'I became closer to my family', 'I became more patient', and 'I found purpose of life', are included. To measure assessment of the negative experience, the scale included items such as 'I felt worse than other people', 'I could not trust others', 'I became more insecure about the future', and 'I became violent and aggressive.' The items are scored on a 5-point Likert scale. Higher

<Table V-5> Positive and negative changes after the crossing

Classification	Items	N	M	SD
Positive change	I became confident about myself to be able to do anything.	194	3.70	0.88
	I got to think about the important things in life.	193	3.82	0.76
	I felt I have grown as a human being.	193	3.49	0.75
	I became closer to my family.	177	3.32	1.08
	I became more patient.	191	3.35	0.82
	I found purpose of life.	194	3.54	0.78
	Mean	195	3.54	0.56
Negative change	I felt worse than other people.	193	2.42	0.91
	I could not trust others.	195	2.63	0.78
	I became more insecure about the future.	193	2.95	0.96
	I became violent and aggressive.	193	2.42	0.81
	Mean	195	2.61	0.57

sum of positive experience scores indicates higher positive assessment and higher sum of negative experience scores indicates higher negative assessment.

As can be found in <Table V-5>, the North Korean refugees view some changes from the crossing experience to be positive. In regards to the positive assessment on changes, the findings reveal that the highest score received was on 'I got to think about the important things in life' with mean score of 3.82. One may question about the appropriateness of interpreting the act of thinking about the important things in life to be a positive change. However, self-reflection on their values and life goals is a necessary process for positive attitude in life. Especially, for the North Korean refugees adjusting to a new society, examining their old values and goals would help them to eventually establish new goals and values.

Moreover, by affirming to the item ‘I became confident about myself to be able to do anything’, the result indicates that the crossing and the settlement process have contributed to the improvement of self-confidence in their life. The findings suggest that the North Korean refugees believe that they have achieved better life they wanted after overcoming many hardships and crisis during the crossing process. That is, the North Korean refugees are assessing their changes in a positive way. The confidence from the positive assessment becomes a very important resource for the refugees in adapting to the South Korean society. Adapting to a new society requires a very positive attitude and belief that they can eventually achieve the goals by being able to overcome the failures and hardships.

In addition, having a life goal, growth as a human being, being more patient, and intimacy with family are some aspects that show the positive assessment of the respondents. The mean score for the 6 positive assessment items are 3.54, which is higher than the median value of 3. Yet due to the high rate of missing responses with high standard deviation for closeness with family members, the item reliability is comparably low. The missing scores may be attributed to the physical and psychological distance with their family members after the crossing.

Meanwhile, the highest score received for the negative assessment was on item ‘I became more insecure about the future (M=2.95).’ This indicates that the North Korean refugees are insecure about their future and worried about adapting to a new society. Though the insecurity of the North Korean refugees may not solely be explained with this score, the insecurity and anxiety of a refugee in a new society seem to be inevitable process of adaptation. The anxiety about the future appeared frequently in the interviews with the North Korean refugees. Yet as for the other items such as ‘I felt worse than other people’, ‘I could not trust others’, and ‘I became violent and aggressive', considerable respondents replied 'Hardly ever' which indicates that the North Korean refugees did not realize much the negative changes asked in the survey. The total mean score for the negative change assessment items was 2.61, which was lower than that of positive change assessment.

The survey result implies that the North Korean refugees do not always consider their experience to be negative; rather they accept it as positive changes. Depending on how one interprets the experience, it can have either positive or negative aspects. Finding the positive aspects from the experience and accepting it can be an important resource for a successful problem solving. As for the North Korean refugees who are put in a situation where they are required to adjust to a new society, the positive attitude may be critical for their successful adaptation.

2. The actual condition of North Korean refugee's adaptation

To examine the adaptation of the North Korean refugees in the South Korean society in more depth, we looked at the socio-cultural adaptation, current difficulties, and satisfaction with life. Socio-cultural adaptation scale evaluates social, cultural, and emotional adaptations subjectively whereas the current difficulty scale asks more specific questions about the actual hardships of the respondents. For example, the socio-cultural adaptation scale asks statements such as 'I have hard time catching up with my work or at workplace' or 'I have difficulty taking part in social activity,' whereas the current difficulties scale ask specific items like 'getting a job' or 'getting along with people at work.' The satisfaction with life scale was used to measure the positive aspects of psychological

<Table V-6> Average lengths of stay after the crossing, in third country, and after the entry

	No. of respondents	M (year)	SD
Period after the crossing	182	4.93	2.30
Period in third country	181	3.02	1.95
Period after the entry	183	1.91	1.54

<Table V-7> Correlations of lengths of stay after the crossing, in third country, and after the entry

	Period after the crossing	Period in third country
Period after the crossing	1.0	
Period in third country	.75***	1.0
Period after the entry	.55***	-.15*

* $p < .05$, *** $p < .001$

health with items such as health condition, work life, relationship with friends, environment in life, and self-satisfaction. These items were measured on a 5-point Likert scale.

In order to investigate the actual condition of the North Korean refugees, the overall tendency of socio-cultural adaptation, current difficulties, and satisfaction with life was examined, and then in-depth analysis was conducted in terms of gender, age, and education level from North Korea. In addition, the length of stay in a third country before the entry to South Korea and the length of stay after the entry to South Korea have been taken into the analysis as well. The average period of the subjects in this study after the crossing is 4.9 years, length of stay in a third country is 3.02 years, and length of stay in South Korea after the crossing is 1.9 years on average. The result shows that on average, the subjects' lengths of stay in North Korea and a third country are longer than the period in South Korea (Table V-6).

The correlation coefficient between the period after the crossing and the period in a third country is .75, the period after the crossing and the period after the entry to the South is .55, and the period in a third country and the period after the entry to the South is -.15. Interestingly, there is a negative correlation between the period in a third country and the period after the entry to South. This finding implies that recently the North Korean refugees' stay in a third country such as China is comparably long. This study analyzes the degree of adaptation to a new society in South Korea depending on the period in a third country and the period after the entry to South Korea (Table V-7).

1) Socio-cultural adaptation

The North Korean refugee's socio-cultural adaptation was examined with a 12 item scale. Each item was measured on a 5-point scale where higher score means more difficulty in adaptation. The result indicates that the respondents of this study showed no prominent difficulties in adaptation. The lowest score received was on the item 'I sometimes avoid contact with people because I have a fear of other people' (M=2.69). and the highest score was on the item 'I feel guilty about leaving my family and relatives' (M=3.36).

The 12 items were re-categorized through factor analysis by four subscales of 'restraints in a social activity', 'personal discrimination', 'emotional difficulty', and 'social alienation'. The restrained social activity subscale consists of adaptation relating to language, culture, and difficulties in social activity. The personal discrimination subscale has to do with prejudices and discrimination from South Koreans, whereas the emotional difficulty subscale deals with homesickness and guilty feeling

<Table V-8> The refugees' socio-cultural adaptation

Classification	Items	N	M	SD
Restraints in social activity	1. I cannot participate in social activities.	192	3.05	1.08
	2. I avoid meeting people from fear of others.	192	2.69	.87
	3. I have hard time understanding unfamiliar language (Chinese or foreign language) that is used in South Korea.	192	3.01	.80
	4. I cannot adjust to South Korean culture.	192	2.80	.68
	Mean	192	2.89	.69
Personal discrimination	5. I feel discriminated by others even though people do not tell me directly.	194	3.10	.75
	6. I have hard time catching up work and work life.	192	3.22	.66
	7. People have bias against me.	193	2.97	.53
	Mean	192	3.10	.63
Emotional difficulty	8. I suffer from missing my hometown.	194	3.11	.62
	9. I feel guilty for the fact that I left other family members and relatives in North Korea.	195	3.36	.91
	Mean	194	3.24	.73
Social alienation	10. I feel I have a low social status due to the fact that I came from North Korea.	194	3.00	.65
	11. I do not feel like I belong to South Korean society.	194	2.90	.61
	12. I cannot adjust to South Korean law system.	195	2.81	.62
	Mean	194	2.90	.61
	Grand mean	195	3.00	.22

for their left behind families. On the other hand, the social alienation subscale consists of social status, belongingness to the South Korean society, and adaptation with legislative aspects. For following analysis, above four categories were used instead of the 12 items (Table V-8).

According to the survey result, the emotional difficulty subscale received the highest average score out of the four subscales which indicates that the North Korean refugees face more emotional difficulties than any other aspects. As they have stated in the interview, it was their family left behind that made it very hard for them to decide the crossing despite the push factor within the North Korean society. According to them, they were afraid of the influence their crossing would have on their family members who are left in the North Korea. The guilt and longing for their family members continuously affect the refugees' psychological adaptation even after the crossing, which works as a driving force to plan and try to bring their family members from North Korea. It is not hard to find the cases where one of the family members escapes from North Korea first, and after the entry to South Korea, the remaining family members in North Korea are brought over to South Korea. The crossing of their remaining family members are sometimes planned beforehand but usually they learn about the brokers or the possibility of crossing for their remaining family members once the refugees arrive in South Korea.

In terms of gender, male North Korean refugees scored higher on the socio-cultural adaptation difficulties than did females. Especially there was a significant gender difference in the emotional difficulty. Males (M = 3.36) face significantly more emotional difficulties than females (M = 3.14). However, there was no consistent pattern or significant age difference in the socio-cultural adaptations among the age groups of 20s, 30s, and 40s.

In addition, when the socio-cultural adaptation was examined in terms of the education level received in North Korea, the college graduate group (N = 51) faced relatively less cultural adaptation difficulties than below high school graduate groups (N = 132). There were no significant differences found in the remaining three socio-cultural adaptation categories (Table V-9).

<Table V-9> Socio-cultural adaptation issues by sex, age, and education level

Sex	Male			Female			t
	N	M	SD	N	M	SD	
Constraints in social activity	79	2.91	.71	106	2.88	.68	.36
Personal discrimination	81	3.19	.60	107	3.03	.65	1.69
Emotional difficulty	81	3.36	.70	107	3.14	.74	2.16*
Social alienation	81	2.95	.59	107	2.86	.62	.96
Age	**20s**		**30s**		**over 40s**		**F**
	N	M (SD)	N	M (SD)	N	M (SD)	
Constraints in social activity	47	2.99 (.83)	83	2.88 (.63)	37	2.62 (.60)	.39
Personal discrimination	47	3.21 (.62)	85	2.99 (.64)	38	3.18 (.68)	2.21
Emotional difficulty	47	3.32 (.84)	85	3.12 (.67)	38	3.39 (.62)	2.32
Social alienation	47	2.80 (.64)	85	2.90 (.56)	38	2.92 (.65)	.51
Education level	**High school or under**			**College**			**t**
	N	M	SD	N	M	SD	
Constraints in social activity	130	2.95	.69	50	2.70	.71	2.24*
Personal discrimination	132	3.15	.61	51	2.97	.71	1.67
Emotional difficulty	132	3.20	.70	51	3.28	.71	-.70
Social alienation	132	2.86	.60	51	3.00	.60	-1.41

* $p < .05$

The correlation between the socio-cultural adaptation, the period in a third country, and the period after the entry to South Korea was examined. The result shows that among the four subscales, limited socio-cultural activity and social isolation were found to have negative correlation with the period after the entry to South Korea. That is, the longer the period of stay after the entry to South Korea, the less they

<Table V-10> Correlations of socio-cultural adaptation and the period in third country and after the entry

	Period in third country (N=181)	Period after the entry (N=183)
Constraints in social activity	.092	-.19**
Personal discrimination	.052	-.093
Emotional difficulty	-.034***	.010
Social alienation	-.076	-.17*

* p < .05, ** p < .01, *** p < .001

experienced the limitation on social activities and social isolation. The period in a third country and emotional difficulty were negatively correlated, which mean that the longer the period of stay in a third country, the less longing and guilt they felt for their family (Table V-10). These results can be interpreted in two ways. First, during the stay in a third country, physical support and contact with the refugees' remaining family in North Korea are made possible which then alleviate the pressure of duty for their family and emotional burden. They have stated that while working during the stay in a third country such as China, North Korean refugees purchase food or clothes with their income to send them to their remaining family members in North Korea. By means of these contact with the family, some of the remaining family members defect, or if not the case, they are kept in touch with information about China or South Korea. Another interpretation could be that simply the emotional difficulties or guilty feeling may have diminished as time passed by.

Meanwhile, the social prejudice or discrimination showed no significant correlation with the period in a third country or the period in South Korea. This indicates that time is an important factor in adaptation, but yet it may have different effect on the degree of adaptation or the tendency for each category of socio-cultural adaptation. The North Korean refugees responded that they felt the improvement of their difficulties in the cultural category and emotional category over time, which was not the case for the social category. This result has significant meaning that the social prejudice or discrimination that the North Koreans feel do not change over time. The cultural and emotional adaptation is something that may be achieved with one's effort, yet improvement in the social discrimination is out of individual's capability. Discrimination or prejudice toward the North Korean refugees is an essential issue to pay attention to since it hinders their psychological adaptation preventing the psychological integration of both societies.

The fact that length of stay in a third country does not have a significant effect on the adaptation in South Korea draws our attention as well. Despite the expectation that the stay in China would work as a buffer period for the culture shock in South Korea, the period in the third country did not have a big effect on the cultural adaptation in a new society. In most cases with the North Korean refugees, China is chosen as the third country to pass through before the entry to South Korea. Yet, due to a big institutional and cultural gap between the Chinese and Korean society, the period spent in China could not be a big help in adjusting to the South Korean society. As the North Korean refugees remember, they had to face the crisis of life and death for many times and living everyday life as refugees was not easy in China. After leading unpredictable and unsteady lifestyle for a long time, recovering orderly lifestyle along with the adaptation tasks may put heavy burden on the North Korean refugees. These results are found to be more evident when exploring the current difficulties of the North Korean refugees.

2) The current difficulties

The study explored the current difficulties of the North Korean refugees on their everyday life problems more in depth. According to the results, all of the 12 items on the everyday life problems scored higher than the median value of 3 point (M=3.47, SD=.39). Especially, the financial difficulties related to employment and livelihood such as child education expense (M=3.82), earning living expense (M=3.81), employment (M=3.78), and medical expense (M=3.67), turned out to be the greatest. On the other hand, issues related to the financial management (M=3.20), using the language of South Korea (M=3.21), making South Korean friends (M=3.25), and health (M=3.27) imposed relatively less difficulties on the North Korean refugees. Adaptation in everyday life to a new society is an important task for the North Korean refugees, in their early, but in fact, financial aspect of the adaptation is ultimately the biggest issue they are struggling to overcome (Table V-11).

The current difficulties of the North Korean refugees have been analyzed in terms of their demographic background characteristics. First, the difficulty in employment and earning living expense was more evident in the male group (M=4.06) than in the female group (M=3.58). In terms of age, each item showed different tendency. As far as the employment is concerned, the 20s (M=4.11) showed the highest score on difficulty, the group of 40s or older (M=3.89) showed the second highest score, and 30s (M=3.58) showed the lowest score. The score on difficulty related to earning living expense and child education expense was the highest in the age group of 40s. There was a significant difference on the difficulties related to health between the respondents in their 30s (M=3.39) and 40s (M=3.39), and respondents in their 20s (M=2.97). Similarly, the respondents in their 20s showed significantly less difficulty in making

<Table V-11> Current difficulties of the refugees

Items	N	M	SD
Employment	190	3.78	.94
Getting along with co-workers	181	3.29	.80
Earning living expense	183	3.81	.79
Health	152	3.27	.72
Medical expense	150	3.67	.76
Finding a spouse or a date	149	3.44	.81
Using South Korean language	178	3.21	.83
Child rearing	132	3.67	.74
Child education expense	130	3.82	.73
Making South Korean friends	146	3.25	.75
Finding someone to open up	180	3.44	.76
Financial management	181	3.20	.63
Mean	195	3.47	.39

South Korean friends than the other two age groups.

These results allow us to see that the refugees' adaptation tasks can be understood in terms of individual or family development perspective. Depending on the time of crossing during individual's life cycle, the personal tasks one has to achieve as a refugee varied. A refugee in his 20s may feel relatively less difficulty in making friends in a new society, yet he might consider employment to be a difficult challenge. These findings can be interpreted in two ways. It may be contributed to the actual labor market in which the employment for the refugees in their 30s is easier than for thoose in their 20s. This assumption is supported by the result of the survey that the refugees in their 40s showed also greater difficulty regarding the employment than the 30s. On the other hand, the reason for the refugees in their 20s to express more concern for employment than the 30s may be that refugees in their 20s consider employment to be the most essential developmental task. Accordingly, more pressure for employment is perceived by the refugees in their 20s (Table V-12).

<Table V-12> Differences in current difficulties by sex and age

Sex	Male			Female			t
	N	M	SD	N	M	SD	
Employment	81	4.06	.91	102	3.58	.89	3.60***
Getting along with co-workers	76	3.38	.77	98	3.22	.81	1.30
Earning living expense	79	4.10	.74	97	3.58	.75	4.63***
Health	59	3.14	.60	86	3.35	.79	-1.84
Medical expense	60	3.68	.72	83	3.64	.79	.35
Finding a spouse or a date	63	3.59	.82	79	3.34	.81	1.78
Using South Korean language	78	3.22	.86	93	3.18	.81	.27
Child rearing	56	3.77	.63	70	3.56	.79	1.62
Child education expense	55	3.76	.72	69	3.81	.73	-.36
Making South Korean friends	67	3.36	.71	72	3.19	.72	1.34
Finding someone to open up	79	3.52	.68	95	3.37	.80	1.32
Financial management	80	3.16	.63	94	3.23	.63	-.75
Age	**20s**		**30s**		**over 40s**		**F**
	N	M (SD)	N	M (SD)	N	M (SD)	
Employment	47	4.11 (.89)	83	3.58 (.94)	37	3.89 (.84)	5.37**
Getting along with co-workers	44	3.34 (.86)	77	3.42 (.73)	37	3.16 (.80)	1.30
Earning living expense	43	3.88 (.93)	82	3.66 (.72)	37	4.08 (.72)	3.39*
Health	37	2.97 (.80)	61	3.39 (.71)	33	3.39 (.70)	4.15*
Medical expense	38	3.68 (.77)	59	3.58 (.72)	34	3.76 (.89)	.66

Finding a spouse or a date	40	3.53 (.72)	58	3.50 (.68)	27	3.37 (1.04)	.35
Using South Korean language	45	3.18 (.86)	76	3.14 (.76)	35	3.46 (.92)	1.81
Child rearing	29	3.76 (.74)	54	3.52 (.64)	32	3.78 (.83)	1.76
Child education expense	30	3.93 (.64)	52	3.65 (.62)	30	4.03 (.76)	3.56*
Making South Korean friends	38	3.11 (.69)	59	3.27 (.67)	26	3.58 (.86)	3.37*
Finding someone to open up	43	3.30 (.96)	78	3.49 (.55)	36	3.56 (.77)	1.33
Financial management	43	3.07 (.67)	80	3.21 (.59)	36	3.39 (.64)	2.56

* $p < .05$, ** $p < .01$, *** $p < .001$

Different tasks are required for individual and family development, and different degree of difficulties are accordingly followed. The difficulties that follow in performing the expected role are different depending on gender and age. In this perspective, the difficulties that the North Korean refugees experience may not solely pertain to the North Korean refugees. Tasks such as earning living expense or child education expense are burdens not only to the North Korean refugees but also to any member of our society who is in their 40s. However, understanding how a refugee interacts with these burdens and challenges may be necessary.

Meanwhile, the education level received in North Korea did not have any significant effect on their current difficulties (Table V-13). This means that the education received in North Korea could not function as a helpful resource in South Korea. That is, regardless of the education level received in the North Korea, the refugees are experiencing similar level of difficulties related to employment as well as in finding someone who

<Table V-13> Current difficulties by education level from North Korea

Classification	High school or under			College			t
	N	M	SD	N	M	SD	
Employment	129	3.83	.96	50	3.70	.91	.82
Getting along with co-workers	122	3.28	.82	48	3.31	.78	-.25
Earning living expense	123	3.86	.79	49	3.69	.82	1.24
Health	104	3.22	.68	38	3.32	.84	-.69
Medical expense	100	3.70	.73	40	3.63	.90	.51
Finding a spouse or a date	102	3.49	.75	36	3.31	.95	1.18
Using South Korean language	120	3.29	.79	48	3.02	.91	1.92
Child rearing	88	3.68	.72	37	3.62	.79	.41
Child education expense	88	3.86	.71	34	3.71	.72	1.09
Making South Korean friends	97	3.24	.77	39	3.38	.71	-1.03
Finding someone to open up	120	3.45	.78	49	3.45	.74	.01
Financial management	121	3.17	.61	48	3.29	.65	-1.19

is close enough to open their mind to. These results show that the public education is hard to be capitalized beyond a socio-cultural background. This provides implication that determining how to value and appraise the education received from North Korean by the refugees is something to be taken into consideration while making policies for the North Korean refugees. Some refugees believe that they are being discriminated for not getting any credit for the education they received from the North. This issue of public education discrepancy comes from the gap between the policy in the North and the South, thus establishing a practical interpretation and a policy understandable by both the North and the South will be the most crucial task.

The correlation between the current difficulties for the North

Korean refugees, and the period after the entry to South Korea was examined, and according to the analysis, the difficulties they face, such as getting along with co-workers, finding a spouse or a date, using South Korean language, making South Korean friends, or financial management, were improving gradually over time after the entry to South Korea. In other words, issues related to everyday life such as relationship problems, language proficiency, and financial management, get better as time goes by. On the other hand, no significant correlation was found between the time and adaptation with issues regarding employment, earning living expense, health, child rearing, and finding someone to open up to. In terms of human relations, relationship with co-workers or finding South Korean friends improved over time, yet the refugees found finding someone to open up to and share innermost concerns to be still very hard even over time. That is, the skills related to initial interpersonal relations or adaptation improve over time, whereas forming a closer bond with someone seems to be a difficult task for the North Korean refugees. Regardless of the origin of country, finding someone to rely on emotionally or discuss issues of life ultimately allows the refugees to settle safely in a society. Thus expansion and deepening of a human relation will be a very important task both in individual level and society level.

On the other hand, significant correlation was found between the period in a third country, and earning living expense and financial management. Interestingly, difficulties related to earning living expense were negatively correlated with the period in a third country, whereas financial management difficulties had positive correlation with the time spent in a third country. The longer the stay in a third country such as China, the less they feel difficulties earning living expense in South Korea, but more difficulties in financial management. The various

<Table V-14> Correlations of current difficulties with the period in third country and after the entry

Items	Period in third country	N	Period after the entry	N
Employment	-.13	176	-.01	178
Getting along with co-workers	.05	168	-.23**	170
Earning living expense	-.16*	169	.00	171
Health	.09	139	-.22**	141
Medical expense	-.14	137	-.06	139
Finding a spouse or a date	-.05	135	-.18*	137
Using South Korean language	.06	164	-.29***	166
Child rearing	-.05	123	.13	125
Child education expense	.01	121	-.15	123
Making South Korean friends	-.01	132	-.21*	134
Finding someone to open up	.10	167	.04	169
Financial management	.21**	167	-.30***	169

* $p < .05$, ** $p < .01$, *** $p < .001$

experiences in China could have been helpful in getting a job in South Korea, yet it seems to have a negative influence on the consumption habits and systematic management of the income. Financial management is a necessary skill that needs to be achieved in order for the North Korean refugees to lead a life with financial stability. The fact that the ability in financial management that is needed for the sake of stability and reliability in everyday life, diminishes with the time spent in a third country needs to be considered in making policies for the North Korean refugee's initial settlement in South Korea (Table V-14).

How can these results about socio-cultural adaption and current difficulties of the North Korean refugees be interpreted? Taking the scores from the survey, the refugees are not voicing up about the negative aspects regarding the socio-cultural discrimination and alienation or emotional issues. It seems that although there are some hardships they experience in adaptation, the refugees think themselves there are no serious problems about them. However, in terms of specific everyday life issues, the refugees express much more difficulties. For example, the survey results indicate that the refugees show less problem with the items like 'People have prejudice about me (M=2.97)', 'I have difficulty in participating in social activities (M=3.05)', and 'I avoid contact with others because of fear for other people (M=2.69)', than the issues relating to specific difficulties such as 'finding someone to open up (M=3.44)', 'finding a spouse or a date (M=3.44)', and 'making South Korean friends (M=3.25)'.

These survey results may vary to certain extent depending on how the questions are written, drawing different reaction from the respondents. When subjective self-assessment about overall life in South Korea was asked, the adaptation level for the refugees does not take neither negative nor positive stance. Yet, these neutral responses do not indicate that the North Korean refugees have no problem in their adaptation since the responses to questions about current difficulties in more detail proved otherwise. This is an implication that answers to general or abstract questions may have tendency to be broad rather than concrete and specific in terms of their thoughts and situation.

On the other hand, the results could be interpreted that the North Korean refugees may not associate their difficulties of their life experience with their status as refugees. That is, the refugees understand that the difficulties they experience related to employment or human relations do not come from the cultural differences or discrimination against the North Korean refugees. As mentioned earlier, the difficulties of life do not only apply to the North Korean refugees. It is a well shared fact that having a job that meets their expectation and education level and living a stable life are very difficult tasks not only for the North Korean refugees but also for the South Koreans. The high youth unemployment and polarization of the hierarchy are becoming a serious problem in the South Korean society, which the North Korean refugees may have well learned through various paths.

However, this line of interpretation may be problematic both for the North Korean refugees and for the society. An interpretation that focuses on the society's general circumstances may blind the view of a distinctive experiences and characteristics of the North Korean refugees. In other words, the symptom of unemployment of youth of the South and of the refugees may be attributed to different causes. For example, conscious or unconscious discrimination against the refugees may have contributed to the unemployment of the North Korean refugees. However, instead of recognizing the distinctive circumstances of the North Korean refugees, attributing the unemployment of the refugees to the general social symptom allows the society to disengage itself from its social responsibility. Moreover, even in the case of unemployment due to refugees' lack of effort to adjust, it enables the individuals to hand over the responsibility to the socio-economical circumstances and neglect their liabilities. In other words, despite many possible causes for the refugee's unemployment such as the social discrimination or irresponsible attitude of the refugees, it is easy to attribute to the general social cause such as bad market condition. This would eventually hinder providing an appropriate response toward the unemployment issues for the North Korean refugees.

3) Life satisfaction

Exploring the aspects of the refugee's adaptation, the degree of life satisfaction was measured. The life satisfaction scale consists of 5 questions relating to health condition, work life, relation with friends, environment around life, and self-satisfaction. The questions were scored on a 5-point Likert scale. As can be seen in <Table V-15>, the satisfaction scores for the North Korean refugees exceeded a little more than 3 in all of the questions. There were different number of respondents for each item, and the question regarding to work life was answered by the fewest respondents with the lowest average score for satisfaction. On the other hand, the item relating to the surrounding environment showed the highest satisfaction score. Although, the difference between the highest and the lowest score was not large.

In term of the satisfaction according to gender analyzing the sum of the five items, male (M=16.47) scored significantly higher than female

<Table V-15> Life satisfaction of the refugees

Items	N	M	SD
1. I am satisfied with my health status.	192	3.12	.74
2. I am satisfied with my work.	182	3.08	.61
3. I am satisfied with a relationship with friends.	192	3.23	.69
4. I am satisfied with myself.	192	3.23	.70
5. I am so far satisfied with my surrounding environment.	192	3.29	.79
Total	176	15.94	2.48

(M = 15.49). As for each item, the male group expressed significantly higher satisfaction on questions relating to health, self-satisfaction, and environment of life than does the female group. Yet there were no significant gender difference on the items relating to work or friends.

In terms of age, the group of 20s showed the highest overall satisfaction level and the group of 30s showed the lowest. In all of the items relating to satisfaction in relations to friends, self-satisfaction, and surrounding environment, 20s showed higher degree of satisfaction than 30s. However, as for the level of education received in North Korea, no significant difference was found both in the overall satisfaction or in each item (Table V-16).

<Table V-16> Differences in the refugees' satisfaction level by demographic backgrounds

Sex	Male			Female			t
	N	M	SD	N	M	SD	
Health	78	3.31	.65	107	2.99	.76	2.98**
Work life	75	3.01	.63	100	3.11	.60	-1.03
Relation with friends	80	3.29	.70	105	3.16	.67	1.24
Self	80	3.35	.64	105	3.13	.73	2.10*
Surrounding environment	80	3.48	.75	105	3.16	.80	2.72**
Overall satisfaction	72	16.47	2.46	97	15.49	2.38	2.60*
Age	**20s**		**30s**		**Over 40s**		**F**
	N	M (SD)	N	M (SD)	N	M (SD)	
Health	46	3.32 (.90)	84	3.10 (.65)	38	3.05 (.77)	1.97
Work life	43	3.11 (.76)	80	3.10 (.56)	35	3.06 (.59)	.23
Relation with friends	47	3.45 (.85)	82	3.06 (.62)	38	3.24 (.59)	3.67*

Self	46	3.46 (.86)	83	3.13 (.62)	38	3.16 (.68)	2.40
Surrounding environment	46	3.48 (.84)	83	3.13 (.76)	38	3.42 (.76)	2.36
Overall satisfaction	49	16.65 (3.07)	74	15.50 (1.97)	30	15.93 (2.66)	3.13*
Education level	High school or under			College			t
	N	M	SD	N	M	SD	
Health	131	3.12	.72	50	3.10	.79	.18
Work life	125	3.06	.61	48	3.13	.67	-.58
Relation with friends	130	3.22	.69	51	3.20	.69	.17
Self	130	3.25	.70	51	3.20	.75	.49
Surrounding environment	130	3.29	.76	51	3.29	.88	-.01
Overall satisfaction	121	15.93	2.36	46	15.85	2.91	.20

* p < .05, ** p < .01, *** p < .001

There was a positive correlation between the degree of overall life satisfaction and the time after the entry to South Korea (Table V-17). That is, the degree of life satisfaction increased over time spent in South Korea. When looked into each question, satisfaction relating to the relations with friends and surrounding environment increased over time since the entry to South Korea. The term, surrounding environment, may have broader meaning than any other items on the scale, such as health, employment, and relation with friends. In fact, it is hard to know how they interpreted the surrounding environment. If the term was interpreted as the physical environment, the result may indicate that the refugees are viewing the physical environment of the South Korean society to be more positive in comparison to that of North Korea or China. In a broader perspective of surrounding environment, it may have been taken as satisfaction in their overall life. In that case, this question may be used

<Table V-17> Correlations of life satisfaction with the period in third country and after the entry

	Period in third country	N	Period after the entry	N
Health	.04	179	.05	181
Work life	.12	169	-.06	171
Relation with friends	-.01	178	.22**	180
Self	-.09	178	.14	180
Surrounding environment	-.05	178	.16*	180

* $p < .05$, ** $p < .01$

as an indicator of comprehensive self-assessment on their lives.

3. Adaptation of North Korean refugees and personal resilience

Through interviews with the North Korean refugees, individual characteristics, such as individualization, self-efficacy, religious nature and attitude, clear goal, positive prospect, meaning for their circumstances and work, and perspective taking ability, have been found to be useful resources and strengths for the refugees in adjusting to the South Korean society. A survey was then conducted to support these attributes from the interview. The survey measured the personal characteristics such as self-esteem, establishment of identity, and internal attribution, and they were analyzed in respect to the socio-cultural adaptation, current difficulties, and life satisfaction.

1) Establishment of self-identity and socio-cultural adaptation

Self-identity refers to establishment of identity about oneself regardless of the situation or time. The survey was carried out to measure the self-identity with 6 questions. A person with a firm self-identity would have a faith in one's being, which can lead to a conclusion that one would face less confusion in adapting to a new society. Conversely, culture shock, conflicting values, and social discrimination are the elements that are expected to have negative effects on self-identity. However, no significant correlation was found among the establishment of self-identity, general socio-cultural adaptation, current difficulties, and satisfaction. These results imply that the participated North Korean refugees in this research have formed relatively stable self-identity in respect to continuity, constancy, and uniqueness during the socio-cultural adaptation process (Table V-18).

2) Self-esteem and socio-cultural adaptation

Unlike the self-identity, self-esteem was found to have significant correlations with the socio-cultural adaptation, current difficulties, and

<Table V-18> Correlations between establishments of self-identity and socio-cultural adaptation

Classification	N	Self-identity
Constrains in social activity	192	-.12
Personal discrimination	195	.04
Emotional difficulty	195	.01
Social alienation	195	-.06

<Table V-19> Correlations between socio-cultural adaptation and self-esteem

Classification	Self-esteem
Constrains in social activity	-.14
Personal discrimination	-.09
Emotional difficulty	-.002
Social alienation	-.16*

* p < .05

life satisfaction of the North Korean refugees. The higher the self-esteem, the less they feel problematic by the social activity restraints and social isolation issues (Table V-19). In terms of current difficulties as well, the higher the self-esteem, the less difficulty they experience in relations with co-workers and making South Korean friends (Table V-20). In addition, as self-esteem increased, scores on all areas of life satisfaction such as health condition, work life, relation with friends, self-satisfaction, and surrounding life, also increased.

This result indicates the fact that self-esteem is a critical resource in the North Korean refugees' adaptation in a new society. As found in Chapter III, self worth and confidence enhance the sense of personalization and self-efficacy exhibiting a positive driving force in one's adaptation. Especially, the self-esteem is an important personal characteristic that is required for the formation and sustaining of a harmonious relationship with others. As self-esteem increased, the refugees expressed less difficulty on relations with the co-workers and making South Korean friends, as well as higher satisfaction in their relationship with friends.

Interestingly, the self-esteem and child rearing related difficulties were found to be positively correlated. In other words, with higher self-

<Table V-20> Correlations between self-esteem and current difficulties

Items	N	Self-esteem
Employment	190	.10
Getting along with co-workers	181	-.20**
Earning living expense	183	.12
Health	152	-.11
Medical expense	150	-.02
Finding a spouse or a date	149	-.07
Using South Korean language	178	.04
Child rearing	132	.21*
Child education expense	130	.20*
Making South Korean friends	146	-.21**
Finding someone to open up	180	-.13
Financial management	181	-.07

* $p < .05$, ** $p < .01$

esteem, parents recognized more difficulties related to raising a child and child education expense. These results could be interpreted that the refugees with higher self-esteem would have higher expectation for their children and child education which leads the parents to recognize more difficulties. That is, parents with higher self-esteem have higher expectation to provide for their children, yet due to limitation of resources or time, the expectation could not be met. In addition, if a child does not meet the parents' expectations, parents with higher self-esteem may take that as a bigger problem.

Positive correlation between the self-esteem and the burden on child rearing provides a direction to predict the causal relationship between the self-esteem and adaptation. Self-esteem can be predicted to have a bilateral causal relationship with adaptation. That is, they pose influence on each other. Higher self-esteem may influence the higher degree of adaptation, and at the same time, higher adaptation may affect increase in self-esteem. There is a limit to predict the casual relationship between the self-esteem and the degree of adaptation if they are not measured with a time interval. However, the fact that positive correlation was found between the self-esteem and the child rearing difficulties indirectly implies that the self-esteem precedes the current difficulties. The interpretation that higher difficulties would cause higher self-esteem is an idea that is hard to accept. Therefore, these results provide evidence to presume that the logical interpretation is to consider the casual relationship of self-esteem affecting the child reading difficulties rather than child rearing difficulties affecting the self-esteem (Table V-20).

3) Attribution and socio-cultural adaptation

Finally, internal attribution and socio-cultural adaptation of the North Korean refugees were examined. Internal attribution refers to a belief that one can control his or her life. In other words, it is a belief that things one experiences do not happen by coincidence, luck, or other people but the process and the results are controlled by one's plan and intention, including the process and the results. This belief that they are in charge of their lives is a very important factor in socio-cultural adaptation of the North Korean refugees.

The higher the internal attribution score, the lower the scores in all of the items such as limitation in social activity, personal discrimination, emotional difficulty, and social isolation. This indicates that a person with a high internal attribution score accepts the current circumstances as the result of his or her choice and will, and at the same time, positively recognizes his or her role as a member of a new society. The fact that refugees with a high internal attribution have less degree of emotional difficulties such as homesickness and guilt for the remaining family shows the positive effect internal attribution has on the refugees (Table V-21).

The positive strength of the internal attribution on the current difficulties for the North Korean refugees was found as well. The North Korean refugees with higher internal attribution score expressed less difficulty on employment, relation with co-workers, health, making South Korean friends, and finding a close friend to open up to. The belief that one can plan and control his or her life is important in many areas, yet it seems to be a more crucial resource in human relations. The higher the internal attribution score, the lower the difficulties on making South Korean friends, finding someone to open up to, and relations with co-workers (Table V-22).

One exceptional relationship to above results would be the relationship with children. Similar to the case of self-esteem, there was a positive correlation between the internal attribution and the difficulties on child rearing. The result that one's faith in having control of one's life is associated with greater difficulties in raising children is remarkable. As mentioned in the overall conditions of the North Korean refugees previously, the refugees with children consider child rearing to be one of the most difficult tasks they face in a new society. The North Korean refugee parents may face greater difficulties due to the conflicting child rearing philosophy and values that they already have with the values emphasized from a new society, and dealing with children whose lives are constructed differently from those of the North. The cost on child rearing and education would put even greater burden on the North Korean refugees without financial stability. Contrary to the other areas of difficulties, issues related to the child rearing difficulties could not be

<Table V-21> Correlations between internal attribution and socio-cultural adaptation

Classification	Internal attribution
Constrains in social activity	-.31***
Personal discrimination	-.21**
Emotional difficulty	-.20**
Social alienation	-.18*

* p < .05, ** p < .01, *** p < .001

<Table V-22> Correlations between internal attribution and current difficulties

Items	N	Internal attribution
Employment	190	-.21**
Getting along with co-workers	181	-.25***
Earning living expense	183	-.10
Health	152	-.20*
Medical expense	150	-.11
Finding a spouse or a date	149	-.10
Using South Korean language	178	-.09
Child rearing	132	.19*
Child education expense	130	.11
Making South Korean friends	146	-.15
Finding someone to open up	180	-.29***
Financial management	181	.001

* p < .05, ** p < .01, *** p < .001

resolved with personal attributes and resilience.

Self-esteem and internal attribution that are found to have a positive effect on the overall adaptations of forming personal resilience could not act as a buffer for the difficulties regarding child rearing but instead had a negative influence. These results have an implication in understanding the adaptation of North Korean refugees that the approach needs to be taken in respect to a family rather than an individual. In order to understand the challenges and tasks of a family in adaptation to a new society, more family-oriented approach needs to be taken. Researches focused on the individuals have limitation in understanding the family life of the refugees and how the family affects their adaptations.

4. Adaptation of North Korean refugees and family

Following the previous studies on the actual adaptation conditions of the North Korean refugees through several items, the influence of a family on the refugees' adaptation was examined. In establishing the definition of a family, the survey first asked an open-ended question: 'Did you accompany any family members when you were escaping from North Korea?' Then, they were to select all applicable choices among spouse, son, daughter, father, mother, father-in-law, mother-in-law, male siblings, and female siblings.

In respect to the question whether crossing accompanied family, the rate of the missing values was high as about 30 respondents did not answer. Out of 165 respondents, 75 (45 %) answered that they accompanied family members as following: spouse (N=16), son (N=23), daughter (N=23), father (N=14), mother (N=23), male sibling (N=17), and female sibling (N=8). The number of refugees who responded that they have remaining family members in the North was 118, which is about 60 % of the total respondents. The remaining family members mentioned were spouse (N=27), father (N=27), mother (N=23), son (N=28), and daughter (N=15).

Meanwhile, the total number of respondents who are living with their family was 76 and the number of refugees who accompanied their family at the time of crossing but not living together was 16 (22 %). The marital status of the total respondents was found to be unmarried (N = 62), living with spouse (N = 27), separated with spouse (N = 44). The case of being separated with spouse includes all the cases such as widowed, divorced, and left in North Korea.

1) Family of North Korean refugees and their socio-cultural adaptation

The socio-cultural adaptation score was measured on several areas in respect to the family-accompanied crossing. The results indicated that the family-accompanied crossing does not have a significant effect on the adaptation. However, household status, which indicates whether the refugees are living with their family or not, was found to have a significant influence on the restraints in social activity among many areas of socio-cultural adaptation. Refugees who are living together with the family, express relatively less fear and experience less difficulties related to the language or culture of South Korea than the refugees who are not living with their family. However, social discrimination, emotional difficulties, and social isolation did not show a significant difference in terms of the household status of the North Korean refugees. This pattern is more noticeable when there are family members under 18-years old living together. Depending on the relationship with the respondents, family members under the age of 18 may be children, grandchildren, or younger siblings (Table V-23).

The three marital status groups were analyzed in respect to the restraints in social activities. The result showed that the restraint level

<Table V-23> Differences in the refugees' socio-cultural adaptation by family variable

Entry status	Family-accompanied			Family-unaccompanied			t
	N	M	SD	N	M	SD	
Cultural adaptation	73	2.79	.76	89	2.96	.65	-1.50
Personal discrimination	74	3.10	.69	91	3.15	.63	-.45
Emotional difficulty	74	3.27	.69	91	3.27	.75	.01
Social alienation	74	2.93	.65	91	2.88	.56	.54
Household status	Living with family			Not living with family			t
	N	M	SD	N	M	SD	
Cultural adaptation	75	2.79	.85	107	2.99	.56	1.81^{+}
Personal discrimination	76	3.09	.71	109	3.11	.59	.23
Emotional difficulty	76	3.17	.75	109	3.30	.75	1.17
Social alienation	76	2.88	.67	109	2.91	.56	.33
Household status-existence of the minors	Having under-age family member			Not having under-age family member			t
	N	M	SD	N	M	SD	
Cultural adaptation	27	2.56	.82	165	2.94	.65	2.67**
Personal discrimination	28	2.99	.64	167	3.12	.63	.99
Emotional difficulty	28	3.25	.66	167	3.24	.74	-.09
Social alienation	28	2.89	.57	167	2.90	.61	.08

$^{+}p < .10$, $^{**}p < .01$

was the highest in 'separated with spouse' group and the lowest in 'living with spouse' group. Yet no significant differences were found among the groups in terms of emotional difficulties and social isolation problems. These results indicate the fact that married refugees who are not living with their spouses, realize more discrimination and prejudice against them and experience more challenges of the restraints in social activities (Table V-24).

<Table V-24> Differences in the refugees' socio-cultural adaptation by marital status

Classification	Single		Married-living with a souse		Married-not living with a spouse		F
	N	M (SD)	N	M (SD)	N	M (SD)	
Constraints in social activity	61	2.84 (.79)	27	2.66 (.81)	43	3.14 (.57)	3.99*
Personal discrimination	62	3.09 (.64)	27	3.05 (.77)	44	3.38 (.53)	3.29*
Emotional difficulty	62	3.24 (.83)	27	3.37 (.55)	44	3.44 (.58)	1.09
Social alienation	62	2.84 (.71)	27	3.06 (.47)	44	3.05 (.59)	1.81

* $p < .05$

The household status having more influence on the restraints in social activity than the family-accompanied crossing is an interesting result. In general, the family-accompanied crossing would be expected to have a positive effect on the North Korean refugees' adaptation since it could provide emotional support for each other with less homesickness and guilt for the remaining family members. In this study, however, the family-accompanied crossing did not have significant relationship with the emotional difficulties for the North Korean refugees. Furthermore, even in the case of refugees accompanying their families, if they are not currently living with their family it did not have any significant influence on adaptation. This may conclude cautiously that for a family to be a positive influence in adaptation, not just being physically close but also having intimate emotional interaction are required.

2) Current difficulties of North Korean refugee families

The areas and degree of current difficulties were examined in terms of the family-accompanied crossing, current household status, and composition of underage family member. First, the family-accompanied refugees expressed greater difficulties related to child rearing and child education expense than sole refugees (Table V-25). Refugees currently living together with the family members expressed more challenges in child rearing tasks, but less difficulties related to the relation with co-workers and finding spouse or date (Table V-26). Refugees living with under age family member witnessed less challenges related to medical expense, using South Korean language, and finding date than did the

<Table V-25> Differences in the refugees' current difficulties by entry status

Classification	Family-accompanied			Family-unaccompanied			t
	N	M	SD	N	M	SD	
Employment	70	3.87	.87	91	3.81	.99	.39
Getting along with co-workers	69	3.17	.79	85	3.38	.82	-1.56
Earning living expense	67	3.88	.81	88	3.80	.78	.67
Health	55	3.25	.75	70	3.19	.71	.53
Medical expense	55	3.76	.84	68	3.65	.75	.81
Finding a spouse or a date	52	3.31	.81	70	3.49	.79	-1.22
Using South Korean language	67	3.15	.94	83	3.25	.76	-.75
Child rearing	56	3.91	.67	58	3.53	.75	2.82**
Child education expense	57	4.02	.77	54	3.69	.61	2.52*
Making South Korean friends	52	3.23	.85	68	3.28	.71	-.34
Finding someone to open up	65	3.34	.91	86	3.55	.63	-1.59
Financial management	65	3.26	.67	88	3.16	.54	1.04

* $p < .05$, ** $p < .01$

<Table V-26> Current difficulties by household status

Classification	Living with family			Not living with family			t
	N	M	SD	N	M	SD	
Employment	72	3.85	.91	108	3.77	.99	-.54
Getting along with co-workers	72	3.01	.87	101	3.44	.71	2.80**
Earning living expense	70	3.93	.77	104	3.79	.81	-1.14
Health	59	3.19	.80	83	3.34	.67	1.22
Medical expense	59	3.81	.84	82	3.59	.70	-1.75
Finding a spouse or a date	53	3.30	.89	87	3.57	.73	1.98*
Using South Korean language	70	3.10	1.00	98	3.31	.66	1.49
Child rearing	57	3.86	.61	66	3.53	.77	-2.60*
Child education expense	57	3.91	.71	64	3.75	.71	-1.25
Making South Korean friends	52	3.23	.83	85	3.31	.71	.56
Finding someone to open up	66	3.32	.90	104	3.54	.61	1.76
Financial management	67	3.22	.57	105	3.21	.62	-.14

* p < .05, ** p < .01

refugees without underage family member (Table V-27).

It can be assumed that living with a family-accompanies the challenges in child rearing, but the refugees living alone may feel the burden of marriage in finding a date or a spouse, or of medical expenses. Taking these findings into consideration with the results on current difficulties in terms of ages shown earlier, refugees in their 20s showed greater difficulty in employment and 40s in earning living expense and child education expenses. Analysis in terms of age emphasizes the differences in tasks at individual's different developmental stages allowing the interpretation accordingly.

Meanwhile, the average age of the respondents of this study was not significantly different depending on the family-accompanied crossing

<Table V-27> Current difficulties by the existence of under-aged family member

Classification	Having under-aged member			Not having under-aged member			t
	N	M	SD	N	M	SD	
Employment	25	3.48	.76	165	3.63	.99	-.12
Getting along with co-workers	26	2.77	.74	155	3.20	.82	1.49
Earning living expense	24	3.59	.68	159	3.68	.78	-.40
Health	18	2.82	.71	134	3.16	.71	.65
Medical expense	17	2.74	.97	133	3.61	.75	2.56*
Finding a spouse or a date	20	2.66	.83	129	3.36	.79	2.33*
Using South Korean language	24	2.52	.85	154	3.13	.76	2.14*
Child rearing	24	3.49	.61	108	3.50	.75	-.61
Child education expense	25	3.22	.82	105	3.74	.61	1.96
Making South Korean friends	22	2.82	.71	124	3.14	.71	.79
Finding someone to open up	27	2.95	.70	153	3.36	.63	1.62
Financial management	26	2.90	.61	155	3.11	.54	.44

* $p < .05$, ** $p < .01$

or household status. This implicates that the family developmental cycle has a significant influence on the current difficulties for refugees as much as the individual developmental cycle. That is, regardless of age, for the refugees living with family, child rearing becomes an important task, whereas for the refugees living without family finding a spouse becomes the current task. Thus, considering both individual life process and family development, we can better understand the current difficulties and tasks of the North Korean refugees are then made clearer.

The current difficulties of the North Korean refugees were examined in terms of their marital status. Three groups of marital status which are unmarried, married and living with a spouse, and married

<Table V-28> Differences in the refugees' current difficulties by marital status

Classification	Single		Married-living with a spouse		Married-not living with a spouse		F
	N	M (SD)	N	M (SD)	N	M (SD)	
Employment	61	3.95 (.99)	25	3.72 (.84)	43	4.26 (.79)	2.89
Getting along with co-workers	58	3.08 (.82)	25	3.12 (.73)	40	3.68 (.69)	7.76***
Earning living expense	56	3.79 (.85)	26	4.08 (.69)	43	4.28 (.63)	5.43**
Health	49	3.00 (.71)	18	3.33 (.59)	35	3.34 (.64)	3.31*
Medical expense	49	3.59 (.73)	19	3.95 (.78)	35	3.94 (.59)	2.17
Finding a spouse or a date	54	3.48 (.84)	17	3.18 (.81)	34	3.71 (.87)	2.31
Using South Korean language	59	3.08 (.86)	25	3.00 (1.00)	43	3.40 (.69)	1.93
Child rearing	40	3.65 (.74)	24	4.04 (.55)	30	3.80 (.85)	1.26
Child education expense	40	3.85 (.77)	24	4.17 (.38)	29	4.00 (.65)	1.79
Making South Korean friends	55	3.15 (.80)	18	3.44 (.86)	32	3.59 (.61)	3.75*
Finding someone to open up	60	3.23 (.89)	23	3.61 (.72)	43	3.65 (.61)	4.27*
Financial management	59	3.02 (.68)	25	3.28 (.54)	43	3.30 (.56)	3.21*

* $p < .05$, ** $p < .01$, *** $p < .001$

but not living with a spouse, were analyzed (Table V-28). The greater difficulties were expressed in many areas for the case of married but not living with a spouse when compared to the other two groups. They complained more about difficulties on getting along with co-workers at work than the other two groups. Also earning living expense and finding someone to open up were considered to be more difficult for them than for the unmarried refugees. In other words, the unmarried refugees displayed the least difficulties whereas the married refugees living without their spouse expressed the most difficulties.

3) Family of North Korean refugees and life satisfaction

The life satisfaction of the North Korean refugees was examined in terms of the family-accompanied crossing, household status, underage family member, and marital status. There was no significant difference in satisfaction on health, work, relationship with friends, and surrounding environment in respect to the structural composition of family members (Table V-29; V-30).

<Table V-29> Differences in life satisfaction by family variable

Entry status	Family-accompanied			Family-unaccompanied			t
	N	M	SD	N	M	SD	
Health	74	3.11	.80	89	3.17	.64	-.52
Work life	70	3.06	.59	84	3.07	.64	-.14
Relation with friends	74	3.27	.73	88	3.19	.66	.71
Self	72	3.24	.76	90	3.21	.66	.22
Surrounding environment	72	3.26	.82	90	3.29	.71	-.21
Life satisfaction	68	15.87	2.77	81	15.96	2.17	1.02
Household status	Family living together			Family not living together			t
	N	M	SD	N	M	SD	
Health	107	3.18	.63	75	3.09	.87	.72

Work life	99	3.06	.57	73	3.11	.61	-.54
Relation with friends	107	3.22	.66	75	3.29	.71	-.67
Self	107	3.25	.66	75	3.25	.74	-.01
Surrounding environment	107	3.34	.79	75	3.29	.78	.36
Life satisfaction	68	15.87	2.77	81	15.96	2.17	-.94
Household status-existence of the minors	Having under-age family member			Not having under-age family member			t
	N	M	SD	N	M	SD	
Health	27	3.19	.84	165	3.10	.72	-.45
Work life	25	3.00	.41	157	3.10	.64	.99
Relation with friends	28	3.36	.62	164	3.21	.70	-1.16
Self	28	3.18	.67	164	3.24	.70	.47
Surrounding environment	28	3.29	.71	164	3.29	.81	.05
Life satisfaction	28	15.57	2.69	167	15.55	2.69	-.04

<Table V-30> Differences in life satisfaction by marital status

Classification	Single		Married-living with a souse		Married-not living with a spouse		F
	N	M (SD)	N	M (SD)	N	M (SD)	
Health	61	3.26 (0.79)	26	2.88 (0.71)	43	3.14 (0.71)	2.31
Work life	58	3.10 (0.64)	26	3.08 (0.56)	39	2.92 (0.58)	1.09
Relation with friends	62	3.34 (0.75)	27	3.19 (0.62)	43	3.19 (0.59)	0.85
Self	62	3.34 (0.77)	27	3.26 (0.66)	43	3.33 (0.68)	0.12
Surrounding environment	62	3.45 (0.82)	27	3.30 (0.67)	43	3.30 (0.80)	0.61
Life satisfaction	61	16.59 (2.65)	22	15.64 (2.52)	36	15.75 (2.47)	0.37

If so, does a family have any influence on the degree of satisfaction of the North Korean refugees? How does a family affect the satisfaction of the North Korean refugees and what are the variables that explain their strengths? In order to examine the routes and methods of family influence upon the adaptation of the refugees, the attributes of family process were approached in respect to resilience. The following section discusses the family resilience by cohesion and adaptability in relation to the adaptation of the North Korean refugees.

5. Adaptation of North Korean refugees and family resilience

The structural characteristics, such as family-accompanied crossing, household status, underage children, or marital status, were not significant factors in explaining the life satisfaction of the North Korean refugees. Therefore, we focused more on the relational characteristics of a family such as cohesion and adaptability rather than looking at the structural characteristics. FACES II scale was used to examine the cohesion and adaptability of family and the results are as follows. Each of the cohesion and adaptability scales included 8 questions and measured on a 5-point Likert scale ranging from 8–40 points with the median value of 24. The average total score for cohesion for the refugees was 27.24 (SD=4.32) and adaptability was 27.63 (SD=4.15) which exceeds a little more than the median value. The cohesion and adaptability scores were not significantly different in terms of gender.

How are the structural characteristics of a family related to the relational characteristics? The analysis indicates that the cohesion and adaptability level had no significant difference in terms of the family-

<Table V-31> Differences in cohesion and adaptability by family-accompanied crossing

Entry status	Family-accompanied			Family unaccompanied			t
	N	M	SD	N	M	SD	
Cohesion	72	27.97	4.25	81	26.95	3.98	1.66
Adaptability	72	28.17	4.21	80	27.71	3.47	1.41
Household status	**Family living together**			**Family not living together**			**t**
	N	M	SD	N	M	SD	
Cohesion	74	27.54	5.11	96	27.38	3.16	-1.30
Adaptability	74	28.11	5.19	96	27.42	5.11	-2.22
Household status-existence of minor	**Having under-age family member**			**Not having under-age family member**			**t**
	N	M	SD	N	M	SD	
Cohesion	27	29.07	3.32	150	26.91	4.40	-2.43*
Adaptability	27	29.11	3.68	149	27.36	4.26	-2.03*

* $p < .05$

<Table V-32> Differences in cohesion and adaptability by marital status

Classification	Single		Married-living with a spouse		Married-not living with a spouse		F
	N	M (SD)	N	M (SD)	N	M (SD)	
Cohesion	62	27.39 (2.80)	25	29.00 (2.84)	43	27.74 (4.44)	2.28
Adaptability	62	27.89 (3.90)	25	28.64 (3.58)	43	28.28 (3.38)	0.33

accompanied crossing, household status, or marital status. However, the presence of family member under 18-years old had a significant effect on cohesion and adaptability levels. According to the result, families with underage children showed higher degree of cohesion and adaptability than families without such children. This finding provides implication of the underage generation's significant role in a family in terms of the cohesion and adaptability of a family. Family unity is created around the younger generation and the adaptability is increased in order to raise the children (Table V-31; V-32).

Crossing with the family members may put the refugees in a greater danger than crossing alone. Nevertheless, we predicted that family-accompanied crossing would be the indicator for cohesion of a family. It can be predicted that emotionally united family with strong bonding would choose to make family-accompanied crossing rather than sole crossing. However, the findings from the analysis demonstrate that the family-accompanied crossing is not a significant indicator for cohesion of the family. There was no significant difference on the cohesion score of family depending on whether it was a family-accompanied crossing or not. This result leads us to assume that the family-accompanied crossing may be a strategic choice rather than matter of cohesion. Refugees may choose to try crossing alone first then plan for additional crossing for their family afterwards.

However, these results allow the future researchers to exclude above strategic choice of sole crossing and avoid the biased results in explaining the socio-cultural adaptation of the North Korean refugees in terms of cohesion and adaptability. Higher cohesion score during the early period of crossing for accompanied family may imply that the positive impact the family has on the refugee's adaptation could refer to the initial attribute of the family. That is, it may be interpreted that the positive strength of family does not arise during or after the crossing process, and yet families with initially higher cohesion even before the crossing adjust better in a new society. Yet, in regard to family-accompanied crossing, if there was no initial difference in terms of cohesion without any other

<Table V-33> Correlations of cohesion and adaptability with the period in third country and after the entry

	Period in third country	Period after the entry
Cohesion	-.200*	.014
Adaptability	-.131	.010

* p < .05

characteristics, and if the living together has a positive effect on the adaptation, these results can be interpreted that living together itself, not any other initial attribute of the family, has an effect.

In attempt to examine the family cohesion and adaptability in terms of the period in a third country and the period after the entry to Korea, simple correlation analysis was performed (Table V-33). The period after the entry had no significant correlation with the family cohesion and adaptability. Interestingly though, the family cohesion and adaptability (p = .09) were negatively correlated with the period in a third country. It is remarkable that the family cohesion and adaptability decrease as time spent in the third countries increases. The fact that the experience in China has a negative influence on a family rather than a positive influence implies that experiencing crisis and adversity could weakens the strong bond and adaptability of a family.

In general, crisis and adversity have a negative influence on individual and family. Otherwise it wouldn't be recognized as a crisis. Even though China was an alternative choice to North Korea, living in China wouldn't have been easy. During the long term escape as refugees, a family may function as a shelter for the family members, and yet sometimes a family may be forced to sacrifice one of its members for the survival of the whole. Sacrificing one of the family members for other members of the family can be the only choice for survival during a crisis, but ultimately it can threaten the strong bond and healthy relationship of the family. The cases of sacrificing one of the family members to preserve the family were testified during the interview. The sacrifice may have been an inevitable choice at that time, but it eventually led the family into a conflict or tension drawing apart the relationship between family members.

1) Family resilience and socio-cultural adaptation

The correlation between socio-cultural adaptation in terms of family cohesion and adaptation was examined. There was no significant correlation found in the family cohesion and adaptability in respect to the limitation on social activity, personal discrimination, and social adaptation (Table V-34). However, the cohesion and adaptability were found to be positively correlated with the emotional difficulties of the North Korean refugees. According to the analysis, higher family cohesion and adaptability mean higher homesickness for their hometown and remaining family, and higher sense of guilt. The results may be interpreted that families with higher cohesion but could not living with the family members due to their circumstances, experience greater emotional difficulties. Perhaps, it can be taken that the refugees who experience serious emotional problems, may consider cohesiveness and bond between the family members to be more important.

2) Family resilience and current difficulties

The family cohesion was found to have no significant influence on the current difficulties in the previous analysis. However, the adaptability of family mitigated the burden on health and financial management

<Table V-34> Correlations of socio-cultural adaptation with cohesion and adaptability

Classification	Cohesion	Adaptability
Constraints in social activity	-.12	.01
Personal discrimination	-.11	-.05
Emotional difficulty	.16*	.25***
Social alienation	.10	.00

*** $p < .001$

<Table V-35> Correlations of current difficulty with cohesion and adaptability

Items	Cohesion	Adaptability
Employment	.05	.09
Getting along with co-workers	.02	-1.00
Earning living expense	.12	.07
Health	-.02	-.23**
Medical expense	-.07	-.08
Finding a spouse or a date	-.06	-.10
Using South Korean language	-.06	-.59
Child rearing	.02	-.15
Child education expense	-.01	-.06
Making South Korean friends	.00	-.09
Finding someone to open up	-.06	-.03
Financial management	-.08	-.19*

* $p < .05$, ** $p < .01$

difficulties. That is, the refugees with higher family adaptability expressed less difficulty on health or financial management issues. Yet, the clear relationship between family adaptability and personal health or financial management was not found. The flexibility and adaptability of a family showed no relevance in socio-cultural adaptation, while they alleviated the pressure on difficulties in health, financial management, and child rearing. These findings indicate that the flexible adaptation of a family plays an important role in resolving difficulties of the North Korean refugees (Table V-35).

3) Family resilience and life satisfaction

Family cohesion and adaptability were analyzed in terms of satisfaction of life score for the North Korean refugees. The satisfaction of life score was significantly correlated with family cohesion and adaptability. First of all, the higher the cohesion score, the greater the satisfaction of life in health, themselves, and surrounding environment. In addition, the higher the family adaptability, the more they are satisfied with health, relation with friends, themselves, and surrounding environment. Among the five areas of satisfaction of life, only the items related to work life did not have any significant correlation with the family cohesion and adaptability. These results demonstrate that the family cohesion and flexible adaptation ability are closely related to the satisfaction of North Korean refugee's personal lives (Table V-36).

So far, the analysis reviewed the effects of family cohesion and adaptability of the North Korean refugees on their social adaptation. The findings from the analysis demonstrate the followings to be the important resources for the family especially during crisis and adversity; emotional bonding of family, communication ability, and flexibility in setting rules and taking roles depending on the circumstances. These resources and abilities of family are not formed in a short period of time nor is fixed without changing. They are developed over time and adjusted with difficult circumstances and challenges.

As the research findings indicate, the family cohesion and adapt-

<Table V-36> Correlations of life satisfaction with cohesion and adaptability

Classification	Cohesion	Adaptability
Health	.22**	.26***
Work life	-.08	.09
Relation with friends	.11	.14
Self	.24**	.31***
Surrounding environment	.14	.23**

* p < .05, ** p < .01, *** p < .001

ability decreased as time spent in a third country incresed. Yet, since the survey did not investigate further on the experiences in a third countries such as China, the exact factor affecting the lowering of family cohesion and adaptability in a third country could not be analyzed. However, taking the positive influence of family cohesion and adaptability to the adaptation in the South Korean society into consideration, long term stay in China may result in a negative effect on the adaptation in South Korea.

6. Social network and support

We have explored the family resilience in respect to cohesion and adaptability in the previous section. In this part of the chapter, the influence of individual's social network and support on the adaptation of the North Korean refugees is examined. It is a well known fact that the support from a social network is an important factor of resilience in overcoming the adversity and crisis, and also acts as the main protection factor. The social network is related to family resilience in two ways. First, the social network formed by a family becomes a supporting resource in crisis for the family. The social network formed by a family means the network established by each role within the family. For example, relations with parents of children's friends, teacher of children, or friends of senior parents are established networks related to the roles within the family. When these relationships are reorganized around the family, the social network then functions as a resource for the family. Secondly, sometimes family members living apart take part in the broader social network of an individual. That is, the network established by the family members or relatives who are not living together, provides support and strength in adaptation of an individual and family.

The social support received by the North Korean refugees from various people in a third country or in South Korea has been mentioned in Chapter III. The social support was mainly from the people they met through official or unofficial routes during the crossing process such as American missionaries, Korean-Chinese, personnel at Hanawon, and detectives. These people are imprinted in the memories of the North Korean refugees since they provided critical support for the refugees' survival during the crossing process. However, the social network of the North Korean refugees on a daily basis may vary from above. A survey was conducted to explore how their close relationships, social networks, and the emotional, instrumental, social, and informational supports are related to the adaptation of the North Korean refugees, and the results are discussed in this section of the chapter.

1) Social network

In attempt to investigate the North Korean refugees' main composition of social network, we inquired the respondents to appoint the two closest people in order from the given list of people. The given examples were father, mother, son, daughter, sibling, other relatives, church or religious organization fellow believer, colleagues from Hanawon, hometown people, personnel at Hanawon, school friend, neighbor, and others. Despite these given examples, there were cases where they wrote family in general or names, which made it hard to distinguish the specific relationship with the refugees. Some of the respondents did not follow the instruction from the questionnaire even though it emphasized on choosing the closest people who are not living together with them.

The closest people mentioned from the survey in sequence are colleague from Hanawon (N=44), parents (N=33), and hometown people (N=17), the second closest people were colleague from Hanawon (N=34), hometown people (N=33), and fellow believer (N=15) in order. The cases of choosing other for the answer were excluded from the listing due to unclear relationship with the refugees. However, after adding up all the answers of parents, son, daughter, siblings, and family, a total of 76 people picked their family to be the closest people, and 52 picked family as the second closest people. Even though the survey emphasized on selecting people who are not currently living together, the instruction may not have been followed carefully, and it is possible that some of the answers may include the people who are currently living together with the refugees. Yet, even if the family members living together were included in the answers, the fact that the refugees selected their family members to be the closest people suggests that the various supports from their family are important resources for the North Korean refugees.

Other than family, the social network formation is actively established within the refugees such as colleagues from Hanawon or people from hometown. The formation of a community by the refugees allows them to exchange information and establish inter-support system. Typically, it is not rare for migrants to settle in a specific area forming an ethnic community. In the case of North Korean refugees, they are

<Table V-37> The refugees' closest person

Closest person	Frequency, firstly mentioned	Frequency, secondly mentioned
Father, mother	33	11
Son, daughter	7	9
Siblings	15	9
Other relatives	2	2
Hanawon colleagues	44	34
People from same hometown	17	33
Church friends	6	15
Hanawon personnel	0	2
School friends	13	3
Neighbors	5	13
Family	14	2
Others	17	23
Total	173	156

assigned to government leased apartments after the Hanawon training, naturally creating the refugee community around the apartment complex. North Korean refugees who participated in the interview knew all the other refugees living in the same apartment complex and introduced others to participate in the research. Apparently, they were very familiar with each other's life through daily interaction.

Besides the family, colleagues from Hanawon and hometown friends, the next closest people were neighbors, fellow believers, and school friends who were not identified whether from the North or from the South. For example, the neighbors could be refugees from the same apartment complex or South Korean people. Also, in the case of fellow believers, since there are churches where a lot of refugees attend, it is hard to distinguish if they are from the North or the South. Nevertheless, it provides an implication that church, school, and place of residence can be important route of social network for the North Korean refugees (Table V-37).

The North Korean refugees establish primary social network centering the family, and at the same time closely interacting with other North Koreans such as colleagues from Hanawon or hometown people. It is a remarkable fact that an important social network is already established during the Hanawon training period and it continues to be maintained after they come out to the society. Hanawon becomes the first place to experience community in South Korea where the refugees share their information and daily lives. The social network from Hanawon becomes subject to conformity for the refugees where they can share and identify their experience with other refugees, and at the same time becomes a critical resource for life and adaptation even after the training period in Hanawon.

The fact that social network is formed and maintained around family or colleagues from Hanawon, suggests that they are living in a relatively limited relational network. These relational networks seem to be natural phenomenon at a glance and yet, it is an indication that the social capital that can be utilized by the refugees for adaptation in the South is only formed around the primary social group. The North Korean refugees reported that maintaining harmonious relationship and making new South Korean friends are not easy tasks. The degree of closeness and interaction with South Koreans can be the indicator for psychological integration of the refugees in the South Korean society. In that sense, the fact that refugees' social network is organized around the other refugees need to be considered in terms of psychological integration.

2) Social support and socio-cultural adaptation

Support received from the closest people for North Korean refugees was examined in terms of different categories such as emotional, instrumental, informational, and leisure areas. The average scores of the four categories were as follows: information support (M=3.60), emotional support (M=3.51), instrumental support (M=3.41), and leisure support (M=3.30). In other words, important decision making is relied upon the information given by the closest people, and exchange of information on how to get along with other people are made most frequently. Meanwhile, leisure support activities such as 'go on an outing or eat out together' or 'visit each other without any cause' were not held as frequently. The four categories of social support have high correlation with each other. Especially, high correlation (r=.68) is found among emotional, instrumental, and leisure support. These findings suggest that support received from close social networks is multidimensionally formed (Table V-38).

Generally, social support is negatively correlated with socio-cultural adaptation difficulties of the North Korean refugees and is understood as the supporting factor and resource in resolving problems for adaptation. In regard to each area of social support, the emotional support is negatively correlated with the limitation on social activities and the social alienation. The instrumental support also has a negative correlation with the limitation on social activities, whereas the informational support has a positive correlation with the personal discrimination, and the leisure support is negatively correlated with the limitation on social activities (Table V-39).

These correlations can be interpreted in terms of the bilateral causal relationship. The emotional support plays an important role for refugees

<Table V-38> Correlations between sub-categories of social support

Classification	Emotional support	Instrumental support	Informational support
Emotional support			
Instrumental support	.68***		
Informational support	.55***	.46***	
Leisure support	.65***	.68***	.50***

*** p < .001

<Table V-39> Correlations of social support with socio-cultural adaptation

Classification	Emotional support	Instrumental support	Informational support	Leisure support
Constraints in social activity	-.30***	-.26***	.03	-.19**
Personal discrimination	-.06	-.01	.15*	.04
Emotional difficulty	.09	.00	.10	-.01
Social alienation	-.20**	-.19**	-.04	-.08

** p < .01, *** p < .001

in participating in social activities and eliminating cultural gap. The leisure support from close relationship alleviates the fear of social life and encourages self-confidence. In addition, it moderates the stress from language difficulties and cultural disparity. The instrumental support has significant relationship with the limitation on social activities and the social alienation problems as well. The instrumental support is received in the means of borrowing money when needed. The fact that refugees have someone who provides physical support functions as a safety net in their social life, helps to provide the sense of belongingness in the society. Yet the effect of instrumental support on adaptation is predicted to be partly attributed to the high correlation it has with emotional support.

The items related to the informational support category are as follows: 'provide me with information on how to get along with people around me', and 'provide me with information for important decision making.' The informational support had positive correlation with the difficulties related to personal discrimination and prejudice. This result suggests that the North Korean refugees seek a lot of advice when they face difficulties related to personal discrimination or prejudice. Considering that the social network for refugees is composed of the families and the advice from the people who share the similar experience would be the primary resource. However, it is hard to estimate how the advice or the exchange of information amongst the refugees would be helpful in the adaptation of North Korean refugees. The informational support had a positive correlation only in the area related to the personal discrimination, and had no other significant effects on the other areas.

As pointed out previously, among the four social support categories, the informational support received the highest average score. Yet, the informational support had the least effect on the limitation in social activities. Incorporating these results together, there arises a doubt about the actual positive effect the internal exchange of information and advice for decision making within the refugee community might have on the limitation in social activities. In resolving above uncertainty, the following aspects need to be explored in relation to the social network of North Korean refugees: how the social network of North Korean refugees is open to the outside of their refugee community, the quality of information exchanged and expanded within the refugee community, whether more information needs to be provided from the outside of their community for better adaptation and integration to the South Korean society.

3) Social support and current difficulties

The support from the social network has a significant correlation with the difficulties of North Korean refugees. The correlation can also be interpreted in terms of the bilateral causal relationship. First of all, the emotional support has a negative correlation with the difficulties in relations with co-workers, making South Korean friends, and finding someone to open up, suggesting the close connection between the emotional support and interpersonal relationship. These results indicate that the refugees gain self-confidence and experience less difficulties in social relationships when they are provided with emotional support from their family or closest people. That is, the formation of a harmonious relationship with co-workers, South Korean friends, and neighbors may be the source of emotional support. These findings lie in the same context with the previous outcome about the emotional support alleviating the limitation of social activities and social alienation.

However, the emotional support showed a positive correlation with child rearing. This can be interpreted that the more refugees experience difficulties with child rearing, the more they seek the emotional support. Emotional support of the refugees was examined with the questions on the visits they receive in times of illness or loneliness, recognition they receive as an important person, and providing consultations to others in times of difficulties. That is, the more difficulties they feel, the more emotional support is required in order to gain back their self-confidence on their value of existence.

The instrumental support was negatively correlated with the difficulties in relation to getting along with co-workers, making South Korean friends, and finding someone to open up. It is unclear whether these results are attributed to the high correlation with emotional support

<Table V-40> Correlations of social support with current difficulties

Items	Emotional support	Instrumental support	Informational support	Leisure support
Employment	.01	-.02	.17*	.02
Getting along with co-workers	-.25***	-.29***	-.09	-.31***
Earning living expense	.00	-.05	.15*	.05
Health	-.08	-.12	-.11	-.16
Medical expense	.08	.07	.12	.12
Finding a spouse or a date	-.76	.00	-.11	-.10
Using South Korean language	-.05	-.10	.04	-.15
Child rearing	.21*	.11	.23**	.17
Child education expense	.15	.06	.26**	.15
Making South Korean friends	-.21*	-.19*	-.04	-.25**
Finding someone to open up	-.21**	-.18*	-.06	-.18*
Financial management	-.04	-.09	-.09	-.15*

* $p < .05$, ** $p < .01$, *** $p < .001$

or to the fact that less difficulty from interpersonal relationship would lead to more frequent instrumental support. Despite the above uncertainty of causal relationship, it is clear that the supports that the North Korean refugees receive from interpersonal relationships include the instrumental support as well as the emotional support.

Unlike the other categories of support, the informational support was found very much correlated with the physical difficulties. The informational support was negatively correlated with difficulties related to finding a job, earning living expense, child rearing, and child education expense. This result should not be interpreted with the simple causal relationship but rather be seen in respect to their needs for more information and advice from close social network as they recognize more difficulties in the above aspects of life.

Finally, the leisure support was negatively correlated with the difficulties related to the relations with co-workers, health, using South Korean language, making South Korean friends, finding someone to open up, and financial management. It showed significant correlations, therefore, in the most number of areas among the four support categories. Interestingly, spending leisure time together without specific purpose had a positive influence on refugees' adaptation. Having someone who can spend their spare time together does not seem to have much relevance with using the South Korean language, health, or financial management. However, establishing a close relationship and social network with other people by spending a lot of time together catalyzes the adaptation of refugees emotionally and instrumentally (Table V-40).

4) Social support and life satisfaction

In all of the four categories of the social support, emotional, instrumental, informational, and leisure support, a positive correlation was found between the social support and life satisfaction of the North Korean refugees. This suggests that the social support is a crucial factor that has a positive effect on the refugee's life satisfaction. The emotional support was related to the satisfaction in work life and themselves, whereas the instrumental support was found to be related to the satisfaction in health, work life, relation with friends, and surrounding life environment. The informational support was related to the satisfaction in health, relation with friends, themselves, and surrounding environment, while the leisure support was related to the satisfaction in work life, relation with friends,

<Table V-41> Correlations of social support with life satisfaction

Classification	Emotional support	Instrumental support	Informational support	Leisure support
Health	.05	.14*	.18*	.12
Work life	.24**	.21**	.15	.20**
Relation with friends	.14	.25***	.30***	.18**
Self	.19**	.14	.36***	.13
Surrounding environment	.06	.20**	.29***	.20**

* p < .05, ** p < .01, *** p < .001

<Table V-42> Regression analysis of social support on constraints in social activity

Classification	Coefficient (s.e)	t
Emotional support	-.47 (.13)	-3.57***
Instrumental support	-.17 (.12)	-1.38
Informational support	.33 (.09)	3.65***
Leisure support	-.01 (.11)	-.07
Constant	3.92 (.34)	11.64***
F	8.78***	

* p < .05, ** p < .01, *** p < .001

and surrounding environment (Table V-41).

However, these results require careful interpretation. As previously mentioned, the four categories of social support are highly correlated each other. That is the social supports received from social network are engaged with each other. Frequent daily encounter creates the basis for exchange of informational, emotional, and instrumental support. Considering the fact that the social network is composed of people who are very close, it is self-evident that the informational support and emotional support are inseparable with each other. Providing the information objectively without relating to others' sympathy or the emotional support does not fit to the intimate aspect of social network. Therefore, the four categories of social support defined in this chapter should not be taken as four separate aspects, rather it should be considered as a whole.

The reason for the emphasis on interrelated areas of the social support is to minimize the interpretational error in considering only the correlation between social support and adaptation of the refugees. For example, the emotional support had a significant influence in limitation in the social activities and personal discrimination, but the instrumental and leisure support did not have any significant effect on them (Table V-42). Therefore, in interpreting the correlations, the fact that all four categories of the social support are integrated with each other very closely is very important to remember.

7. Adaptation of North Korean refugees and limitations of the study

This chapter explored the North Korean refugees' socio-cultural adaptation by analyzing the quantitative data obtained by the survey. Chapter III concentrated on listening to the North Korean refugees about their lives and adaptations, whereas this chapter focused on finding the patterns that could generalize the experiences from a larger group of people. The participated North Korean refugees included males and females of various age groups. The collected data analyzed have a number of important implications about refugees' adaptation.

First, when the actual condition of limitation on social activities were investigated and analyzed qualitatively, no serious limitation was revealed. On the one hand, these results may be based on the limitations to the study. The tendency for the North Korean refugees to respond with the median value of scales throughout the survey must be attributed to their socially encouraged attitude of not taking sides but showing socially normative reaction rather than expressing of their experience and thoughts honestly.

On the other hand, however, these results allow us to ponder about the possibility of overstating the adaptation problems of the North Korean refugees based on the extreme cases introduced in the media. Most of the North Korean refugees do experience the adaptation challenges. Yet, anyone who comes across a new culture and lifestyle faces adaptation problems. Thus, understanding the peculiar problems and adaptation pattern specific to the North Korean refugees during the adaptation process is a critical task. In addition, more attention is required on how these refugee-specific experiences would influence the integration of society.

VI

Adaptation and Social Psychological Integration of North Korean Refugees

Koreans in the North and the South have lived together under the same cultural backgrounds for several millennia. As a result, they share many similarities in terms of cultural aspects such as language, values, perspectives, and food. And yet, North and South Korea have undergone severe differences culturally from each living under different political structures without any cultural interchange during the last sixty years. Such differences are evident not only in the economy but also in the language, food, values, and inter-personal relationships. This study, in exploring the effective ways for the North Korean refugees to adjust after the entry to South Korea, focuses on their adaptation process and tries to describe a task of integration in terms of social psychological aspects and a direction for policy making.

For these, we will examine a general model of acculturation and concepts related to the model, and analyze acculturation process undergone by the North Korean refugees in South Korea by the name of integration. In addition, problems and overcoming tasks that would arise in the adaptation process of North and South Koreans in times of post-unification are to be discussed. In the latter part, a direction to policy making that would be helpful in forming a social and psychological integration of North Korean refugees and South Koreans, will be presented briefly.

1. Task of a social and psychological integration

It is possible to think that a better way to live in South Korea is immediately discard their life styles under the North Korean political system, get financial support from the South Korean government, and obtain appropriate jobs simultaneously. Thus, it can be assumed that educating the North Korean refugees on the South Korean cultural factors such as system, language, food, religion, and inter-personal relationship, is in prompt need to help the North Koreans to adapt well to the South Korean society.

However, previous studies have shown the complexity of adaptation process. First, does adaptation in a cultural aspect work in one-way direction? In terms of this question, supplementary questions come along: Does acculturation for the North Korean refugees refer to acceptance of the new life style and values in South Korea? Would this one-way direction be better for their mental health and psychological adaptation, and furthermore, is it appropriate for the development of the South Korean society with the North Koreans in times of the post-unification? If so, the main education recipient or subject to change would be the North Korean refugees while they settle in South Korea and the sole responsibility is theirs for their maladaptation to the South Korean society. However, previous studies on acculturation provide some different views.

Second is the problem of inquiring what would be the desirable formation for people from two different cultures to live together? In other words, is it desirable that a group live in total assimilation of the other group's culture, and is that possible? Or, is it rather desirable one should sustain its identity without being assimilated? If assimilation is the most desirable way for the North Korean refugees to adapt to the social culture of the South, they should discard all of their lifestyle and values that were familiar to them, and fully accept the social culture of South Korea. However, after examining results from previous studies on acculturation and interview materials on the North Korean refugees, it seems neither desirable nor realizable for one to discard one's every cultural backgrounds. If the North Korean refugees cannot assimilate entirely to the South Korean social culture, selecting an adaptation strategy for the two groups to coexist should be carefully considered.

Third is the problem of whether acculturation is a group process, an individual process, or an integration of the two processes. The importance of this problem is that the method and degree of intervention for unity and coexistence of the North and the South Koreans differ by which perspective is taken in examining acculturation. In addition, when there occurs an inevitable problem in acculturation process, it presents where to focus between the individual and the group to solve the problem.

In order to examine questions described earlier, we will clarify the concept of acculturation, and examine the acculturation process' theoretical models and results from the previous studies. Concepts and models presented in this chapter will provide conceptual framework in understanding the social culture adaptation by the North Korean refugees.

1) General process of acculturation

(1) Definition of acculturation

According to Social Science Research Council (1954), the term acculturation may be defined as 'cultural change that is initiated by the conjunction of two or more autonomous cultural systems. Acculturative change may be the consequence of direct cultural transmission: it may be derived from noncultural causes, such as ecological or demographic modifications induced by an impinging culture; it may be delayed, as with internal adaptations following upon the acceptance of alien traits or patterns; or it may be a reactive adaptation of traditional modes of life. Its dynamics can be seen as the selective adaptation of value systems, the process of integration and differentiation, the generation of developmental sequences, and the operation of role determinants and personality factors'.

Above definition has clear meanings and thus, it is agreed by many scholars. However, the concept of acculturation is often used interchangeably with other terminologies. In order to clarify the concept of acculturation in this study, similar terms need to be distinguished. First is adaptation. 'Adaptation' is a general and umbrella term which implies all the acculturation process and its results (Dubos, 1965). Studies on 'adaptation' indicate that adapting strategy and adapting level to a culture differ by individuals, and such difference can be divided into three stages which are adaptation, reaction, and withdrawal (Berry, 1976).

First stage is adaptation, which refers to a change toward reducing environmental conflicts by finding a way to harmonize individual and environment together. Thus, this strategy is the closest term to broader meaning of 'adaptation'. Second is 'reaction', which refers to an active change of surrounding environment or newly experienced mainstream culture by actively and rebelliously responding to the cultural influence in a relationship with the environment. As a result, it can increase consentaneity or suitability of the environment and the individual, and yet it differs from adaptation in that it tries to change the environment suitable for the individual rather than the other way around. Third is withdrawal, also a change that can reduce pressure from the environment. It refers to reducing pressure from the environment by withdrawing from the adaptation process without further interaction with the environment. To sum up, withdrawal cannot be accepted in terms of the true meaning of adaptation, and reaction also is hard-to-succeed adaptation since only few people in the adaptation process can resist from the pressure of cultural adaptation. As a result, adaptation is often a sole alternative in a situation where one encounters a new culture and conflicts arise as a consequence (Berry, 1988).

Second term to be distinguished is enculturation. Enculturation refers to the process by which the developing individual learns the culture (language, norms, values, etc) of his or her group (Berry et al., 1992). Together with socialization, enculturation forms part of the mechanism of cultural transmission within a culture. In contrast, acculturation refers to the second-culture acquisition through a contact with different cultures.

Third term to be distinguished from acculturation is 'psychological acculturation'. Graves (1967), the first person who identified the term, expressed that acculturation at the population level should be distinguished from acculturation at the individual level. According to Graves, acculturation refers to changes in social structure, economic base, and political organizations of the groups involved in the acculturation process. On the other hand, psychological acculturation refers to changes in behaviors, attitudes, values, and identities of the individuals from a group undergoing acculturation process. He proposed that by distinguishing

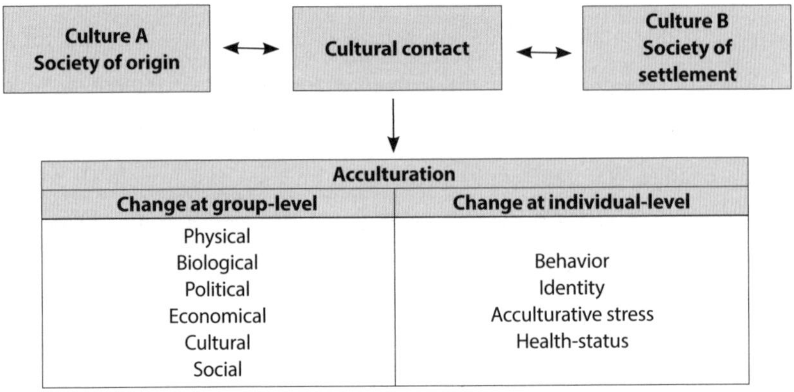

<Figure Ⅵ-1> Acculturation process (Berry, 1988, p. 42)

between acculturation and psychological acculturation, a researcher may have the clear subject and level of a research, while able to account not only for the individual differences on acculturation within a cultural group, but also for the systematic relationships between the population-level and individual-level phenomena.

Acculturation of an individual in one culture does not absorb the surrounding culture's regulations and matters as they are, but rather it is a phenomenon of bidirectional cultural change from encountering two or more different cultures. Moreover, the change occurs not only at the population-level but also at the individual-level. <Figure VI-1> illustrates the process of acculturation.

According to Berry, who has studied acculturation process in depth, acculturation is a process of change through contact with a different culture and the change occurs at various levels. Types of change can be defined into a change at population level and a change at individual level.

The changes at population level are as follows;

- Physical change: Acculturation on changes in physical environments such as residential area.
- Biological change: Acculturation on changes in nutrition, disease, and food.
- Political change: Acculturation on changes in political status such as losing autonomic rights under the new residential area's government.
- Economical change: Acculturation on changes in economical status, familiar economic system, economic value, or methods to create economic value.
- Cultural change: Acculturation and acquisition of the new language of relocated place, and abandonment of religion, traditional value structure, educational system, and traditional skills.
- Social change: Change in the relationship within groups and individuals, the appearance of new ruling class, and the traditional social status.

Changes at individual level are as follows;

- Behavioral change: Occurrence of different behavior patterns than that of the past for survival and changes in value, belief, and motivation.
- Identity change: Establishment of new identity by equating themselves with the new societal group and rejecting the original one. Change in self attitude that includes subjecthood of self and group.
- Acculturative stress: Stress experienced during the process of adjusting to a new culture.
- Heath status change: Change in both physical health and mental health related to the acculturative stress.

As a whole, acculturation can be defined as in “acculturation comprehends those phenomena, which result when groups of individuals having different cultures come into continuous first-hand contact with subsequent changes in the original culture patterns of either or both groups (Redfield, Linton, & Herskovits, 1936, recited by Castro, 2003)”.

(2) Acculturation concept and models

a. Acculturation types

Much of the research on acculturation in recent decades has been guided by two distinct models. One of which is Linear-Bipolar Models (e.g., Gordon, 1978) and the other is Two-Dimensional or Acculturation-biculturalism Model (e.g., Berry, 1988) (Castro, 2003).

Linear-bipolar models are based on the assumption that immigrants or ethnic minority members absorb into the dominant culture. As a result, acculturation occurs in a unidirectional process and immigrants’ and ethnic minority members’ value, attitude, behavior, and identity become similar to that of the dominant society. This concept is commonly used with the term of assimilation. Gordon’s assimilation model is one of the Linear-Bipolar models. His model is based on the process of American ethnic minority members assimilating into the main American culture. He proposed that when immigrants settle in a new nation, changes occur in their social structure, cultural patterns, and psychological features from one generation to another. This change is called assimilation. There are seven types of assimilation which are described in <Table VI-1>.

This model, traditionally well accepted, proposed that acculturation is an one-sided, unidirectional process, where the ethnic minority members lose their cultural identity as they adapt to the larger society. Acculturation, however, turned out to be not only a process of changing

<Table VI-1> Gordon (1978)'s model of assimilation

Type of assimilation	Subprocess
Cultural assimilation or acculturation	Change of cultural patterns to those of host society
Structural assimilation	Large-scale entrance into institutions of host society
Marital assimilation or amalgamation	Large-scale intermarriage
Identificational assimilation	Development of sense of peoplehood based exclusively on the host society
Attitude assimilation	Absence of prejudice
Behavioral assimilation	Absence of discrimination
Civic assimilation	Absence of value and power conflict

the ethnic minority members' original culture as they adapt to a larger society but also a process of changing the dominant culture. And the issue that the loss of ethnic minority members' identity is not at all an efficient adaptation process raised the advent of Two-Dimensional Models.

Contrary to the Linear-Bipolar Models, Two-Dimensional Models assume that the immigrants maintain their original cultural identity while developing a positive identification through forming a social network within the new culture. One of the leading Two-Dimensional Models was developed by Berry et. al. (1984). According to Berry, immigrants are faced with two important questions in the process of adapting to a new culture: Is it considered to be of a value to maintain the cultural identity and characteristics? and Is it considered to be of a value to maintain relationships with the other ethnic groups? These are 'yes' or 'no' questions, and the forms of adaptation can be drawn based on the answers to these questions. Adaptation can be classified into the following four modes: assimilation, integration, separation, and marginalization <Table VI-2>. Since these forms of adaption imply decision-making when adapting

<Table VI-2> Two-dimensional model (Berry, 1986, 1988)

<table>
<tr><td colspan="2" rowspan="2"></td><td colspan="2">ISSUE 1:
Is it considered to be of a value to maintain cultural identity and characteristics?</td></tr>
<tr><td>YES</td><td>NO</td></tr>
<tr><td rowspan="2">ISSUE 2:
Is it considered to be of a value to maintain relationships with other ethnic groups?</td><td>YES</td><td>I
Integration</td><td>II
Assimilation</td></tr>
<tr><td>NO</td><td>III
Separation</td><td>IV
Marginalization</td></tr>
</table>

to the new culture, they can also be referred to as the acculturation strategies.

As can be seen in <Table VI-2>, the integration strategy describes a mode of maintaining an ethnic identity and tradition while holding a positive relationship with the new society. The assimilation strategy describes a mode of seeking and preferring a relationship with the mainstream culture without a desire to maintain one's cultural identity. The separation strategy describes a mode of avoiding the mainstream culture while maintaining a strong cultural identity and tradition. The marginalization strategy describes a mode of losing cultural and psychological contact with both one's ethnic group and the larger society.

There are a few things to consider at this point. Firstly, the strategies or modes preferred at a group level may be different from those at an individual level (Berry, 1997). In other words, a particular group might prefer the integration strategy while some individual within the group might prefer the marginalization or the assimilation strategy.

Secondly, these acculturation strategies are not only adopted by the ethnic minority members or nondominant groups but also adopted by the dominant group members regarding how the nondominant groups should acculturate. That is, the nondominant group tries to adopt the integration strategy whereas the dominant group requires them to adopt the assimilation or separation strategy. Moreover, the dominant group may choose how they approach the nondominant group when they are in the process of adapting to the nondominant group. That is, the dominant group can choose which strategies to adopt regarding their attitudes and behaviors toward the nondominant group regardless of the nondominant group's attitude. This phenomenon appears because the acculturation is in fact bidirectional.

Thirdly, the acculturation modes are not only adopted by the members of nondominant or dominant groups, but also are reflected by the political ideologies or long-term policies of the larger society (Berry, 1988). For instance, a nation can employ a policy that encourages assimilation, integration, separation, or marginalization. In the case of Canada, the federal government adopted a platform of "multiculturalism" to officially encourage the integration strategy (Berry, 1988).

In brief, the acculturation modes are distinguished into the Linear-Bipolar Models and Two-dimensional Models by the theory. The Two-Dimensional Models, which hold a perspective that the ethnic minority groups should maintain their cultural identity while adapting to the new culture in the process of acculturation, are adopted by many researchers. These acculturation strategies are available to both the dominant and nondominant groups. Individuals and groups may choose to adopt different strategies, or a nation can adopt a strategy as a policy through people's consent.

b. Characteristics of acculturating ethnic groups

Characteristics of an acculturating group are also an influential factor in the process of acculturation. Berry and Kim (1988) categorized acculturating groups into immigrants, refugees, natives people, ethnic

<Table VI-3> Type of acculturation group (Berry, 1988)

Mobility \ Voluntariness	Voluntariness	Involuntariness
Immobility	Ethnic groups	Native people
Mobility	Immigrants (relatively permanent)/ Sojourners (temporary)	Refugees

groups, and sojourners by their mobility and voluntariness with cultural contact. These are illustrated in <Table VI-3>.

People who are voluntarily involved in the acculturation process (e.g., immigrants), experience less difficulty than people who are involuntarily involved (e.g., refugees and native people). The reason is because they adopt relatively positive attitudes toward cultural contact or change. In addition, sojourners who are temporarily involved in the acculturation process without continuous social support system will hardly adjust to the new society. Categorization of the acculturating groups implicates how each individual should acculturate (Berry, 1988).

c. Acculturation and stress

Stress in acculturation process is a stress that is caused by factors in the acculturation process and it leads people to behave in particular ways. People who had undergone extreme stress, experience reduction in mental health status (confusion, anxiety, or depression), feeling of marginalization and isolation, increase of psychosomatic symptoms, and confusion of identity (Berry, 1988). Acculturative stress does not necessarily lead to mental health problems. In some cases, it destroys a life of an individual, and yet that, in turn, gives a great opportunity in one's life and promotes mental health. That is, acculturation experience can cause stress factors and

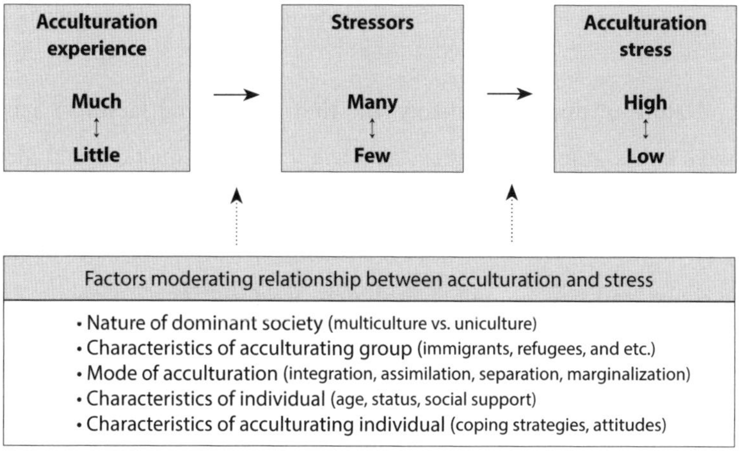

<Figure VI-2> Factors related to stress in acculturation process

these factors cause stress to individuals during the acculturation process. Relationship among acculturation experience, stressors, and individual's stress is differentiated by several moderating factors. These moderating factors include 1) nature of the dominant society (multi-culture vs. uni-culture), 2) characteristics of acculturating groups (immigrants or refugees), 3) mode of acculturation (integration, assimilation, separation, marginalization), 4) individual's demographic and sociological characteristics (age, sex, social status), and 5) individual's psychological characteristics (coping strategies, attitudes). The following figure illustrates these relationships (Figure VI-2).

Factors moderating relationship between acculturation and stress

- Nature of dominant society (multiculture vs. uniculture)
- Characteristics of acculturating group (immigrants, refugees, and etc.)
- Mode of acculturation (integration, assimilation, separation, marginalization)
- Characteristics of individual (age, status, social support)

• Characteristics of acculturating individual (coping strategies, attitudes)

Nature of dominant society, the first moderating factor of acculturative stress, refers to whether the society adopts a multicultural ideology (e.g., level of acceptance of diversity) or an ideology pursuing assimilation (or pressure to follow unicultural standard). Findings in previous studies indicate that social and psychological problems are less likely to appear in a society with a multicultural ideology (Murphy, 1965).

Characteristics of acculturating group, the second moderating factor, are classified into immigrants, refugees, ethnic groups, native people, and sojourners. Considering the fact that these groups were distinguished by their level of voluntariness and mobility, stress level for the native people or refugees, who encountered the new culture involuntarily, might be greater than that of the ethnic groups or immigrants, who encountered the new culture voluntarily.

Acculturation mode, the third moderating factor, should distinguish not only whether it is for a nondominant or dominant group, but also whether the mode is for a group-level or individual level. In general, however, the integration mode is the most desirable adaptation mode over assimilation, separation, or marginalization mode. Therefore, it can be assumed that individuals or groups of both dominant and nondominant groups that adopt the integration mode will experience less stress.

The fourth and the fifth factors are generally categorized as a psycho-social factor. This includes sex, age, prior experience before the resettlement (e.g., war, torture, famine, and etc.), knowledge of the new culture, marital status, social support, and 'cognitive control' towards acculturation. Among these factors, individual competence (stress coping ability) plays a critical role in dealing with significant change in life (Lazarus & Folkman, 1984) and leads to different stress levels, as a result for different individuals in the acculturation process.

d. Summary

Followings are the summary of various models and studies presented by many scholars.

- •Acculturation process is a bidirectional process rather than an unidirectional process. Thus, the dominant culture not only influences the members of nondominant group, but also is affected by the nondominant culture as well.
- •Acculturation occurs in various levels from a group and systematic level to an individual and psychological level (refer to <Fig. VI-1>). That is, changes in the group level include physical, biological, political, economical, cultural, and social aspect of changes. Changes in the individual level include behavior, identity, stress from adaptation, and health-status aspect of changes (Berry, 1988).
- •There are two models explaining the acculturation process: Linear-Bipolar Models and Two-Dimensional Models. According to the Two-Dimensional Models, acculturation mode is classified into integration, assimilation, separation, and marginalization, in which the integration mode (or strategy), generally, is the most effective in adaptation (Castro, 2003).
- •Acculturation mode can 1) be chosen differently by individual and groups, 2) be chosen not only by the members of nondominant cultural group but also by the members of dominant cultural group, and 3) be chosen politically by a nation and be reflected in a long-term policy.
- •Acculturation mode and its result are differentiated by the acculturating group which is categorized through its voluntariness and mobility.
- •There are three stages to acculturation: physical adaptation, adaptation

to official social structure, and socio-cultural adaptation. The adaptation process can be completed when the socio-cultural adaptation is adopted.

- Moderating factors in the acculturation process are 1) nature of dominant society, 2) characteristics of acculturating groups, 3) acculturation modes, and 4) individuals' psycho-social factors, in which the stress coping strategy is considered the most important.

2) Attributes of North Korean refugees and task of social and psychological integration

Previous studies point out that while the North Korean refugees had less difficulty in political and ideological aspect, they differed a lot by each individuals in regard to the economical adaptation in the process of adapting to the South Korean society. On the other hand, most refugees had greater difficulty in psychological adaptation (Kim, H., 2004; Jeon, 1999). We will focus to discuss the policy for the North Korean refugees' acculturation, and social and psychological integration. To begin with, we will explore the attributes of the North Korean refugees to apply concepts and models of acculturation process discussed earlier to them.

(1) Attributes of North Korean refugees

North Korean refugees who entered South Korea have the following attributes in comparison to the other groups undergone acculturation.

a. North Korean refugees lived in an extremely closed society.

North Korean refugees lived not only in a politically closed society, but also in a society which emphasized uniculturalism. As described earlier, in order to efficiently adapt to a new culture, integration strategy of accepting the identity of new culture along with one's original identity is needed. Such attitude can be acquired easily in a multicultural country or in a country where such strategy is enforced. However, since the North Korean refugees lived in and adapted to, for long, a politically and socially closed society which emphasizes the uniculturalism traditionally, they might be unfamiliar to the integrated acculturation. As a result, there is a high possibility of maladaptation to the South Korean culture.

b. Likewise, mainstream culture (South Korean society) has an ideology of uniculturalism.

South Korea as the mainstream culture which the North Korean refugees adjust to, also traditionally valued homogenous nation and uniculturalism. For this reason, integrated acculturation might also come as unfamiliarity. In addition, the South Koreans think of the North Korean refugees as people who used to be in the same population, and thus the South Koreans might pressure them to assimilate into the mainstream culture instead of applying integrated acculturation method. That is, the possibility that South Koreans request the North Korean refugees to change their values and lifestyle to those of the South not accepting their experiences and cultural identity, values of the lifestyle formed in North Korea and in a third country, and lifestyle developed by overcoming difficulties is high.

c. North Koreans settled in South Korea, a politically hostile country during the last fifty years.

North and South Korea were not only familiar to their own traditional cultures but also were in a hostile relationship during the last fifty years. As a result, constituents of each society couldn't accept the other's political beliefs and values. Accepting such values meant a threat to the existence of the country. When this perception continues, it will be hard for South Koreans and the North Korean refugees to share their values. Especially the older generations of South Korea, who extensively received anticommunist education after the Korean War, will not only reject the situation when they are influenced by the population of minority culture (North Korean refugees) and adapt to the changes, but also require the North Koreans to take the 'assimilation' strategy instead of the 'integration' strategy. A friction might arise with the older generations who are politically conservative, if the nation tries to establish an acculturation policy favorable to the North Korean refugees.

d. North Korean refugees have negative impression of the group they left from.

North Koreans have difficulty taking positive perspective of the North not only due to their experience of starvation and inferior socio-economic situation, but also due to disenchantment of high-level officials in North Korea for intentionally providing negative information about the South Korean economy and social level. As a result, they would take an adaptation method that requires assimilation to the South Korean society and culture rather than taking an integrated method that requires acceptance of the South Korean culture while maintaining their positive identity. Yet, confusion may arise by unconsciously interpreting the North Korean situation positively due to extreme brainwashing experience from the North. For example, there were some cases in which the refugees got confused during the interview because while having strong antipathy toward North Korea, they unconsciously responded with respect in questions about Kim, Il-Sung or Kim, Jong-Il.

e. Degree of culture shock differs by individual.

North Korean refugees' different psychological and social experiences during the crossing process lead to different degree of culture shock experienced by each individual. Some experienced shock from loss of a family member or migration from a sudden and impromptu escape from North Korea. Contrarily, some precisely prepared crossing by exploring the northern border several times or asking a friend to report him dead for the safety of the remaining families. Moreover, some had life threatening experience of getting caught by the Chinese police before entry to South Korea, where as some made entry to South Korea in just two days. This indicates that psychological shocks and fears experienced by the North Korean refugees differ by each case. In addition, it seems different in terms of how fast they adopt to the South Korean capitalistic value for the refugees who lived in China before the entry to South and for those who entered South Korea directly from the North.

> Yes. It took me short period of time to enter South. (...) By doing so, it was harder for me to adapt to South Korea than others. China is more toward to capitalism and since I came here directly from North Korea, it was hard for me. I didn't know much and I was so naïve. I think I learned a lot by living. But it is still hard for me to live here. (K-1)

North Korean refugees who lived in China before the entry to South are familiar to the capitalistic value in which people earn as much as they work, whereas refugees who entered rather directly from the North were unfamiliar with the idea.

f. North Korean refugees are categorized into the refugee category due to their involuntary move.

Among types of groups undergoing acculturation, the North Korean refugees are not considered 'racial group' since they are not different from the South Korean race. Moreover, they are not a 'native group' since they did not originally live in South Korea. Nevertheless, they cannot be considered 'immigrants' nor 'sojourner' whose entry is from free-will and positive factors. Therefore they are close to 'refugee' among 'immigrants', 'refugee', 'sojourner', 'native', and 'racial group' since their cultural contact had been made involuntarily. Refugees face several difficulties in interaction with the mainstream culture and one of which is change in evaluation of them over time. For example, Vietnamese refugees who once were welcomed by the Germans are now regarded with jealousy as 'refugees on welfare aid' (Emminghaus, 1988). This kind of phenomenon can be found also from the North Korean refugees. Following is the description of interview on refugee education related personnel #6.

> Children had more problems. Children in the South couldn't accept the North Korean refugee children. That's because the children in the South heard that children in the North are very poor and die from starvation and yet they see the North Korean refugee children spend much money in the South. By seeing that, the children in the South became very frustrated. (related personnel #6)

Accordingly, the North Korean refugees in the initial stage were welcomed by the South Koreans but as they live in bad materialistic culture by spending their settlement funds in leisure or buying expensive materials, they have been regarded with jealousy.

g. There is a great possibility that the North Korean refugees become a target for psychological projection by the South Korean and vice versa.

In addition to sharing the same language, North and South Korea are both geographically located in the Korean Peninsula. For this reason, they share cultural resources and information on each other greatly. On the other hand, for being politically and geographically separated for the last fifty-so years, their information on each other has been seriously distorted. That is, in spite of many distorted information or different cultural experiences, they might think they know about each other well because the share resources. In fact, difficulties of exposing the cultural characteristics of the North Korean refugees put the North and the South Koreans in a relationship where they do not understand each other. When this happens, severe psychological projection between the two groups or people within the group may occur. In other words, people believe what they want to believe. They do not attempt to understand others nor acknowledge their ignorance toward the other's cultural backgrounds because they believe that they know the other very well. In such case, the two groups have more difficulty of understanding each other truly than groups of total strangers do.

h. North Korean refugees are recognized differently by organizations or their subgroups belonging to the mainstream culture.

North Korean refugees' identities are recognized differently by organizations or groups they contact. In other words, organizations or groups that are in contact with North Korean refugees, understand them differently by their needs and project their different desires to them. For example, China legally considered them 'illegal migrants' or 'nomads', whereas missionaries considered them 'humanitarian refugee' or 'food refugee'. Personnel in the Ministry of Defense who inspect their motive for crossing, consider them a 'spy' initially and then suddenly treat them as a 'crossing hero' or 'crossing brother'. Sometimes through a media, they are considered a 'hero', who crossed by laying their life on the line, or an 'expert', who knows crossing process well. Moreover, in religious groups, they are respected as the 'special one', who have escaped religious persecution by the help of God and accepted God. However, when they returned to normal life, they are considered a 'recipient of government subsidy' or 'the unemployed'. Police treat them as a 'subject to surveillance' or people under 'probation'. At school, they are treated as a 'backward student' or 'trouble maker'. Likewise, by continuously contacting public institutions and groups that have different perspective on the North Korean refugees, they form a confused identity of not knowing who they are in the South Korean society (Jung, 2003).

To sum up, in contrast to the Vietnamese refugees, Eastern Germans, and American immigrants who were in need of acculturation from refuge or sudden migration, North Korean refugees are different from other groups considering that they are the same race, and yet had lived in an extremely closed society which was hostile toward South Korea, and that the mainstream culture group (South Korean society) is also familiar to the tradition of uniculturalism. Although they seem to know much about each other from sharing the same history and cultural tradition, they are in relations to provoke many projections from distorted understanding, which make the North Korean refugee group very unique from other groups such as the American immigrants or Vietnamese refugees. Tasks and obstacles to overcome for the integration of refugees with such uniqueness are described next.

(2) Task of social and psychological integration

Social and psychological integration holds two kinds of perspectives. One of which is establishing an individual identity through individual's internal integration. The other is establishing an independent and yet, cooperative relationship from inter-understanding in interpersonal relationship. That is, the former can be done by solidifying one's identity through fully accepting one's characteristics or strengths and weaknesses, acknowledging one's individuality, and establishing one's future. The latter refers to a relationship of acknowledging each other as a separate and different individual while admitting the commonalities between them and strengthening the understandings of interpersonal relationship.

When this theory is applied to the North Korean refugees, the North Korean refugees and South Koreans need to establish mature relationship by not projecting each other and establish a group cultural identity of the North Korean refugee and South Korean to accomplish the social and psychological integration between them. Deep understanding of the refugees has to come prior to the establishment of both. This part will explore who the refugees are, in order to help establish their identity and a comprehension method that helps them to establish their identity.

a. Understanding the North Korean refugees

Understanding the North Korean refugees as they are by the South Koreans or even by themselves is most needed in establishing the identity of North Korean refugees. In other words, the refugees should not view themselves as a people who need to be assimilated to a new society by discarding their old experiences or being under control of the surrounding people after the entry to South Korea. In addition, the South Koreans who belong to the mainstream culture, should not customize North Korean refugees by their ways of understanding of the refugees. As mentioned earlier, the North Korean refugees will have hard time establishing their identity if many institutions understand the refugees with only their own perspectives and require the refugees to become appropriate to their desires.

For example, a public lecture and confession of faith could be a good opportunity for a North Korean refugee, who came by laying his or her life on the line, to be recognized as an 'expert' of the crossing and or as the 'special one' who survived by the help of God. As this happens repeatedly, however, one realizes that others' recognition or expectation of him/her is limited to the political or religious interests. And one tells a story to fulfill other's expectations, he/she may experience emptiness and lose one's identity. When psychologically reviewing a case of a North Korean refugee who drinks heavily every night after he gives a confession of faith, his act is from appeasing oneself for losing his identity.

In order to achieve the North Korean refugees' social and psychological integration, they should establish their own identity as a North Korean refugee regardless of others' thoughts. Most North Korean refugees isolate or marginalize themselves from the mainstream culture in fear of exposing their North Korean identity. On the other hand, some people reveal their identity to others. In case H-4, the refugee acknowledged his status and after accepting the difficulty of experiencing a new society and culture, he used an active coping strategy to overcome the difficulties.

> (Interviewer: Did you have any difficulties at school?)
> Well, I had difficulties from lack of knowledge. It was easy to be intimidated because I didn't know the culture here but I thought to myself that it is natural that I don't know because I came from the North Korean society. I got very lonely from not being able to get along with friends. I suffered tremendously from psychological stress because I was a loner at school. I regretted coming to South Korea. Then I realized that the root of the problem is my lack of knowledge of the culture. It's

> not a surprise that I don't know the culture and it not something to be ashamed of. Once I realized it, I tell other refugees that they only need to learn the culture. It might be hard to interact with friends because of this and yet they shouldn't suffer from it. (...) In many cases, refugees fall down from such problem. I was about to fall down then I stood up. (H-4)

Similar to this, M-2 suffered from a social structure when she first came to South Korea. However, when she realized the fact that her reality has changed in the South, rather than missing her advantages or resources she had in the North, she overcame by facing her loneliness.

> I believe early realization is important in adaptation. In order to adjust quickly, I need to know where I stand in this society and set a goal. Previously, I didn't have a goal nor knew the meaning of life. It was very difficult. Nobody cares for what I do here. I have to do everything on my own. People don't adjust to this when they first arrive here. I feel like an abandoned person and wanted to go somewhere and kill myself. I didn't know what to do and there was no one to tell me what I should do. (...) In my case, I suffered a lot because nobody helped me out. (However)That helped me out greatly in settling here. If people helped me out from a pity, I would never have realized so early. I would never have realized that I have to be in charge of my life. Every tears I shed and every effort I made, paid me back.When people first come to South Korea, they come with many dreams.They feel like their lives will turn out nice and stuff. People need to break out of that dream. I think it was difficulty about a year and a half for me and once I set my goal, I now believe every difficulty is worthwhile. (M-2)

Such process is never easy. These cases show an individual acknowledgment of one's current situation and accepting the situation as it is. Along with this, the North Korean refugees should give themselves some credit for surviving and adjusting during the adversity in order to accomplish the social psychological integration in the South. Anyhow, they overcame many hardships before arriving to South Korea. They are people who survived the life in North Korea and China, and never gave up their life. Although they are suffering temporarily from adjusting to a new place, they should recognize themselves as a strong-minded people who can overcome anything, and so should the South Koreans.

b. Integration within a relationship

Key thing to remember to establish a social psychological integration within a relationship between the North Korean refugees and South Koreans, is that the acculturation is bidirectional. South Koreans might have hard time accepting the concept that North Korean refugees are not the only group assimilating to the mainstream culture, and they also need to change while living with the North Korean refugees. Since it has been more than fifty years since the separation, the North Koreans' cultures and thoughts have changed. The North Korean refugees entering the South bring a culture, that is distant from that of the South, and it will have some impact on the South Koreans. If this does not happen, then the North Korean refugees will experience a psychological and emotional maladaptation and they will not be able to integrate to the South Korean culture groups. Thus, to build a social psychological integration between the refugees and South Koreans, an attitude of understanding each others' identities is crucial.

Second factor needed for building the integration within a relationship is an understanding that the integration means 'accepting the difference' rather than 'becoming one'. Two groups from two different cultures living in a culturally integrated society means they 'agreed on a principle of accepting the difference'. Moreover, the refugees' lives do not assimilate to the South Korean culture immediately after they arrive the South. We cannot expect the refugees to solve their problems in a way that South Korean would do. They had their own lifestyle since their time in North Korea and during the crossing period. Thus, the South Koreans should understand that the North Korean refugees need time to learn the new society's system as new born babies do.

Case L-1 expressed that he wants the South Koreans to understand the refugees as they are and not judge or urge them. According to him, the South Koreans should not have bias against the refugees that they are slow in adaptation or lack adaptation skills. He continued by saying that to achieve a thorough understanding of the acculturation process of the refugees, the South Koreans should stop comparing the refugees with themselves but should rather compare the refugees with the South Koreans who crossed into the North. His story shows the frustration he had for not being understood by others.

> Time is a crucial influential factor in adaptation. It's not that we don't know how to adjust. A genius does not graduate college in a month. Even a genius needs 4 years to graduate college. A minimum of three years are needed to know the South Korean society. (…) An idea that we don't adjust well just because we are 'North Korean refugees', is the South Koreans' standard. In that case, we should be compared to people who crossed into North Korea. Do you know what happens to them? They all end up in a prison. Why? That's because they do not adjust to the North Korean society. When in Rome, do as Romans do. They just say whatever they want to say as if they are still in a democratic society. They curse and drink whenever they want. Is it fair now? I can even

> write a thesis out of this. There are many people who crossed into North Korea since the Korean War. Why can't they adjust to the North Korean society? (L-1)

This does not implicate that the North Korean refugees should be understood as 'special beings' for most people treat others as 'special beings' based on their own projection. Instead, the refugees should be viewed as an 'ordinary people' who went through an 'unique experience'. They are not 'special', 'especially strong', 'piteous', nor 'pathetic' people. For example, people who were willing to help the refugees, staffs at Hanawon, teachers, or Catholic priests, viewed the refugees as 'piteous people' at first. However, with time, they reported to have some distance from the refugees because having a pity perspective on the refugees did not help establishing a relationship.

> Well… these days, I'm having a second thought. I have a deep remorse. At first, I wanted to give them all of my housekeeping. I gave out cosmetics, and sometimes my child's old clothes when they had a child. (…) Every teacher here goes through this process. Newly joined teachers are full of enthusiasm. Teachers who have been here for long think 'you should experience it for yourself, and you will soon realize you should keep a distance from them'. Go by the regulation. You will get hurt if you give all of your heart but at the same time you shouldn't keep yourself from caring. That's the know-how. At first, we love them and then we hate them, and finally we keep just the right distance from them. I think most staffs here go through the same process as I did. (Personnel #2)

The story described above shows that people hold two contradicting views on the refugees: ‘piteous’ and ‘not simply piteous’. Defining and approaching the refugees as ‘piteous’ people is based on helpers’ projection of their own desires or emotions. It does not include true understanding of the refugees. As a result, although the refugees get help, they still feel like get help without being fully understood by their helpers. This interview possibly indicates that a helper realized that the refugees can be a disappointment because they sometimes are ‘very strong’ but also ‘very mean’ when protecting themselves.

Careful examination of interviews of the refugees, North Korean refugee-related personnel and South Koreans suggests the followings in order to hold a long-term relationship with the refugees.

First, most North Korean refugees escaped the North not for their ideological reason but for very practical reasons such as constant life threats and extreme poverty. Famine and life threats from instability of political identity in North Korea, and unstable identity and risk of arrest in China lead the refugees to enter South Korea. Prior to understanding their experienced anxiety and threats, they should not be judged as betrayers and as people who are able to betraying whenever they face instability and psycho-social stress as they did from the North. Judging the refugees with such bias prevents the refugees from establishing their own identity by doubting themselves and as a result, they will have hard time adjusting to this culture or have positive opinion of the South Korean society.

Second, most North Korean refugees desired to settle in China. The reason for coming to South Korea is not because they liked South Korea but instead because China was a difficult place to settle than they had imagined and going back to North Korea was impossible. South Korea was not their first priority but rather it was an unavoidable choice they had to make during the process of solving their practical problems. In fact, some would never have decided to defect North Korea in the first place if they had known they would end up in South Korea.

> People would not defect if they know they are going to South Korea in the first place. We heard so many bad rumors about it. We thought we would be killed if we get caught. But I changed my mind once I came here. (laugh) (N-1)

They arrived in South Korea which was driven by their situation and yet South Korea still welcomed them. The South Korean government helped them to settle by providing settlement funds and a place to live. This indicates the high possibility of the refugees to be thankful of the South Korean government and people for accepting them. Providing such financial aids, however, does not authorize us to change their ideology as we wish. We can provide aids to the refugees because we are 'brothers (or one nation)' and yet, expecting to be treated as a 'brother' in return is too much to ask. If such demand is asked while helping the refugees, the help is not to help them but to fulfill our own desires and projected purposes. The refugees will change their ideology and attitudes toward the South Koreans through experiencing freedom and positive factors as they live in South Korea. We cannot force them to erase their past ideology and accept the new one right away while they are still experiencing the ideological confusion. The more we force them to change, the more pressure they feel from the South Korean society which might hinder their opportunities to be free. The fact that the refugees didn't choose South Korea as their priority destination should be understood fully.

Third, the decisions to defect North Korea and make entry to South Korea were for very practical reasons. It was not decided for a political reason or only with a 'courage' as to be called a 'crossing hero', nor was it decided because the refugees were called by God as expected by the religious organizations. Whether or not they brought family members, bribed soldiers, or were a victim of human trafficking, the choice was made within a very practical and urgent situation. Regardless of the crossing process, their decision should be understood as a practical choice to escape from the life threats and anxiety. If the refugees' decision is understood as an ideological or religious choice or other South Korean's projections are applied to understanding of their behavior, the South Koreans will never truly understand them, and eventually the refugees will also loose the sense of who they are.

Lastly, the refugees hold ambivalence. Ambivalence refers to having simultaneous and contradictory attitudes or feelings toward an object, person, action, or thought (Kaplan & Sadock, 1998). Analysis of ambivalent conflict structure of the North Korean refugees (Jeon, 1999) shows following ambivalence: Are they special people or ordinary people?; Are they independent or dependent on the South Korean government?; Do they take money seriously or lightly?; Should they forget or remember remaining family members in the North?; and Are they South Koreans or North Koreans? Such ambivalence hinders establishment of the refugee's identity.

Jeon (1999) presented following suggestions to help the refugees to overcome such psychological conflicts.

First, a policy should not be carried out in way that encourages ambivalence of the North Korean refugees.

Second, the refugees should be provided with an appropriate education that teaches about their prestige and role.

Third, a policy to support the refugees should not be carried out unilaterally to encourage their dependency.

Fourth, churches and civic organizations should not only provide the financial aids in supporting the refugee group. Financial aids should be paid in return for their labor. For this, a systematic support for the refugees' psychological and mental health should be established politically. At the same time, the South Koreans should be trained to understand the refugees' ambivalence.

Fifth, the refugees are people who overcame adversity but at the same time, they don't understand their own existence and feel lonely and isolated when others do not understand them as who they are. They are in need of understanding from the surrounding people to fight off such isolation and loneliness. Moreover, they want the South Koreans to have genuine understanding of them.

Sixth, there is a big individual difference among the refugees. As previously described, individuals and their groups might experience different types of acculturation. Thus, in understanding North Korean refugees, we should acknowledge that their preferred acculturation type, their crossing experience, and decision making process at a critical point are different for each refugees. For example, case F-1 appreciated resources he received at Hanawon whereas others perceived Hanawon as an unpleasant place. One refugee believes he has been looked down by the South Korean based on only one question he was asked, whereas another accepts it as a fair response and tries to start from the bottom. Acknowledgement that such difference exists among the refugees, is critical when approaching them. It is important to note that a way to understand one refugee cannot be applied in understanding another.

Seventh, the North Korean refugees had undergone a life or death experience. This fact has to be remembered always when establishing a relationship with the refugees. The reason is that such experience provides essential resource for them and at the same time, it takes up a part in forming their identity. From this experience, the refugees can be identified as a 'unique people' if not 'special people'. South Koreans and the refugees need to figure out a way to utilize these experiences as their resource. It can be a way to raise their self-esteem. For example, encouraging statements at Hanawon, such as 'You went through a lot from hunger and poverty', or 'Forget everything you learned in North Korea and start new in South Korea', are still important. However, at the same time there is a need to educate them about giving meaning to their hardships and adversity during the crossing period, and things to boost up their confidence in the future.

Eighth, the North Korean refugees should recognize themselves as people who will carry out important matters in the future. They should be taught that they can act as a resourceful people after the unification even though it might be hard for them to realize at this moment. Case H-4 establishes his/her own identity after such realization.

> I tell people that the unification isn't nonsense. It is a way for our country to develop. In the process of making it better, we would have to go through the unification. In order to carry out the unification in a right way, we have to know North Korea. For the development of our country, people need to understand North Koreans and learn to live with them. (…) In that sense, the North Korean refugees are an essential people for the unification. Every time I go talk to other refugees, especially children, I remind them how important they are in South Korea. (H-4)

3) Issues after the unification of the North and the South

Phenomena and issues that would arise post-unification are hard to forecast from the North Korean refugees' data because we don't know yet about how the unification will be accomplished. For example, the process of the unification might be like that of Germany which had a large-scale migration at once or it might be accomplished through a long-term goal of maintaining two political structures until the economy of North Korea gets stable while allowing visits from the two countries. Forecast on the post-unification, however, implicates that the acculturation will occur anyhow, whether as a big or small group, and thus the data from the refugees are the best data to rely on. From the data of refugee interviews, previous studies on the acculturation, and tasks for social psychological integration of the refugees, the following suggestions can be made to prepare for the post-unification.

First, an important question of whether the South Koreans are willing to accept the North Koreans as ‘our people’ need to be addressed, and a social consensus should be reached. There is a big difference between providing aides to financially deprived citizens with a social welfare policy and absorbing people from outside the South Korean societal boundary by providing education for the acculturation. Currently, the government does not provide a clear logic for the unification of the South and the North other than an ideological reason that they all belong to ‘one nation’. The government must develop logical and practical reasons for the unification, and seriously address whether each citizen can share the economical, sociological, and psychological burden for the acculturation process and draw a social consensus. If the North Korean migration group is absorbed to the South Korean society without such process, serious confusions will arise not only within the relationship between the South and the North Koreans but also within the South Korean society itself.

Second, the government should remember that the acculturation is a bidirectional and not unidirectional process. Adaptation of the North

Koreans in the South Korean society is important. But the South Koreans' adaptation toward the refugees or North Korean migration group is crucial as well. Thus, a policy for educating the South Koreans should be established while preparing an acculturation education and training programs for the refugees or North Koreans after the unification.

Third, the government should deeply consider which acculturation strategy to apply to the refugees (or foreign workers and North Koreans in the future). South Koreans need to choose which acculturation strategy to use toward new immigrants. A critical point to consider is whether to let the new immigrants to choose their own strategy or approach them with a certain strategy which the government has chosen. Traditionally, Korean peninsula has been known for its antialien characteristic toward other cultures or foreigners. Considering this special characteristic of Korea, the government needs to predetermine, to avoid a chaos, which type of strategy, assimilation, separation, marginalization, or integration, to apply as a policy and educate the citizens.

Fourth, a policy needs to be constructed considering that the North Korean immigrant group after the unification will be different from the North Korean refugee group. First of all, the refugee group is relatively small, and therefore it is rather possible that they accept the idea of assimilating to a bigger society. In contrast, inflow of the North Korean immigrant group after the unification will be relatively large making it unnecessary for them to assimilate to the mainstream culture. Consequently, the latter group will more likely show a strong resistance to the acculturation process, and instead attempt to change the mainstream culture. Secondly, the refugee group might accept the 'assimilation' policy of the government more easily become they might think that they were rescued by the South Koreans from the extreme anxiety and stress they experienced during the crossing process. North

Korean immigrant group, on the other hand, will show less receptive attitude. Therefore, the government must prepare for more complex social psychological adaptation policy than that for the refugee group.

2. Policy for social and psychological integration

1) General direction

One critical consideration is needed in establishing a policy for the social and psychological integration of the refugees: understanding the refugees and their culture shock experiences from a social and psychological perspective rather than from a clinical perspective (Emminhaus, 1988). A clinical perspective is mostly used by clinical psychologists, and they view refugees as ordinary patients without any exceptions. In this perspective, the refugees with paranoiac characteristic that arise as a result of encountering a new culture or anxiety from losing every familiar social symbols that existed in the homeland, are interpreted as 'patients' who experienced intermediate to severe culture shock. Such perspective, however, was criticized for several reasons. First, it only focuses on the internal psychological conditions by examining psychological problems. Second, only individuals with problems were included, and third, a refugee is identified as a patient.

On the contrary, there is another perspective that views acculturation as a social skills learning process. This perspective newly defines culture shock as 'an individual's specific experience and behavior in a novice environment' (Higginbotham & Tanaka-Matsumi, 1981). This perspective starts to consider the social environment systematically without associating every problem to individual's pathology. This allows to understand refugees' experience through interaction between culture and individual, and it is defined by a cross-cultural encounter. As a result, in setting a policy direction, a policy for social and psychological integration should be balanced by both the clinical and social skills learning perspectives.

2) Policy for child and family

(1) Reconsideration of North Korean refugees' spatial decentralization policy

North Korean refugees are spatially decentralized because if many of them were crowded in Seoul or other metropolitan cities where there is high competition for employment, it would lead to high unemployment rate among the refugees (Kim, 2001). Spatial decentralization policy is believed to be set based on an economical reason. On the other hand, the socio-cultural perspective considered the policy as problematic in a way that it weakens the social support system. America's policy to decentralize the Vietnam refugees to different places received criticisms. Such is because the policy did not consider the Vietnamese's cultural features. Unlike Western people, Vietnamese get lots of social support from their family. Therefore, flexible spatial decentralization policy is necessary which allows people to live near other family members if needed while the refugees are decentralized as a whole.

(2) Educational support for the refugee's family

Some problems within a family are anticipated as the refugees adjust to South Korea. That is, the children of the refugee families assimilate to a new culture quickly and excessively whereas parents do not fully assimilate to a new culture, which leads to a 'separation'.

Consequently, parents and children experience tensions and conflicts, and parents might lose their authority over the children in the process. Moreover, spouse relationship might be in jeopardy if a wife adjusts to a new society faster than a husband, or a wife is better off financially than a husband. Following considerations are needed to prevent such problems.

First, the refugees should be informed and prepared that each individual has different speed in adjusting to a new culture, and problems may arise from such differences. Children adjust to the South Korean life and acquire new values quickly through life in school whereas parents or other family members cannot catch up with the speed of children. They need to be informed beforehand that such gap will bring conflicts between generations.

Second, training the refugees on how to cope with the problems arose from the gap between family members is necessary. According to Jeon (2000), followings need to be taught: parents and children need to understand each other; they should not give up communicating with each other even if the problem is not solved after one or two tries; they should solve one problem at a time rather than trying to solve the problems all at once, and misunderstanding does not mean denying fundamental love between the parent and children. The government should provide an educational system, which allows such training.

3) Social and cultural policy

Early literature on the North Korean refugees presented following policies for socio-cultural integration of the refugees: improvement of Hanawon education; providing consultation from professional counselors; establishing systematic network between the government and religious organizations; introducing covenant relationship between the government and private organizations; and establishment of welfare center. Additional suggestions are presented as following.

(1) Integrative policy making for the process of acculturation

In order to trigger the integration strategy in the process of acculturation, South Koreans should not force the refugees to fit into the South Korean culture. South Koreans' acknowledgement of the refugees' cultural resource, identity, and value of their special experience is necessary and they should try to live together. For this, acculturation education should not only be taught to the refugees but also to the South Koreans in a way that would help them to understand the refugees better. In addition to training the refugees on the South Korean system or culture, another education process for both the refugees and South Koreans, which will help to stimulate interaction between them, should be developed.

Historically, Korea had been influenced by various cultures from being surrounded by the Great Powers. The reason for emphasizing 'homogeneous race' is because it is a strong psychological asset that helps to build our own identity from various cultural influences by the Great Powers. In this special circumstance, the culture of North Korea or foreign workers might come as a threat to maintaining our own cultural identity. Recently, however, the Korean Wave culture played a role of securing our cultural identity in the Southeast Asia. Taking this as a base, the government should develop a policy that confirms our identity. By doing so, we will not take away the opportunity to apply the integration strategy on the refugees while unnecessarily emphasizing our cultural identity to them. Instead, reestablishment of our identity through this process is necessary.

(2) Work training and employment policy

Most desirable support that the refugees want among many settlement supports they receive, including a direct financial support, is employment (Kim, 2001). Such request can be constantly seen in interviews with the refugees. Employment is both positive and practical way to help the refugees adjust and settle quickly to the South Korean society. Among employment policies, an establishment of work training school for the refugees and spatial decentralization of the refugees (Kim, 2001) were suggested.

Another suggestion is to adopt a policy that allows the refugees to work in a field that is somewhat related to their previous jobs in North Korea. In other words, when a refugee is choosing between a job that is out of his/her related field but pays better salary now and a job in a related field which has greater potential in the future but pays less, one should be encouraged to choose the latter. For example, people who showed efficient adaptation in the South Korean culture and society had similar jobs with the ones they had in North Korea. Therefore, employment counseling should be encouraged to connect the refugees' jobs to their past jobs in North Korea.

(3) Arrangement of a support system for psychological interaction between North Korean refugees and South Koreans

For integrating the acculturation process not only for the refugees but also for the South Koreans, an opportunity for them to interact with each other need to be arranged in addition to preparing education specifically for the refugees. Spending time and psychologically interacting with each other will prevent problems arising from projecting their own problems to others. Correction on such projection is possible

<Table VI-4> Examples of how the South Koreans and the refugees project each other

The refugees' projection of South Koreans	Facts that can be confirmed
South Koreans change their attitude towards me as soon as they hear my intonation and the reason is that they look down on me.	Change of attitude is not because the South Koreans look down on us but rather it's because they do not know how to interact with the North Korean refugees.
When I get less wage than the Chinese workers, I feel like I have been belittled and I don't want to reveal my North Korean identity.	The owner of the company does not have any intention of ignoring the North Koreans. But rather the owner doesn't want to take a risk by paying beyond the new employ's capability.
When the refugees make a testimonial in public offices or religious organizations, audience has certain expectation on what they want to hear from the refugees.	There might be some expectation toward the refugees' speech but they don't want the refugees to feel empty. In fact, honest story can touch one's heart.
South Korean's projection of the refugees	**Facts that can be confirmed**
The North Korean refugees came to South Korea because they want to be here.	It's somewhat burdensome to think that way. South Korea wasn't bad but the refugees preferred China.
They must be extraordinarily brave to cross the border.	The refugees were rather scared than brave. Nothing could have been done but to cross the border and it was the best plan.
We should encourage the refugees to eat a lot because they probably suffered a lot from hunger. In this way, they would understand how much we care for them.	They don't like to be viewed as pathetic people.

through group process such as group counseling. Honest interaction during the process of projection correction provides deeper understanding of each other. <Table VI-4> illustrates a list of possible projections and things found out through interactions with each other.

(4) Promote positive impression of North Korean refugees through mass media

Mass media might be the most efficient method to raise higher understanding of the North Korean refugees. One of the ways to build social and psychological integration by understanding and firmly establishing the identity of the refugees is to promote positive impression of the refugees to the South Koreans through the mass media. Interviews with the refugees, however, reveal that the mass media has not yet played such a role. According to them, the mass media has put a negative impression of the refugees on the South Koreans. Negative attitude of the mass media prevented the refugees from establishing their own identity and kept the South Koreans from providing the refugees enough time to adjust. Mass media should support the refugees to build their positive identity and help the South Koreans to be more lenient toward the refugees by emphasizing the positive aspects of the North Korean refugees.

References

Ahn, G. (1986). Guinseonghwang, Jigakhakguppoongto Mit Do Byuninui Sanghojakywongi Haksuptaedowa Hakupseongchie Michinun Young-hwang. Chungang University unpublished doctoral dissertation.

Ahn, Y. (2002). A Qualitative Study on Family Culture of North Korean Defector. Catholic University of Korea unpublished master's thesis.

Anthony, E. J. & Cohler, B. J. (1987). *The Invulnerable Child*. New York: Guilford Press.

Berry, J. W. (1976). *Human Ecology and Cognitive Style: Comparative Studies in Cultural and Psychological Adaptation*. London: Sage.

Berry, J. W. (1986). Multiculturalism and Psychology in Plural Socities. In *Ethnic Minorities and Immigrants in a Cross-cultural Perspective*. (Ed.). L. H. Ekstrand. Berwyn, IL: Swets North America.

Berry, J. W. (1988). Acculturation and Psychological Adaptation: A Conceptual Overview. In *Ethnic Psychology: Research and Practice with Immigrants, Refugees, Native Peoples, Ethnic Groups and Sojourners*. (Eds.). J. W. Berry & R. C. Annis. Berwyn, PA: Swets North America.

Berry, J. W. (1997). Immigration, Acculturation, and Adaptation. *Applied Psychology: An International Review*, 46, 5–68.

Berry, J. W., Portinga, Y., Segall, M., & Dasen, P. (1992). *Cross-cultural Psychology: Research and Applications*. Cambridge: Cambridge University Press.

Buriel, R. (1993). Child-rearing Orientations in Mexican American Families: The Influence of Generation and Sociocultural Factors. *Journal of Marriage and the Family*, 55, 987–1000.

Castro, V. S. (2003). *Acculturational and Psychological Adaptation*. Wesport, CO: Greenwood.

Cha, J. (2000). Tongile Itseo Simlijeok Tonghapui Jeonmangwa Gwaje. Nambukhanui Simlijeok Tonghap–2000y hanguk simlihakhoi chungyeo simpojieum, 1–18.

Chae, J. & Han, S. (2003). Influence of North Korean Defectors' Selfenhancement Bias to their Psychological Adaptation in South Korea. *Korean Journal of Psychological and Social Issues*, 9 (2), 101–126.

Cho, B., Lee, J., & Han, S. (2005). The Relationships among Home Environment Locus of Control, Social Supports, and Behavior Problems of Korean-Chinese Children in Yanbian. *Journal of the Korean Home Economics Association*, 43 (3), 91–104.

Chosunilbo (2007). April 7. Talbukjayeonhaphoi. 'Saeteomin' Yongeossjimalra.

Conger, R. & Elder, G. H. Jr. (1994). *Families in Troubled Times: Adapting to Change in Rural America*. New York: Aldine De Gruyter.

Dubos, R. (1965). *Man Adapting*. New Haven: Yale University Press.

Elder, G. H. Jr. (1974). *Children of the Great Depression: Social Change in Life Experience*. Chicago: University of Chicago Press.

Emminhaus, W. B. (1988). Refugee Adaptation: Basic Research Issues and Applications. In *Ethnic Psychology: Research and Practice with Immigrants, Refugees, Native Peoples, Ethnic Groups and Sojourners*. (Eds.). J. W. Berry & R. C. Annis. Berwyn, PA: Swets North America.

Eom, T. & Lee, K. (2004). The Relationship among Social Problem Solving Capability, Social Support and Depression of North Korean Defectors. *Mental Health & Social Work*, 18, 5–32.

Fraser, M. W., Richman, J. M., & Galinsky, M. J. (1999). Risk, Protection, and Resilience: Toward a Conceptual Framework for Social Work Practice. *Social Work Research*, 23: 131–143.

Garmezy, N. (1993). Children in Poverty: Resilience despite Risk. *Psychiatry*, 56, 127–136.

Gordon, M. (1964). *Assimilation in American Life*. New York: Oxford University Press.

Graves, T. D. (1967). Psychological Acculturation in a Tri-ethnic Community. *South-western Journal of Anthropology*, 23, 336–350.

Greene, R. R. (Ed.) (2002). Resiliency: An Integrated Approach to Practice, Policy, and Research. Washington D.C.: NASW Press.

Han, I. (2001). Depressive Traits of North Korean Defectors. *Mental Health & Social Work*, 11, 78–94.

Han, I. & Lee, S. (2002). North Korean Defectors Depressive Traits, Alcohol and Tobacco Consumption and their Perceived Well-being. *Korean Journal of Family Social Work*, 10, 121–142.

Han, M. (1999). Tukjib: Nam, Bukhan Mit Jungguk Joseonjok Haksuldaehoi Balpyononmun (Yeonbyeondaehakgyo changlib 50junyeon ginyeom haksulhoiui); Saecheonnyeonul hyanghan josunjokui hyunhwangwa mirae/1990s hanguk gyoyukui banseongkwa gwaje. *Minjusimingyouknonchong*, 4, 51–63.

Han, Y. (2005). Bukchehe Yangdaegidoong, Jeongbojeongchi-gongpocheongchi. www.dailynk.com/.

Higginbotham, H. N. & Tanaka-Matsumi, J. (1981). Behavioral Approaches to Counseling across Cultures. In P. Pedersen, J. G. Draguns, W. J. Lonner, & J. E. Trimble (Eds.), *Counseling Across Cultures*. Honolulu: University of Hawaii Press, pp. 247–274.

Jain, A. & Belsky, J. (1997). Fathering and Acculturation: Immigrant Indian Families with Young Children. *Journal of Marriage and the Family*, 59, 873–883.

Jang. H. & Kim, Y. (2000). Bukhanitaljumanui Gajokanjeong Mit Sahoijeokungka Eyeoseongui Eyeokhwal. *Hangukyeosunggaebalwon Yeongubogoseo*, 240-13.

Jeon, B. (1974). Jaagaenyeom Chukjeong Ganongseonge Gwanhan Yeongu. *Yeonsenonchong*, 11, 107–130.

Jeon, B. (2003). Talbuk Adong·cheongsonyeonui Namhansahoi Jeokungmunjewa Daeungbangan. Talbuk Cheongsonyeon Gyoukjedoui Hyeonhwang Mit Jeeon. Bukhanitaljoominjiwon Mingandanche-hyupuihoi Adong·cheongsonyeonboongwa Seminar Balpyojaryo (pp. 2–10) (10.10.2003). Bukhanitaljumin Jiwon Mingandanchehyupuihoi.

Jeon, W. (1997). Review of Adaptation and Mental Health of Refugees and Perspectives and Counterplots in Korean Reunification Process. *Journal of the Korean Neuropsychiatric Association*, 36 (1), 3–18.

Jeon, W. (1999). Talbukjaui Boho Mit Gooknaejeokung Gaeseonbangan. Je32hoi Gooknaehaksooldaehoiui (11.30.1999) Balpyononmoonjib (99-05) (pp. 40–64). Tongilyeonguwon.

Jeon, W. (2000). *For the South and North Korea Ppeople's Unification*. Seoul: Olum.

Jeon, W. (2001). Can Two Peoples Get along?: The Prospects of Unification of the Psychology of South and North Koreans. *Korean Unification Studies*, 5 (2), 47–67.

Jeon, W., Hong, C., & Eom, J. (2003). Survey of the North Korean People's Social Consciousness Study on North Korean Defectors in South Korea. *Journal of Korean Neuropsychiatric Association*, 42 (5), 631–643.

Jo, Y., Jeon, W., & Min, S. (2004). The Religious Orientation and the Ego Defense Style of North Korean Defectors. *Korea Journal of Christian Counseling*, 8, 279–299.

Johunbeotdl (1999). *Dumangangul Geonneoeon Saramdl*. Seoul: Jeong-tochulpan.

Jong-Seok, L. (1996). Bukhanjumin Euisikgujo Mit Gachigwan Josa. Tongil-yeonsoowon.

Jung, B. (2003). Talbuk Adong·cheongsonyeon Namhansahoi Jeokungmunjewa Daeungbangan. Talbuk Cheongsonyeon Gyoeukjedoui Hyeonhoangkwa Jeeon. Bukhanitaljuminjiwon Mingandanchehyeopeuihoi Adong·cheongsonyeonbungwa Seminar Jaryojib. Bukhanitaljuminjiwon Mingandanchehyeopuihoi: 2–10.

Kalil, A. (2003). Family Resilience and Good Child Outcomes: A Review of the Literature. Centre for Social Research and Evaluation. Ministry of Social Development.

Kalplan, H. I. & Sadock, B. J. (Eds.) (1998). *Synopsis of Psychiatry*. 8th Edition. Philadelphia, PA: Lippincott Williams & Wilkins.

Keum, M., Kwon, H., & Lee, H. (2004). The Acculturation Process of North Korean Adolescents Refuges. *The Korean Journal of Counseling and Psychotherapy*, 16 (2), 295–308.

Kim, H. (2004). A Study on the Actual Conditions of the North Korea Refugees and the Policy of Management. Wonkwang University unpublished Master's thesis.

Kim, I. (2005). Talbukja Hyunhwangbunseok: Talbuk, Jungkangichak, Jungchakggajiui Chongchejuk Bunseok. *Minjokyeungu*, 14, 6–34.

Kim, M. (2004). Talbukeso Ibgukggaji: Takbukja Ibgukjiwon Gwanryun Beoblyulgaehung Jaryojib.

Kim, S. (2001). Bukhanitaljuminui Namhansahoi Jungchakul Wooihan Daehanbogoseo: 'Sanhsanjuk Jeokoongkwa Jungchak'. *2001yeondo Gukgamjaryojib (I)*. Tongilwoigyotongsangwooiwonhoi kimsungho-wiiwonsil.

Kim, T. & Noh, C. (2003). North Korean Female Defectors' Voices: Hermeneutical Phenomenological Analysis of the Lived Experiences in China. *Journal of the Korean Home Economics Association*, 41 (8), 1–17.

Kim, T. & Noh, C. (2003). The Lived Experiences Focused on Survival Strategies in China = North Korean Female Defectors' Voices (II). *Journal of the Korean Home Economics Association*, 41 (12), 229–243.

Kim, Y. (2000). Bukhanitaljuminui Gajokmunje. *Sahoigwahakyeungoo*, 9, 102–117.

Kim, Y. (2004). Bukhanitaljuminui Hyunhwangwa Jaesahoihwa Munje. *Sahoigwahakyeungoo*, 12 (1), 118–148.

Kim, Y., Park, J., & Lee, Y. (1996). Bukhanitaljuminui Sahoijeokunge Gwanhan Yeongu: Siltaejosa Mit Gaeseonbangan. Minjoktongilyeonguwon.

Lazarus, R. S. & Folkman, S. (1984). *Stress Appraisal and Coping*. New York: Springer.

Lee, J. (1996). Bukhanjumin Euisikgujo Mit Gachigwan Josa. Tongilyeonsoo-won.

Lee, K. (1991). Bukhanui Tongchiideolrogiwa Yeoseong. Sonbongsook·Lee-kyeongsook·leeonjook·kimaesil. *Bukhanui Yeoseongsaenghwal*. Seoul: Nanam: 11–36.

Lee, K. (2000). Talbukjagajokui Namhansahoi Jeokunggwajung. Gajoksahoi-bokjihakhoi chugeoihaksuldaehoi balpyomoon.

Lee, K., Lee, K., Lee, E., Yi, S., Kim, D., Park, Y., & Choi, Y. (2001). *Tongile Apseo Bonun Bukhanui Gajeongsaenghwalmoonhwa*. Seoul National University Press.

Lee, S. (1997). A Study on Acculturative Stress among North Korean Defectors Residing in South Korea. *The Korea Journal of Youth Counseling*, 5 (1), 209–247.

Lee, S. (2002). Bukhanitaljumin: Hyunhwangwa Daechaek. *Ibheobjeongbo*, 72,

1–28.

Lim, H. & Jung, Y. (2005). *Towards Unified Korea in 21th Century: The Dialectics between the Division and the Unification*. Seoul: Seoul National University Press.

McCubbin, H. I., McCubbin, M. A., Thompson, A. I., Han, S. Y., & Allen, C. T. (1997). Families under Stress: What Makes Them Resilient?

Ministry of Unification (2005). Daebukjeongchaekchojeom. Saeteomin-gwanryeon tonggyeo.

Ministry of Unification (2005). Saeteomin (bukhanitaljumin) gwanryeon tonggyeo. http://www.unikorea.go.kr>Tongilsosik>daebukjeongchaekchojeom.

Ministry of Unification (2006). Gukjeonggamsajaryo (Sahoimunhwagyoryubonbu).

Moon, S., Kim, J., & Lee, M. (2000). A Study on the Motive of Escape from the North Korea and the Life Situation of Female Fugitives in China-based on the Interview with North Korean Female Refugees in Yenben Province. *Journal of the Korean Home Economics Association*, 38 (5), 137–152.

Murphy, H. B. M. (1965). Migration and the Major Mental Disorders: A Reappraisal. In M. B. Kantor (Ed.). *Mobility and Mental Health*. Springfield, CA: Thomas.

Ok, S. & Sung, M. (2004). Divorce and Post-Divorce Adjustment of Divorced Men and Women in their 20s and 30s. *Journal of the Korean Home Economics Association*, 42 (12), 141–160.

Park, H. (2003). *Temporary North Korean Society and Family*. Paju: Hanul.

Park, M. & Lee, J. (1999). Talbukgajokui Namhangajok Jeokungsi Geuknun Eoryeowoomgwa Gettalun Daecheobangahn. *Sukmyungyeojadaehakgyo Tongilmunjeyunguso Tongilnonchong*, 17, 3–74.

Park, S. (1995). Bukhancheongsonyeonui Saenghwal. Gongbocheo.

Park, S., Kim, M., & Doh, H. (2000). The Relations of Acculturation and Parenting Behaviors of Korean-Chinese Mothers in Yanbian Area to Adjustment of their Children. *Journal of the Korean Home Economics Association*, 38 (12), 159–175.

Patel, N., Power, G., & Bhavnagri, P. (1996). Socialization Values and Practices of Indian Immigrant Parents: Correlates of Modernity and Acculturation. *Child Development*, 67, 302–313.

Redfield, R., Linton, R., & Herskovits, M. J. (1936). Memorandum on the Study of Acculturation. *American Anthropologist*, 38, 149–152.

Rosenberg, S., Ward, D., & Chilton, S. (1988). *Political Reasoning and Cognition: A Piagetian View*. Duke University Press.

Rutter, M. (1987). Psychological Resilience and Protective Mechanisms. *American Journal of Orthopsychiatry*, 57, 316–331.

Social Science Research Council Summer Seminar (1954). Acculturation: An Exploratory Formulation. *American Anthropologist*, 56, 973–1002.

Tarter, R. E. & Varyukov, M. (1999). Re-visiting the Validity of the Construct of Resilience. In M. D. Glantz & J. l. Johnson (Eds.), Resilience and Development: Positive Life Adaptations. New York: Kluwer Academic/ Plenum Publishers.

U.S. Committee for Refugees and Immigrants (2006). World Refugee Survey; China 2006.

Walsh, F. (1998). *Strengthening Family Resilience*. New York: Guilford Press.

Williams, C. & Berry, J. W. (1991). Primary Prevention of Acculturative Stress among Refugees: The Application of Psychological Theory and Practice. *American Psychologist*, 46, 632–641.

Yang, O., Choi, S., Song, I., Kwon, J., Yang, H., & Yeom, T. (2004). Sahwoibokjiwa Tanleukseong. Nanumijip Chulpansa. (Ed.). R. R. Greene. *Resiliency: An Integrated Approach to Practice, Policy, and Research*. National Association of Social Workers Inc.

Yi, S. (1996). Gajokjoouiwa Jibhabjui, Seongchuijihyangwa Yangyuk Gachigwanui Gwangyei-Jyungryuchong Abeojirl Daesanguro. *Hanguksahoihakhoiji*, 30, 545–573.

Yi, S. (1999). Bukhanui Joochesasang Sahoihwa Jeongchaekui Wonliwa Gu Hangyeo. *Gyoyukhakyeongoo*, 37 (4), 120–136.

Yi, S. (2005). *Red Devil and Worldcup*. Seoul: Seoul National University Press.

Yoon, I. (1999). Talbukjaui Namhansahoi Jeokungsiltaewa Jungchakjiwonui Saeroun Jeopgun. *Hanguksahoihak*, 33, 511–549.

Yoon, I. (2000). The Case for Defectors in South Korea = North Korean Defectors and their Social Adjustment. *North Korean Studies Review*, 3 (2), 123–184.

Yoon, I. (2005). Nambukhan Sahoitonghapui Jogeongwa Jeonmang. *Jeong-*

chaekgwahakyeongu, 15 (1), 99–144.

Yoon, I. & Kim, S. (2005). Health and Medical Care of North Korean Defectors in South Korea. *Bogeongwa Sahoigwahak*, 17, 149–182.

Yoon, Y. (2004). Jaewoitalbukja Siltae: Hyunhwangwa Daeahnul Joongsimuro. *Je7gi Bukhaningweonnanminmoonje Academy Jaryojib*. Bukhaningyeonsiminyeonhab.

Index